Charles Marine

Poems, heart songs and ballads

Charles Marine

Poems, heart songs and ballads

ISBN/EAN: 9783744736909

Printed in Europe, USA, Canada, Australia, Japan

Cover: Foto ©Thomas Meinert / pixelio.de

More available books at **www.hansebooks.com**

POEMS

HEART SONGS AND BALLADS

BY

CHARLES MARINE

INDIANAPOLIS, IND.

1896

POEMS, HEART-SONGS AND BALLADS.

BY CHARLES MARINE.

ANDRE MAR.—A MEDLEY.

1

Sweet Rose Lander came over the hill
  Singin' a song o' love;
I sat me down by the forest spring
  An' moaned with the moanin' dove.
Sweet Rose Lander gave me her heart
  When the heather was purple yesteryear;
Now her heart is cloyed with love for another
  An' my joy runs out in a streamin' tear.

2

I sat me under the silent moon
  To think o' the joy I once did know;
But a dark cloud passed o'er her pale, calm face
  An' I said, Likewise was my joy my woe.

3

There's an old tombstone an' a sunken grave,
  Under the hill by the great black stones,
An' a gray-haired man with a wrinkled brow,
  Comes at the even an' weeps an' moans.
I read on the headstone these chiseled words,
  That the sun had seamed an' the rain had fret,
"The purest heart that virtue knows
  May fall with the burden of regret."

4

I went sailin' o'er the sea,
  O'er the sea o' mystery,
An' a maid sat dreamin' on the isle o' my quest
  That I touched when the sun was low in the west.
I took her hand in a tender way
  An' said, this truly is paradise :
I kissed her lips an' my soul ran out
  An' melted away in her sweet, sad eyes.
Oh, beautiful isle; 'tis woman's heart;
  Oh, beautiful sea, for love thou art;
But, oh, for the bliss that will never be—
  To return to that heavenly isle in the sea.

5

The lover came to the forest spring
  Where a maid sat moanin' her grief at eve,
"Oh, let me, maiden, to you sing
  A song your sadness to relieve :
'Hearts that grow cold when love is young
  Are better than hearts fate does sever.
Bitter the pain in the hearts thus stung,
  But weepin' will ease them never.
'Hearts that are true that fate does part
  We mourn for at morn an' at even ;
Naught can relieve a broken heart
  But the angel tears o' heaven.'"
Her sweet, sad eyes toward him do move
  An' her lips grow pale an' quiver;
The lover cries, "My love! my love!
  Oh, the angel tears deliver!"

6

"Youth is fickle," the old dame said ;
  "Love in the cupboard is very poor bread.
An' oh, an' oh, an' so, an' so,
  For woe, for woe, we know, we know,
Comes to the young an' the old,
  The fickle an' wise, to be sure ;
But an old man's pocket
  That jingles with gold
Is better than youth who is poor."

THE CAPRI MAIDEN'S SONG.

I met a Capri maid in town
  With wavy locks of jet
And glintful eye whose liquid depths
  I never shall forget.
But oh, she sang a song to me
  With voice so sweet and low,
I turned my head away from her
  For the tears began to flow;
I turned my head away from her
  For the tears began to flow.

She sang to me of love grown cold
  And a maiden's broken heart,
And I wondered as she sang, if she
  Of her song could be a part ;
But I hoped she sang of another's fate
  With pain to her heart unknown ;
But when she turning saw me weep,
  She wept,—"It is all mine own!"
But when she turning saw me weep,
  She wept,—"It is all mine own!"

I took the Capri maiden's hand
And spoke a kindly word,
Her tender bosom rose and fell
With deepest anguish stirred;
She took the gold I gave to her
And mingled with the throng;
But, oh, I never shall forget
The Capri maiden's song;
But, oh, I never shall forget
The Capri Maiden's song.

WHEN THE SONG O' THE ROBIN.

When the song o' the robin is heard in the
   wood
An' the dew on the young grass is gleamin',
An' the first blue o' spring 'gins to smile in
   the sky
'Tis then that a lover goes dreamin',
'Tis then that a lover goes dreamin',
'Tis then that a lover goes dreamin',
When the robin does sing at the first blue o'
   spring,
'Tis then that a lover goes dreamin'.

When the tulip springs up by the old garden
   wall
An' the warm sun the earth is a-lovin',
An' the path o'er the hill 'gins to fade into
   green,
'Tis then that a lover goes rovin',
'Tis then that a lover goes rovin',
'Tis then that a lover goes rovin',
When the hill-path is green, an' the tulip is
   seen,
'Tis then that a lover goes rovin'.

When the musk o' the wild rose blows sweet
   o'er the lea
An' the dove on the cot is a-cooin',
An' the full flush o' summer comes balmily on,
'Tis then that a lover goes wooin',
'Tis then that a lover goes wooin',
'Tis then that a lover goes wooin',
When the musk o' the rose, o'er the summer
   lea blows,
'Tis then that a lover goes wooin'.

When the wind thro' the chinks blows sough-
   in' an' cold
An' few o' the summer birds tarry,
An' the flowers lie scattered beneath the first
   frost
Then it's time for a lover to marry,
Then it's time for a lover to marry,
Then it's time for a lover to marry,
When the flowers scattered lie an' the birds
   homeward fly,
Then it's time for a lover to marry.

JEAN.

When weary days were o'er us, Jean,
   In the long-gone-by,
With little hope before us, Jean,
   But many days to sigh,
I gave you then my heart an' vow—
I loved you then—I love you now.

An' when the sky in beauty, Jean,
   Brought us more prosperous day
An' chastenin' rod an' duty, Jean,
   Drove trouble far away,
Still then my heart was yours an' vow—
I loved you then—I love you now.

An' yet I am confessin', Jean,
   As in the days o' yore,
That love's the choicest blessin', Jean,
   Alway—forevermore.
Are ever yours my heart an' vow—
I love you now—I love you now.

PLUMP BILLY MARTIN

Plump Billy Martin, tiptoe fine,
You can't steal this heart o' mine;
So don't come courtin' with your smiles
An' pretty sayin's an' your wiles;
I read you as I read a book;
Long since I've hung you on the hook.

Plump Billy Martin, do you mind
That once with love you were stone blind,
An' thro' the breaky country drove,
With dapple grays your lady love
Till all at once—you found, alack,
Her wealth had flown—you jumped the track!

An' now you come a courtin' me;
But I'm heart whole an' fancy free.
These broad, green fields I share with none,
So you had just as well be done;
No husband buyin' lot for me,
Plump Billy Martin, do you see?

OH, MOANIN' GALES.

Oh, moanin' gales that haunt the night,
   My heart goes moanin' with you;
The wild clouds rob the sky o' light
   An' grief my life to myth you.
Oh, moanin' gales o' midnight moan
Your grief to mingle with my own.

You come to me from that grim vast
   O' frozen void with laden breast;
Your deep-set woe will end at last
   With mine, when we at length shall rest—
You 'neath the smile o' southern sky
An' I beneath the sod shall lie.

WHAT SHALL WE SING?

What shall we sing? Of the heart's bitter pain
We have sought long to soothe, but shall ever remain?
Shall we sing of the joys that memory gives,
Or the first love of youth that in heart sweetly lives?

What shall we sing? In low plaintive air,
Of the maiden that knew of the pangs of despair?
Or, say, shall it be of the dead hopes of yore,
And the faces we knew, but shall see nevermore?

What shall we sing? Of the love that grows cold
When fair youth has vanished and we have grown old?
Shall we sing of the days that were brightest and best,
Or the joys far beyond in the eternal rest?

What shall we sing? Shall it be that sweet song,
We knew in our youth and sang all day long?
Shall we sing of the brightness the future may bring?
Let us sing a song sweetly; but what shall we sing?

IN THE RYE.

I met a maiden in the rye,
In the rye, and she was sweet;
She looked askance and in her eye
I saw a little sparkling fire,
And so I drew a little nigher,
The maiden in the rye to meet.

Low, to the maiden in the rye,
I bowed in gallant courtesy.
I took her lily hand, for high,
The golden rye did lift its tips,
And kissed and kissed her nectar lips
And pressed her closer unto me.

Nor this sweet maiden in the rye,
Ne'er said a word, nor sought to go:
"O sweetest love, there's no one nigh."
Her only answer was a blush;
So in the ecstacy and hush,
We let our sweetest passions flow.

SONG OF THE LOTOS-EATER.

O, there is a place where mortal can dwell
And be free from this bickering world of care,
Nor the soul e'er know the meaning or tell
Of sorrow or pain, of sin or fear.

Where, as time runs on and life is sweet,
And the spirit all light and happiness,
There will never be aught that the heart may greet,
But that it will love—but that it will bless.

And there does linger the smile of love,
Not the vain pretence here in disguise;
But a love that's likened to that above—
Not the vaunted look of lying eyes.

O, sweetly the heart of mortal can rest,
For there, nevermore, does run life's sand,
And the heart never dies but forever is blest,
And the soul roams in rapture this strange, sweet land.

CHRISTMAS ONCE A YEAR.

Christmas comes but once a year—
Day of peace and day of cheer;
Day of hope and day of prayer—
Christmas comes but once a year.

Christmas comes but once a year;
Oh, the joy that it does bear
To expectant hearts when near—
Christmas comes but once a year.

Christmas comes but once a year;
Hearts are gladdened when 'tis here;
May it never bring a tear—
Christmas comes but once a year.

Christmas comes but once a year.
To the hearts we love, 'tis dear
To give tokens love does bear—
Christmas comes but once a year.

Christmas comes but once a year.
Christ, the poor, O, may they share
Thy rich blessings everywhere—
Christmas comes but once a year.

Christmas comes but once a year;
May its joy spread everywhere,
Till hearts of every clime revere
Christmas coming once a year,

THE BIBLE.

Holy Book, that teaches how to live
And grow stronger with the years:
Holy Book, that teaches how to die
And conquer all our fears.
A mighty truth that lifts the woe

From weary souls, and makes the heart
Rejoice, the lips sing sweeter song,
And bids dark images depart.
Each word, each line, computes the love
That God bestows on us who rove,
This wilderness of dark despair.
O Grand old Book! let poets bless
Thy presence in this world of care,
And form their tasts from nothing less.

THE BAD TINKER.

You spoilt my watch, you wizen botch
You, winkin' wise, deceived me;
The time o'day has sped away:
I've lied to whom believed me.
The bob-tail car, with bell and jar,
Swings round the second corner,
Now I must wait on limpin' fate,
To disappointment mourner.

POLL AND SALL.

SITTING OVER THE FIRE TALKING

Law, me! don't ask me that, Sall:
The number I'll speak nor pen,
For it's twenty times twenty an' over,
An' twenty times over again,
An' twenty times all o' that, Sall,
If I guess without notch or chalk,
When I was young—but hush, Sall,
We're gittin' too old for such talk.

Yes, indeed, we're to old for such talk, Sall,
But when I was young, as I said,
My cheeks were as red as the roses,
You know, Sall, when I was wed:
An' I was plump an' round, Sall,
I could stand a sight, you know;
But we'd better be readin' our bibles, Sall,
I think, than to be talkin' so.

An' John was ruby an' white, Sall,
You know, an' built so square;
It was nip an' tuck between us, Sall,
I can tell you, for many a year:
But his back was growin' round, Sall,
As the years went flyin' by,
An' he tottered a bit as he walked, Sall,
An' the fire went out o' his eye.

But I seemed pert at sixty;
I could stand a sight right sure.
Eh! but I often have wondered
How much, Sall, I could endure.
Of course, my John was a good man—
Broad an' strong as could be;
But he's gone, an' I am left, Sall,
He wa'n't quite a match for me.

An' your man went to the war, Sall;
But he didn't go amiss,
For he was too cold o' nature, Sall,
For you, all passion an' kiss:
Besides he had sickness you know, Sall,
An' could never do his part;
Of course, you grieved when he fell, Sall,
But it didn't break your heart.

For you know the next spring found you
Married to good Milton Prow—
Broad, an' tall, an' handsome, Sall,
Without a blemish, I'll vow;
An' I'll guess that your longin' wa'n't stint Sall,
After you passed to his hands,
For I believe he possessed every virtue—
Every virtue, Sall, that is man's.

Law, goodness! but who would have thought, Sall,
That he'd been the first to doubt?
I've often studied it over, Sall,
But never could make it out.
I could see as the years went by, Sall,
That his chances were gittin' less;
First I had many a fear for you, Sall,
But your timber was toughest, I guess.

Now, let's hush, for it's wrong—it's sinful!
For such old things as us
To be talkin' like this ; but I guess, Sall,
It's better to laugh than to fuss ;
Then, we grew up girls together,
An' one's secrets were t'other's, you know,
But we'd better be thinkin' o' heaven, Sall,
Than to be talkin' so.

A FUNNY MAN.

I know you as I knew you when
Your buttocks showed thro' ragged gear,
Thro' all the seasons of the year,
And scoffed at by far wiser men.

But born of egotistic spleen,
And with a store of shallow wit,
And tho' there are who laugh at it,
The wiser mind calls crude and green.

To put to shame some honest hind
The mimicking some luckless gump—
The pastime of a silly chump,
With not a pennyweight of mind.

And you are funny—funny, hey?
And like old Egypt's pyramids,
You think your reputation bids
Well to stand eternally.

I will not prophesy. A kind
Will bear you onward with their grace,
And, though they twit behind your face,
You think you have a mighty mind.

WEARY DAYS.

How sad it is to think of life
With all its seasons of despair.
The heart-pains, disappointments, strife;
Even with old friends, whom we thought
The foundation of all our joys ;
Even mild-eyed love grows cold
And taunts us—selfishly destroys
The last fond token of the heart.
The woes of indigence, vice and crime,
Death; aye, worse, a daughter or son
Hath fallen and grovels in the slime
On the dark streets of hell! O, tears
Of the widowed mother : her child,
Luckless outcast, hath for life,
Misery's inheritance. Beguiled
Were sweetly its first rosy days ;
But death hath closed the scene—
The mother died ; hunger drove it forth.

The sparkling wine doth cheer the heart.
A father sips at eve, for business prest
Him sore all day. Lo! when his hair
Was silvered, life should needs be best;
They laid him in a drunkard's grave :
Fair wealth had flown, and thus apart
The family breathed the fetid air
Of woeful slums! E'er thus we strive
With fated life's behest,
And hope. The weary soul cries, "Rest."
Few pleasures come ; but sorrow stays :
True, life is full of weary days.

CARES.

Be strong and grieve not any
Nor let your heart be sad,
For the cares of life are like the chaff
That the winter winds have had ;
They fall on the weak, and on the strong ;
They fall on the rich, and poor;
But they fly away if you give them way,
Like the chaff from the thrashing floor.

Your heart may bow with its load of care,
And your life seem lost to peace ;
Do not despair ; be strong and bear ;
There will come a calm—'twill cease :
You will lift your eyes to a brighter morn,
After the long night of unrest,
And your cares, like chaff, will have blown past,
Ere the sun does sink in the west.

DRESS.

But give me those more staid, nor prone
To drift in vanity, and dabble in the rosy
Hues of fashion till their minds
Are lost in vulgar modes.
For what more vulgar to the sight
Than paint and gewgaw in old age?
And what more clever to the sight
Than modest dress in youth or maid?
Choose then the dress that suits the age,
Nor silks or satins cast aside,
Nor those of color, shade or kind :
But shun all wantoness.

A DIRGE.

There grief, and pain, and sorrow end,
Low buried with the heart at rest.
Wreathe round the grave the sweet, white rose,
'Twas the flower she always loved the best.

Take not the pain to your own young heart ;
But lift your eyes to her home above ;
Heaven is glad, and all is well :
There's a link that binds you, a link of love.

And hers is a fairer home than this—
A home of peace and eternal light ;
A home where the weary pilgrim rests,
And the cares of life can ne'er affright.

And hers is a joy so sweet and long—
A sweeter joy than e'er we knew ;
O, may we know this sweet, sweet joy,
When we're sleeping as she 'neath the sod and dew.

JENNY BY YOUR TESTY LOOKS.

Jenny, by your testy looks,
I know you're on the tenter-hooks ;
But I am off for Dover Hill
My Mary Ann to wed.
You needn't try to gin an' gloze,
You make me queasy with your woes ;
My God! you're growin' from your clothes
You'd better go to bed.

I never knew you, Jenny; tho'
You lied I wooed you to your woe,
An' set the neighbors quizzin',
An' a-blinkin', an' awry ;
But they can't me to mercy shame,
For such a blowzy drab's good name ;
Go find my wily worse, the blame
Is his, an' with him lie.

MARGARET.

I am whom thou sadly longest for;
I am he thou longest for in vain,
            Margaret.
Yet I am he that giveth only pain,
Since Thou to me art like to yonder star,
            Margaret,
Too far above, too bright, too great a prize;
Just let me look once more into thine eyes,
            Margaret.

FOUR SEASONS.

Spring came and it was fair;
  Summer brought a grander bloom;
Autumn, next, all things mature;
  Winter, then, with cold and gloom.
And thus the world goes on—
  On forever till the last;
Spring, summer, autumn then,
  The dreary days and winter's blast.

Infancy, the prattling child;
  Youth, O, beauty, still more fair;
Manhood in perfection shone;
  Then old age and hoary hair.
Thus, our transient lives run on—
  On forever—on alas,
Till the sand-glass of all time
  Writhes and lets the last grain pass.

TIME.

Returnless Time, thou wast too fleet
Of wing, too prone to lead astray;
Too transient was thy infancy;
Too brief thy restless stay.

Lo! thou hast bound remediless,
Round weakening limbs unyielding stocks
That bind me closer unto thee,
Bowed head and hoary locks.

Invincibly thou runest thy race;
  To thee I'm ready to resign;
In resignation to thy will,
  I humbly sink supine.

But when my ashes bear death's mark,
  My spirit in survivency,
Will fly to God nor fear thee not,
  O, Time, eternally.

THE PALACE.

A palace stands in a crystal sea;
  No mortal save I knows this sweet paradise;
A white hand opens its gates for me,
  And I dream in the light of beauty's eyes,
In the palace that stands in the crystal sea.

O deep is the eye that on me does shine;
  O sweet is the smile I see;
Love leads delight to her passioned shrine,
  Where the richest of gift is for me,
In the palace that stands in the crystal sea.

A palace stands in a crystal sea,
  And high is the palace wall;
But I kiss the lips that welcome me;
  O my love is fair and tall,
In the palace that stands in the crystal sea.

There soft delights and perfume meet,
  And mingle with love and sleep;
O white are the arms that twine me sweet;
  I die in the bliss of a sin so deep,
In the palace that stands in the crystal sea.

MINNIE HAS A BLUE EYE.

Oh, Minnie has a blue eye;
  A rosy cheek an' soft white hand;
An' Minnie wears a pretty dress,
  A-ridin' by my daddy's land.

Her mammy sent my mammy Ann
  Her own receipt for weddin' cake,
An' mammy tried it for my luck,
  An' found it made a soggy bake.

I whistled by the field o' rye;
  I caught the eye o' Minnie fair;
But she lent on a townsman's arm
  An' rode behind a dapple pair.

But as they dashed along the road,
  She shot a glance at me behind,
As much to say, The devil take
  The townsman I am leadin' blind.

'Twas Minnie with the blue eye
  That fooled her townsman wooer;
Tho' rich as a Jew in love with her too,
  He couldn't win fair Minnie Moor.

TOM CROOK.

Did you ever hear tell o' that Real Estate man,
Whose name was Tom Crook, or hear o' his plan

How he tried to rob his old friend who came
    from the West
With a bag full o' money he had to invest?

Well, this man Crook tried to rob came back
    to his town,
An' to find his old friends he went up an' down.
He found some that knew him and his hand
    gladly shook;
But the gladdest amongst them was this fellow
    Crook.

Well, this man Crook tried to rob, said he'd
    been out West,
An' had come back a rich man an' wanted to
    invest
In a fine country-place somewhere thereabout,
Handy for him to come in an' go out.

"I've got just the place," says Crook as he
    smiles,
"A beautiful place, out o' town a few miles.
You can buy it dirt-cheap, o' that there's no
    doubt."
So next mornin' this man Crook tried to rob
    started out.

He took the hack out—it ran every day,
Yet often the hack had been robbed on the way.
That mornin' he rode to the place an' half back
When a man with big pistols rode up to the
    hack.

Well, this man Crook tried to rob, was given
    his choice
To shell out his silver or his daylights, bejoice!
But this man Crook tried to rob had a mighty
    clear head,
An' quick as a flash shot the bold robber dead.

Well, this man Crook tried to rob, an' the
    hack driver took
The dead robber to town, an' found it was
    Crook;
He was all in disguise, an' his horse disguised
    too,
An' for years had been robbin' in the way I
    tell you.

Now wasn't it funny, this Real Estate man
Had robbed an' got rich on such a slick plan?
But, Tom Crook fell at last an' o' course it was
    best,
When he tried to rob his old friend who came
    from the West.

OLD DADDY DURBIN.

When old Daddy Durbin
    Comes a-limpin' down the street,
It's worth a half a dollar
    The old man to meet.
Such a very clever fellow
    You seldom ever see—
Always crippled up an' limpin'
    Yet as happy as can be.

He's a clever old man
    With long frosty hair,
Old Daddy Durbin
    Who lives over there.
He always goes smilin'
    An' limpin' about
An' shakin' an' scrapin'
    Whenever he's out.

"Oh, how are you this mornin'?"
    You will hear the children say,
"Why, lawsy mercy on you,
    I'm feelin' mighty gay!
'Cept I've got the roomytiz
    An' a stitch here in my side,
But t'otherwise I'm feelin'
    Happy, well an' satisfied."

I DREAMPT LAST NIGHT.

I dreampt last night old friends were by me—
    Old friends passed by so long;
No joy of old did they deny me,
    With toast and happy song.
My heart was light, my laughter merry,
    I knew not grief I bear;
I spent an hour of time unweary,
    With old-time friends so dear.

I dreampt last night, old friends were by me
    But wakeful hours misprove
The joy, and leave no comfort nigh me,
    But the memory of their love;
Yet, better far, if in our dreaming,
    Though wakeful hours prove vain,
To greet old friends in blissful seeming,
    We ne'er shall see again.

MARY.

O, the kindness of her heart;
O, the patience of her soul.
My life was wrapt in darkness when away;
But with her, divine sunshine:
For she purified my soul,
And I felt myself a true man,
Which, God knows, was not before.
When alone, how often I have wept—
She seemed an angel child;
So inexperienced, so frail, so good;
And I, poor and uncouth, so unworthy her;
But I loved her, O, so fondly.

I lived for her, but in living grew miserable,
For I could not give her what I would.
She was a diamond, I a rough unhewn stone,
Insignificant and poor of kind,
While her brilliancy only augmented my nothingness,

LOVE BIDES A WISH-A-DAY.

Love bides a wish-a-day
　Fancy beguiling,
Only to pass away
　With beauty smiling,
And ere the days have sped
　Through one brief season,
Hearts chide what love has said,
　Oft with good reason.

Transient the maiden's rest—
　She who is dreaming,
On her fond lover's breast,
　In blissful seeming:
Tho' sweet the seeming is
　In love's bright hour,
Vain, vain the dreaming is
　In Cupid's bower.

There is a love that lives—
　An never dying;
But it's the love that gives
　Weeping and sighing;
'Tis in the hearts that fate
　Severs forever:
That is the love that dies
　Never, oh, never.

FAIR WOMAN.

Fair woman, fair woman my heart is thine
　Yes, ever thine while life shall last;
Fair woman, fair woman wilt thou give me thine,
　Or shall I in sorrow go past?

Fair woman, fair woman while life shall last,
　I'll love but thee and think thee best;
Fair woman, fair woman throw off thy mask
　And let thy heart speak its request.

Fair woman, fair woman naught else is there
　To bring more joy than love of thine;
Fair woman, fair woman O, truly fair,
　Unlike thy beauty so divine.

MAM BLEACHED HER FLAX SHEETS.

Mam bleached her flax-sheets
　When the wild-thorn did blossom
An' let them hang out
　For the neighbors to see,
But I stole them at night
　With no fear in my bosom,
To spread in the bramble
　For Charlie an' me.

O, Charlie was coo
　With a brow white as cotton,
An' he wheedled my heart
　An' set me awry;
An' he left me a grief
　That shall ne'er be forgotten,
An' took all the glint
　From my merry blue eye.

SHORE OF THE DARK NO MORE.

I stood on the shore of the dark No More
And the waves leapt high on my breast
And pierced to my heart like a cruel dart
　And moaned in their wild unrest.
I stept in my boat with a grief-cloyed throat
　For I saw a loved face on an isle far and lone,
I battled the tide to its storm-beaten side
　To find but a cold grave-stone—
　To weep o'er a cold grave-stone.

I sat in the gleam of love's young dream
　And the daisies bloomed under my eye;
But the summer past, nor the dream could last
　And the daisies had bloomed to die;
And I saw thro' a mist a sweet face kist
　And I felt a soft hand in my own;
But hope passed by with a tear-dimmed eye
　As I mourned o'er a cold grave-stone—
　As I prayed o'er a cold grave-stone.

GRANDMOTHER TRIP.

Low bent in her anility, Grandmother Trip,
Came trudging down the road with a budget on her hip,
And she muttered and she chuckled as she passed by,
"I'll live forever—I'll never die."

And the house-dog sunning himself by the gate,
Bristled up with a snarl and a growl of deep hate,
As her threadbare skirts with a sickening smell
Swept by the place he was resting so well.

"Old Mother Trip is going to the fair;
Seventy years old and not a gray hair;
Other folks can't get around like me;
No indeed, no indeed, he! he! he!"

I watched her along the dusty road go,
With her air of joy and her picture of woe.
Who she was, whence she came, no one could
    tell,
When the crowd gathered round where the old
    woman fell.

Trampled to earth by the hoofs of a horse!
"Living forever," perhaps had been worse;
But she said as she turned her old eyes to the
    sky—
"They are singing up yonder, 'I never will
    die.'"

FROM PILLOW TO POST.

From pillow to post, from pillow to post;
What is the profit? little at most;
Little at most for there's little to earn,
Many to keep an' the fire must burn,
For the winds are raw an' the children cry
An' the good wife's comfort is but a sigh.
Work-a-day, work-a-day o'er an' o'er;
God give us strength if we must be poor.

From pillow to post, from pillow to post,
Tho' breathless the heat an' cuttin' the frost:
What profit the sighs—the tears that we weep
When tired, too tired an' weary to sleep?
An' the sad heart throbs an' the lips breathe
    low
The fervent prayer that the poor but know—
O, Lord, O, God give us strength to endure,
For little the comfort there is for the poor.

DOUBT.

Doubt, to thy frozen paradise,
    Far to the ice-bound waste so drear,
    Nor coldness ever feels the clear
Warm rays of light of happy eyes.

And there resign thee to thy fate
    And wail thou with the frozen gale
    That pitiless doth e'er assail
The wasting souls that death await.

But O, my soul, while yet there be
    A little left of blessedness,
    Left to thy lot, O let it bless
And still and comfort lowly me.

I hear the sighs above the day
    And see the ghost of hope pass by;
    It looks on me with sunken eye
And fades in yon strange far away.

And tho' I feel the good design
    Of noble gift and greater prize,

I turn me oft from tender eyes
That longing pity me and mine.

O, Thou, transcendent in thy reign
    Of underlying scope of light,
    Withhold the vengeance of thy might
From weakness unto carnal stain.

POLLY.

O, Polly lives over yon gay summer hill—
    My Polly, sweet Polly,
Where the stream winds around by the old
    gray mill—
    My Polly, sweet Polly.
She's as fair as the lilies that smile by her
    door
And her song charms the wild bird that goes
    flying o'er
Her cottage that sets by the stream's bloomy
    shore—
    My Polly, sweet Polly.

    Then it's o'er the hill to Polly,
    O'er the hill to Polly,
    Winding along to her echoing song,
    O'er the hill to Polly.

O, Polly is waiting and watching for me—
    My Polly, sweet Polly,
'Neath the boughs of the wide-spreading old
    forest tree—
    My Polly, sweet Polly.
Her heart is as true as e'er did impart
The lesson of love to a fond lover's heart
And her sweet eyes' reflection is purity; not
    art—
    My Polly, sweet Polly.

OLD WASHINGTON ST. BRIDGE.

You're worthy all respect, old Bridge,
Your timbers still reflect, old Bridge,
The honest hearts that hewed them
    An' pinned them tight an' fast.
Like old things you are best, old Bridge,
By your sister gayer dressed, old Bridge,
You, modest an' old-fashioned,
    Even now may longer last.

SISSIE.

O, Sissie you are fair an' young,
    Your hair is even parted;
Your glintful eye has been my woe
    An' I am broken-hearted.

When summer decked you withered glen
  With many a musky flower,
I chose the fairest, sweetest one
  To rue in sadder hour.

Your eye has cut me oft an' cold,
  I wander off to sadness;
Your new-found love with silver free
  Does promise greater gladness.
You stole away my happiness
  Ere cruel fate did sever:
O, Sissie once so good an' kind,
  You've ruined me forever.

THE PARTING.

You have sought to gull an' cheat me
  An' by trader's tricks to beat me,
As a smilin' saint to greet me,
  You a coward, thief an' that.
Now I leave you; mark our level:
I to peace—you to the devil!
Severed thus in joy I'll revel
  While you're yieldin' up your fat.

JOHN ALLEN.

John Allen, O, John Allen,
  I never shall forget
When you shouldered your old musket
  An' left me in regret,
An' marched away with the Twenty-first
  An' kissed your hand good-bye;
O, even now the thought of it,
  John Allen, makes me cry.

But you came marchin' back again
  With only one leg on;
You were not the man I knew you once
  For part o' you was gone!
John Allen, O, John Allen,
  My love you still did beg,
Tho' I refused when legs you'd two
  I couldn't with one a peg.

FIRST LOVE.

O, Willie you're a gay love;
  Your songs are lusty sweet!
An' many a maid you've queered, love,
  An' left her at your feet.
Your brow is like the snow, love,
  Your hair is wavy black;
I'll ne'er forget the first love,
  But dread to call it back.

The first love, the last love,
  An' O the best an' worst love,
I may forget the last love,
  But never can the first love,

Your cheek is velvet-rose, love,
  Your hand is white as snow;
Your eye is soft an' blue, love,
  Your voice is sweet an' low;
O, many a maid you've queered, love,
  An' many a heart you've broke;
I'll ne'er forget the first love;
  But weep to hear it spoke.

WHEN SOFT THE WINDS.

When soft the winds o'er bloomy trees
  Are blowing—blowing,
And bird-song fills each balmy breeze
  With wooing—wooing.
O, then, O, then are happy times:
The poet's thoughts all run to rhymes
And fill his soul with sweetest chimes
  Of music.

When violets in their musky nook
  Are springing—springing,
And frisky darts the laughing brook
  A singing—singing.
O, then, O, then are blissful days,
The poet for them ever prays,
His harp is tuned to sweetest lays
  Of music.

WHEN I WAS ON MY FIRST LEGS.

When I was on my first legs
  An' long o' wind an' timber,
I could whistle while I ran a mile
  I was so strong an' limber;
I could jump a fence nor touch a rail,
  An' few there were could throw me.
I was withy, couth, a giddy youth;
  But now you'd hardly know me.

For now I'm on my worst legs,
  My stiff an' crippled nursed legs;
They're nothin' like my first legs
  When I was young an' limber.

When I was on my first legs
  An' growin' from my breeches,
I could swing a girl an' toe a whirl,
  Nor cared for fame or riches:
I could sing a song an' draw a bow,
  'Twas few that could outdo me;
My whistle wild a witch beguiled;
  But now you'd hardly know me.

THE WITCH.

Eh! but the moon is wan to-night
  An' the owl hoots in the oak;
The lizards crawl o'er the cold grave-stones
  An' my old cat cries at a spook!
The white cow's milk has turned to blood
  An' the sheep die on the hill.
Eh! but the moon is dim to-night
  As I pass by the old gray mill.

Alack! for the miller; he crossed me thrice,
  An' lied when I asked him for flour;
Alack! for the miller; he lied to my face;
  But he didn't know my power.
I read his heart an' I read his head
  Ere the lie fell from his lips.
Eh, eh, eh! but he didn't know
  There was death in my finger tips!

An' his wife took sick ere he went to bed
  An' his child's death nobody knows—
Nobody knows but—eh, eh, eh!
  Nobody knows the cause.
My old cat tells me the mill is dry
  An' her tail is a flame o' fire!
Eh! how it crackles among the grain bins
  While the smoke rolls higher an' higher!

Alack! for the miller; he crossed me thrice
  An' lied when I asked him for flour;
Alack! for the miller; he lied to my face,
  But he didn't know my power.
Eh! but the flame licks mighty clean!
  An' the miller is sound asleep.
Let him dream on of the morrow's gain
  To wake to his grief an' weep!

ADAYS, WHEN SUMMER'S MUSKY BUDS.

Adays, when summer's musky buds
  Perfume the zephyrs mild,
I love to wander 'neath the thorny boughs
  Where young love first my heart beguiled
    Till rapture ran it wild,
And all my being thrilled with sweetest vows.

I love to read the carved names
  The old oak treasures yet;
They hallow in my heart the days of yore;
  Tho' some be shrouded in regret,
    How can I e'er forget
The hearts whose names I read but see no more?

But, O, I bow in deepest grief
  When to the grass-grown mound
I stroll to read the graven name thereon;
  I twine the roses that abound
    O'er dead hopes in the ground
And weep for one that's gone, forever gone!

WHY?

Why, that no proof but I must needs deny,
As much, in truth, as twice one are not two,
That, there was in the age we do decry,
A creature we call man, but would eschew?
Why, then, do proofs confirming science, be,
And great evolving cycles come and go?
I can not say, I saw as now I see;
I can not say, I were as I am now;
I can not say, this tree I sit beneath,
Was not an acorn once; nor can I say,
That man's dominion was what we'd bequeath
To dogmas trite, and threadbare hearsay.
If I be wrong—misled by my own light—
I pray some kindly power teach me the right.

TOM OWEN.

Your brow is fair an' smooth, Tom;
  Your hair is wavy brown;
Your cheek is like the rose, Tom;
  Your hand is soft as down.
But O, you broke my heart, Tom;
  But little blame to you,
For the heart that loves awry, Tom,
  Alas, does love to rue.

I brushed your black silk hat, Tom,
  Also your moleskin coat;
I gave you finest linen, Tom,
  An' jewels for you bought;
I gave you rosy wine, Tom,
  With little thanks from you;
But the heart that loves awry, Tom,
  Alas, must love to rue.

You used to kneel to me, Tom,
  When I was young an' free;
You used to sigh but for a smile
  An' said you'd die for me;
But fate has turned the wheel, Tom;
  I'm dyin' now for you;
But the heart that loves awry, Tom,
  Alas, must love to rue.

A PICTURE.

A long, thin nose, with scarlet end;
  Three curls hung in their auburn grace;
And eyes, pale unto buttermilk,
  Bulged from the freckled, hatchet-face;
A saffron neck and coral beads;
  Two silver rings; a green sun-shade;
Calm, solemn as Dyspepsia's ghost,
  She stood and viewed the grand parade.

THE MOURNER.

The days pass on, the days pass on,
  And still I wait, and watch, and pray,
And when the evening slowly comes
  And finds me as of yesterday,
I kneel and pray that coming dawn
  May bring my one sweet joy to me,
To lighten up my soul's dark home,
  So full of misery.

The days pass on, the days pass on,
  And hour by hour my lease of life
Doth shorten with the cheerless days;
  But let them speed and let the strife
Between my soul and woe be drawn
  To closer battle, fiercer fight,
To end; and with the coming dawn
  My spirit take its flight.

The days pass on, the days pass on;
  O, could I count them all in one.
O, could I rest my tired heart
  And know life's weary race was run.
For thee I wait, Eternal Dawn,
  For now my robes are spotless white.
O, that these links were burst apart—
  These earthly links, so tight, so tight.

The days pass on, the days pass on;
  I'll watch and pray while keepeth life;
I wait for thee, Eternal Peace,
  For here is constant trouble rife;
And all my earthly joys are gone;
  My life is like a lifeless clod;
My sweetest hope is that 'twill cease;
  My spirit fly to God.

I WOULD YOU WERE WITH ME.

I would you were with me, my own Sissie darlin'
To hear your sweet voice, like the zephyrs o' May,
To see the warm light in your eye soft an' glintful—
My own Sissie darlin' from me far away.

Lonely I sit 'neath the wood-dove that's moanin',
An' tears dim my eyes an' joy takes its flight,
An' hope fades away in the hush o' the gloamin'
To leave but the shadows o' lonelier night.

O, tarry no longer my own Sissie darlin',
Too lonely the hours when we are apart.
O, leave me not longin' for you broken-hearted,
Come back with your smiles to your true lover's heart.

COME TAKE A GLASS O' OLD-TIME BEER.

Come take a glass o' old-time beer
  For old acquaintance, Rocksy,
The fiz o' it will whiz a bit
  An' make you feel so foxy
'Twill bring the twinkle to the eye
  An' cheer the heart that's laggin';
Come, take a glass o' old-time beer
  While trouble goes a beggin'!

'Twill help recall the happy times
  Before the days o' sixty,
Ere we to fight with muskets bright
  Marched bravely down to Dixey.
'Twill help recall the old-time joys
  When you an' I, so jolly,
Drank to the health, an' smiles, an' songs
  O' pretty waiter Polly.

An' jovial Davy 'hind the bar,
  With portly sides a-shakin';
Let's call him up to take a sup
  While we our glass are takin'.
You wandered east; I wandered west;
  We're back from where we started;
Come, take a glass o' old-time beer
  For friendship broken-hearted.

Let's amble back to old-time days,
  When gaily we together
Danced many a tune in this old room,
  With hearts light as a feather.
Come, take a glass o' old-time beer,
  One glass for heart a laggin',
One glass to light the tear-dimmed eye
  While trouble goes a beggin'!

OLD RAIL FENCE.

So oft in my dreaming of bright, happy days,
  Ere sorrow had furrowed my brow,
My heart breaks away from its trouble and strays
  To old scenes so dear to me now.
But dearest of all in my memory yet
  Is where sweetest joy did commence—
Where sweet little Mary and I often met—
  Down by the old rail fence.

Oh, oft to the old fence so crooked and long,
  When bloomy the meadows were gay,
We strolled in the morn ere the dews dried away,
  To list to the lark's happy song.
And oft with her pail as she came from the spring,
  As beneath the old oak, wide and dense,
I rested at noon, a cool drink she'd bring
  To me at the old rail fence.

And at evening when moonbeams so softly did
    fall
And the nightingale sang in the wood,
We sang in the rapture, we dreamed in the
    spell
That nothing but love understood.
But time brings its changes for joy or regret,
And hope oft a sad consequence;
But of all the dear places in memory yet
Oh, spare me the old rail fence.

INNOCENCE.

A little child at play, on a bright summer day,
    Sang this little song: "O how I love to play
    While the flowers are in bloom,
    Still 'tis sweeter far, to pray
    Here beside my mother's tomb."

Yet, this little child at play, had not any trace
    of care;
    Her heart seemed wrapt in joy; she sang
        with lightsome air :
    "O the roses in their bloom,
    Were never half so fair
    As those on mother's tomb!"

I said, "my little child, is your mother buried
    here?"
    And with bright eyes full of joy, she answer-
        ed with no fear:
    "O, sir, she is, she is;
    O, 'tis sweet to be so near—
    Nay, 'tis more, sir, it is bliss!"

But, I said, "my little child, 'tis strange that
    you're not sad,
    Since your mother now is dead!" "O, sir,"
        she said, "I had
    No mother but this one;
    O, should I not be glad
    To be near her though life's gone?"

MAID O' WABASH BANKS.

The cricket broke its lance o' sound
An' sang a song o' warnin',
An' dark the river slept beneath the moon ;
I saw her white arm 'round him wound
In farewell till the mornin',
An' swift the boat swung off to merry tune.

    Oh, silent an' deep is the river that flows
    Beside the low cot where the wild-flower
        grows,
    An' the willows bow down to the waters
        to weep
    With the maiden whose lover was lost in
        the deep.

The rock rose high with craggy side,
    The whirlpool raged about it,
An' inky o'er the bright moon frowned the
    cloud;
His boat shot o'er the waters wide
    His strong arm none could doubt it,
Till from the tide he called in vain so loud!

The mornin' breaks o'er Wabash shores
    Bedecked with bloomy summer,
An' merry birds sing gladly as before;
The fisherman does bend his oars;
    The maiden waits the comer;
But waits and weeps to see him never more.

THE JALAPA MAID.

Thine eye is blue as the skies above
    Thy mountain-home and stream;
Thy cheek is like the velvet rose;
    Thy brow the richest cream;
Thy silken hair falls in thy lap;
    Thy sweet song ne'er disproves thee;
O, may forever blessings fall
    On thee and he who loves thee.

Thy step falls like the soft moonbeams
    In stilly midnight hour;
Thy voice is like the nightingale
    Within the orchid bower;
Thy smile is like the smile of morn,
    And tender passion moves thee ;
O, may forever blessings fall
    On thee and he who loves thee.

'TIS BEST.

O, give me what I would, sweet Hope.
    And I shall ever constant be,
    And love thee tho' on land or sea ;
    Through life ; aye on eternally ;
O, give me what I would, sweet Hope.

"What would I ?" only this, sweet Hope :
    Wisdom, vast, that I may know,
    To conquer every vice and woe
    That to the flesh is heir below;
"What would I ?" only this, sweet Hope.

If thou wilt give me this, sweet Hope,
    I'll touch each paining heart for thee ;
    I'll calm the surges of life's sea,
    And conquer every misery ;
If thou wilt give me this, sweet Hope.

"O, child of earth, if this thou hadst,
    What would be left for me but death ?
    Who then would sigh with fevered breath,
    And worship at my shrine till death,
O, child of earth, if this thou hadst ?"

"Live on, O, child of earth, 'tis best
To know of want, of pain, of woe,
And find a comfort sweet to know,
At my e'er bounteous shrine below;
Live on, O, child of earth, 'tis best."

SUMMER RAIN.

The rain on the green sward is falling;
'Tis a day of sunless rest.
All the forest wide is singing:
"'Tis a day of nature blest."
Running brook swells with a chorus,
Sweeter than its former lay—
"Whither away, O, rain of summer,
Whither away?"

The bee is hid in the sweet magnolia,
Its buzz is hushed in sweet perfume;
Yellow and bold is the ox-eye daisy;
The rose does blush with a sweeter bloom.
"Thou art our strength, O summer rain,"
Sing the forest, vine and spray—
"Whither away, O, rain of summer,
Whither away?"

AUNT ELLEN.

Yes, child, I've walked life's weary way,
Thrice and ten over thy bright years.
Once I were fair and young like thee,
And few were sorrows and few were tears.

I, too, did dream the dream of love,
I those sweet days of long ago,
And all my heart and all my soul,
Thrilled with the bliss I then did know.

As thou, beneath yon old oak tree,
I've sat with one at eventide,
And looked across the misty fields,
And lived in rapture by his side.

And he would say:—(I think I hear
His soft, sad, earnest voice again,)
"Dear Ellen, I am all thine own;
O, may the future bring no pain."

But, none can read the future, child,
For scarce had summer cast its bloom,
When troops were marching by the door,
And cannon roared and all was gloom!

And as he lingered at the gate,
That sweet, sad evening, 'twas the last,
He placed this ring upon my hand,
And held me to his bosom fast.

"I will return," he said, "before
Gay Christmas-time, our wedding day."
Our wedding day! the words were sweet,
But, O, it seemed so far away.

And then came weary days, dear child,
And anxious at the window there,
I looked for postman day by day,
For word or message he might bear.

Thus time ran on; our wedding day
Grew close to hand—just three days hence.
The old world smiled me back to joy,
And filled me with sweet confidence.

And then the postman stopped again,
His anxious eye too plainly said:
"I bear no message now of joy—
I come to tell thee of the dead!"

O, ask me not what followed, child,
My words can never tell it thee;
But wonder not that I should weep:
Ah, Christmas-time is sad to me.

Yes, he was slain! yet I am true.
O, child, I call this after life,
For is it not an after life
Since I a maiden live a wife?

A wife in heart, a wife in thought,
A wife through all my sacred vows,
A wife in all its noble worth—
Pure love forever lives and grows.

But, this, thy wedding day, dear child,
Gay Christmas-time, thou art so glad,
I'll wear a winter rose to-day,
And try, for thee, to not be sad.

AMY DEAN.

Amy Dean, with sad, sad eyes,
Sad and dreamy, sad and sweet;
Amy Dean—no smile, no song
Comes to thee. Lo! we greet
Thee with tokens of true love;
Ever sweetly sad, yet mild;
Ever dreaming of something—
Sadness hath for aye beguiled.

Amy Dean, thou spokest to me;
But thy words were low and sad;
Ah, they seemed to me as sighs;
Yet, they made my heart so glad.
I had thought of many things
I were going to say to thee;
But, alas, thy low, sad voice,
Made me dumb as yonder tree!

Oft on yonder fallow-hill
   I have sat at eventide,
Looking down on thy fair home,
   Yonder 'neath the poplars wide;
Oft at eve I've seen thee glide,
   Phantom like, passed plat and urn,
To the pool beneath the hill—
   Lost in shadows—ne'er return.

Once waited I 'neath yonder oak,
   Gnarled and lightning-cleft and old,
Till the moon hung pale and low,
   And the virgin morning rolled
Through the crystal dews of night,
   When from pool and misty stream
Came sweet voices to my ear!
   Amy, was it all a dream?

Amy Dean, what mysterious spell
   Maketh thee for aye so sad?
Is there virtue in true love
   That can make thy heart grow glad?
Amy, O, one smile from thee
   And my life is life again;
Amy, couldst thou, wouldst thou love;
   Have we loved thee all in vain?

AN OLD STORY.

'Twas in a sylvan spot we met,
     Long ago,
To plight our troth and vow our vows,
     Sweet and low;
And she was fairer than all in life,
And the full ripe passion of love was rife,
     Truly so.

Words with a thrilling love's impress,
     Spoke we there;
Laved in the lucent rays of bliss,
     All was fair.
Ne'er were there sweeter moments in life;
In heart a husband, in heart a wife,
     Each did share.

Distance and time, alas! 'twas fate,
     Still too true,
Smote in twain our troth and vows,
     Silent rue;
And now is that dear old scene of life,
That sweet, pure face through bitter strife,
     Lost to view.

Naught but a mound of earth is left,
     That is all;
There by that shady spot we met,
     Lone and pall;
But if bitter tears could give her life,
And bring her back in heart a wife,
     Sweet their fall.

SHOW ME THE VINTNER.

Show me the vintner who sells a wine—
   Wine of life, to soothe the heart,
That takes away the sting of woe,
   And bids it e'er depart.

Is his shop in the busy town,
   On the street where care does rove,
Where we find more work than rest,
   Where we find more woe than love?

Or is he where grim hunger preys,
   On weak vitals of the soul,
Where are poverty and vice,
   Where life knows naught else but dole?

Say his shop is o'er the sea,
   In some brighter clime than this—
Far off where immortals dwell,
   On the shores of heavenly bliss?

My eyes grow dim, my pulses weak,
   My soul is cramped in fettered life,
My heart does pain, and swell and throb,
   And bitter tears are always rife.

Suffer me not this woe endure,
   Show me the vintner with the wine,
That soothes the heart and calms the soul
   And gives a joy divine.

FALLEN.

O, let thy sad, sad heart dream on
Of things that ne'er shall be:
Drink thou the nectar hope doth brew,
Thus, soothe thy troubled breast,
For little happiness is thine
Since love shall ne'er return;
But O, to know not of the hour
When pleasant dreams have left thee lone,
And hope hath flown away.

O, mayst thou dream the hours away,
Though there's a bitter truth that lies
Deep hidden in thy breast—
A truth that naught can overcome—
The sequel of an unwise love;
Though beauty covers with a smile;
Though day dreams picture future joys;
Alas, for thee! alas, for thee!
Thou loved not wisely, but too well.

O, think not of the end,
The sad, sad, bitter end!
The end when hope lies dead,
And day dreams melt away like dew,
And thou hast wakened to the truth—
The bitterest of all truths,
Which cryeth from the inmost soul,
And ever to the grave!

I would thou wert the fair, the pure
Whom virtue doted on and crowned
The fairest queen, and parent blessed,
And man felt deeply in the soul
A purer feeling as thou passed,
And loved thee—aye he who rules
And sits in lordly state—he
Whom fortune favored with broad fields,
And mansion and all goodly things.

He lingered near to take thy hand,
To love thee on through life;
And make thee happy wife of his,
And if a mother, soothe thy cares,
And give thee wealth and station;
But he was cast aside; no thought
Was given to thy future lot—
Thou wast to live for this!

Thou lingered at the wanton feast,
Where sparkling wine did charm thy heart,
As serpent charms the bird for prey;
Thou lingered till the mellow light
Of morning tinged the window pane,
And then turned slowly from the ball,
At which thy form was closely pressed
By arms controlled by impulse vile,
Fired by debauchery.

The sequel? Ah, 'tis just the same
Old story that we all know well:
Some scoundrel met; a misplaced trust;
And then, too late, the bitter truth:
A promise of some future day
To ease thy grief and thus escape
Responsibilities—Aye, dream—
Hope on—'Twill soothe thy breast;
But, O, the bitter truth!

FAME.

To make a mark in life—
Climb round by round
The ladder of proud Fame
And confront, bound
By high ambition and vanity,
Which nothing short of death
Can damp, the ten thousand
Obstacles of fate, whose breath
Cries unto us as we strive,
The mockery of renown,
The hollowness of fame,
And over which frown
Jealousy, hatred, selfishness, and all
The torments of fame
And the life that weds it.
But, at the summit! Name
You a grander reward
Than that bright garland of honor—
That world-lauded largess, *Fame!*

There wreathed in brightness?
The donor, as we gain the last round
With tired, weary limb,
Aching brow and care worn
Through gazing in dim
Protracted vacancy, then
Arises, meets us, cries,
"All honor be thine; receive thou
The gift that never (?) dies!"
So drop we full lowly at the shrine,
And on our pates,
Made hairless prematurely
By our over anxious thoughts, the Fates,
Who determine all things,
Acting according to their wise wish,
Set the crown--of what? not what we would,
Alas! a sounding brass—a shallow dish
Of honor, on which we are rhymed
To live upon through life. Seeing it
We say, "I would I had not climbed!"

THE POET.

Tune thy harp and sing a strain,
  By this stream, while the night dews fall;
While the moon is young in the east,
  And the fir tree shadows are long and pall.

Sing, to soothe thy heart to rest,
  For thou art aweary, O, poet strange;
The hush of eventide hath come,
  And the yeoman returns from the grange.

Sing while the quiet shadows fall,
  O, poet, for thou art aweary now,
A song of constancy and love,
  To lighten thy heart and brighten thy sad brow.

Thou art to love, but for thee none,
  It dwelleth not for thee, O, poet, here.
Tho' thy heart is young in years,
  Sad and full old hath waxed it, poet drear.

Things more pure art thine than these,
  Thou meetest here in vile array,
O, cease thy sadness, poet strange,
  And pass thy weary life in song away.

I will not disturb thee, poet;
  Sing on to the young moon thy strain,
Till she stands full o'er thee, then
  Adown to sleep and dream of joy that's vain.

FRIENDSHIP.

Friendship is to the heart
What sunshine is to the flower—
Without which it withers and dies;
So, too, the heart that knows no friend.

DADDY'S HOOKY PIPE.

Daddy bought a hooky pipe
  An' paid a silver dollar,
He put it on the mantel-piece
  An' daddy is a scholar;
He put it on the mantel-piece,
  With windin' stem no lack O,
An' after supper by the fire
  He smoked his good tobacco.
    With a puff, puff, puff!
    An' a pull, pull, pull!
The smoke would curl o'er daddy's head
    Till the room was full!

One day I thought the hooky pipe
  I'd try myself for pleasure;
The folks had gone to town to trade
  So I didn't stint the measure.
I filled it an' I lit it an'
  I smoked—my story's ended!
I couldn't tell how long I lay
  Ere my condition mended.
    'Twas a hump, hump, hump!
    An' a pull, pull, pull!
An' I humped an' dumped O, lawsy me!
    Till the room was full!

OLD DYSPEPSIA.

Here he comes with sallow face,
Trembling hand and sunken eye;
All his life is a dreary blank,
None greeteth him, but passeth by.
  He's full of trouble; let him alone;
  He's full of trouble; he maketh but moan;
    He dreadeth to-morrow
    With tears and with sorrow,
    For he feareth some horrow
      Will swallow him up!

All day long he mopeth about
Under his heavy burden of care;
All night long he dreameth wild dreams,
And walketh his silent chamber and drear.
  "I'm full of trouble," he maketh his moan;
  "I'm full of trouble; all hope is gone!
    But, alas, for to-morrow
    With its care and its sorrow,
    And the thoughts of the horrow
      That filleth my cup!"

Sadly he turns from the busy mart
Sadly he turns and his old bones creak;
The warmth and joy of vigorous life
Bringeth no glow to his sunken cheek.
  And he moans in his trouble "Life is vain;
  Oh, why with a smile should I hide my pain?
    When cometh to-morrow,
    It bringeth but sorrow,
    I would I could borrow
      Some rest from my woe!"

Where'er he goes none greeteth him,
In all his woe their pity lend;
A parasite to life is he;
No joy hath he nor any friend;
  And he wept as he passed a bright school
    miss,
  "How varied and changeful a world is this!
    Thou knowest not sorrow,
    O, mayest thou not borrow,
    From subtle to-morrow,
      The grief that I know!"

GOOD NIGHT.

I saw the sun set o'er the hill,
  And the sky grow red the while;
I felt the dew upon my cheek,
  And the harvest moon did smile;
I heard the cricket sing a song,
  And woe was the song it sang;
I heard the far off watch dog bay,
  While the village church bell rang;
But, O, the sad, sad thoughts that rose
  As I passed the lonely grave;
And, O, the bitter tears I shed
  For the dead hopes none could save;
The dead hopes slept in the narrow tomb;
  But the voice of their spirit lingered o'er,
And breathed on the air as I passed by:
  "Good night, good night, forevermore."

TALENT.

This I would say, my friend,
  Truth you will find it;
Each one I'd recommend
  Ever to mind it:
Do what the heart does bid
  Hallowed by virtue;
Talent you strive to crush
  Can not but hurt you.

Each has a sphere to fill—
  Oh, it's a duty;
Work, then, with earnest will;
  Perfect work is beauty.
Reward will surely come,
  Though long the coming.
Never night was so long,
  But came the morning.

It's a far better thing,
  Has said the poet,
If that which we would sing,
  Others may know it.
Not like the unwise man,
  Old, old in story,
Through fear his talent lost,
  With it his glory.

O, TROUBLE NOT MY USELESS DUST.

O, trouble not my useless dust
When given to the worm.
Bring not thy trophies nor thy tears,
When lifeless is my form.
O, pass me by, as now thou dost,
Unmindful of my worth or trust.

Yet, knoweth to the latest, hence
Goeth out my love to thee,
Nor umbrage lingers for a wrong,
Nor progress thou wouldst bar from me.
Just pass me by as now thou dost—
The pure of heart as vilest must.

And, yet, remember, unto those
Who fain would class me as the crude,
I give a broader, deeper love,
That time may turn to something good.
I ask them only pass me by
And let my useless body lie.

Then trouble not my useless dust
When given to the worm;
Tho', not till then doth waken
The heart that would me harm.
I love thee as I love the best;
I pray thee turn and let me rest.

CAN LIFE WITH ALL ITS PLEASURES?

Can life, with all its pleasures,
Give to the longing heart
One joy from all its treasures,
When love does take no part—
When love from love is flying,
On wings so strong and fast,
And the passion's sadly crying,
That all will soon be passed,
That life is short and bitter,
And love's its only balm;
That wealth can only glitter
On the surface when 'tis calm?
Can the heart then scorn its duty—
Forfeit all for wealth's fair hand,
And be happy with its booty
Leaving love to run its sand?

Oft we grasp it in its brightness;
But our joy soon turns to tears,
When we see, too late, its lightness,
In the coming sadder years,
And we say: O, love was duty;
But I chose in lighter thought,
Rather things of transient beauty,
Casting love away as naught.
O, 'tis sad to thus be severed,
To hope and weep alone,
Vainly sadness has endeavored
To soothe with sigh and moan;

THE OLD CHURCH TOWER.

To the old church tower with its ivy vines,
How often I've climbed in the midnight still,
And sat on the beam where the old bell swung
And looked o'er the silent town on the hill.

When the moon was pale, and the old owl's
  hoot
Sent a mysterious thrill to my weary breast,
And the night winds sighed through the climb-
  ing vines;
It seemed 'twas the only place of rest.

I loved, when the clouds hung low and pall,
To climb to the old church tower so gray,
And play on my flute some old love air
Long years ago I used to play.

And it seemed when my heart was sad, and I
Had climbed to the still old dusty tower,
I was above the sins of a wicked world,
And my soul was free from its awful power.

And there I'd rest for many an hour,
And touch the lips and sing the song,
And live again the joys long passed,
With one that's long been gone.

HER GRAVE.

In the chill, damp air of a still midnight,
I stood by a fresh made grave;
The pale moonlight, through the leafless trees,
Fell on the head stone, and the breeze
Whispered low this mournful song:
"Do not rave, do not rave,
Soothe thy heart with hope that's bright;
Life will not be long!"

In the fresh made grave there a fair form lay,
And I dug in the cold, damp ground,
For one more look in her calm, sweet face,
For one more kiss and last embrace,
Ere ceased my quick and fevered breath—
Lonesome place, doleful sound,
As I dug the cold, damp clay
From the grave of death!

In the wan moonlight, with the earth piled
  high,
I opened the coffin lid;
I looked in the face so still and cold,
I kissed the lips and the ring of gold,
I held her fast—my pulses fell!
Life had gone! and amid
Angels I beheld her nigh,
Saying—"All is well!"

THE RUIN.

Wild roses, gay in bud and bloom,
  Bedeck the ruined pile of glory,
And long gone hours seem to rise,
  In melancholy song and story ;
The matted ivy 'round the base,
  Does smile o'er long-forgotten beauty—
Perchance the sacred resting place
  Of hearts that lived for love and duty.

Borne up by fancy, lofty halls—
  Trod by the beauties of old fame,
And gallant knights with sword and plume,
  And warriors of proud name—
I view with pictured walls, and men
  In quaint coats, and waiting maids,
And all the pomp of buried time,
  Arises from the shades.

A silent, sweet, romantic scene ;
  So old in story, new withal ;
So deep in mystery—Ah ! the tales,
  Perchance, could issue from the wall :
Dark crimes—stories of broken hearts—
  A youth that smote a parent, fled
With his fair love from casement high—
  But, hush ! they are all dead.

THROB, THROB MY HEART.

Throb, throb, my heart ! while flow these bitter tears ;
Throb, throb, my heart ! thou hast known this grief for years.
  Do not look back o'er the past
  For the past is gone for aye ;
  But thy sadness e'er shall be
  Till my soul has passed away. !

Throb, throb, my heart ! for the heart thou caused to throb ;
Throb, throb, my heart ! for the soul that thou didst rob—
  Rob of all that's dear to life—
  All, and even hope at last ;
  Ah ! you waken to repent,
  But, too late—too late—'tis passed !

Throb, throb, my heart ! thou shalt never know but pain ;
Throb, throb, my heart ! nor hope for peace again,
  Nor the touch of a gentle hand,
  Nor the smile of a sunny face,
  Nor the love that shone in those trusting eyes,
  Nor those tender words of grace.

Throb, throb, my heart ! thou shalt know but the pangs of woe !
Throb, throb, my heart ! while I weep on my pillow low.
  Through the long, long dreary night,
  Through the toil of the weary day,
  Thou shalt throb with the sorrow of the past
  Till my soul has passed away !

FAR OFF LAND.

We sailed one night, my heart and I,
We sailed, and the moon did light our way,
  To a land, a far off land,
  Where hearts do slumber, and soft winds fanned
My fevered heart till it grew so cold,
So death-like cold, in that far off land.

We loved that land, my heart and I ;
We'd be content to ever stay
  In that land, that far off land,
  Where the heart can rest and the cruel band,
That binds it here, can be severed there—
Severed for aye, in that far off land.

We'll go again, my heart and I,
'Twill be not the moon that will light our way
  To that land, that far off land,
  Where hearts do slumber and soft winds fanned
My fevered heart—'Twill rest forever—
Ever at rest, in that far off land.

THE OLD MAN'S SONG.

Just leave me here and let me sing,
  And dream of other days,
  And wander in my fancy
  In the good old-fashioned ways,
And dabble in the old brook,
  That ripples with bubble and spray;
On its sandy banks so yellow,
  Is where I used to play.

Let me sing away the hours,
  And think of things long past ;
Let me do as fancy prompts me,
  For I am failing fast.
My step is not so firm, my voice
  Does tremble and my eyes
Have weakened, and my heart does know
  The bitterness of sighs.

Just leave me here and let me sing,
  Some good old-fashioned song ;
'Twill cheer my poor old weary soul,
  It won't be with you long.
Just let me drive the spell away
  That time has wrought on me,
By singing with a feeble voice
  Some old-time melody.

THE OLD LOVERS.

Yes, many years, have come and gone
And we've grown old, my own sweet dear,
Old in heart but young in love,
And young in all that love does give;
For life has been a summer day,
And like a summer day been long,
Long and sweet and full of warmth,
Full of light and clouds withal.

Anna, she, our eldest born,
Brought a joy that could not last—
Ah, between our souls we know
Days agone were fraught with pain—
Pain—it clings unto us yet—
Pain that ever shall abide;
Edna, O, my darling wife,
His, 'tis well, His will be done.

She's at rest! O, vainly she
Strove against the subtle ill;
But the long scourge of disease
Smothered out the spark of life.
And her soul's at rest, dear wife,
Yet her spirit gives us strength—
Ah, His will be done, dear wife;
We have found His love is vast.

And Willie—Ah, sometimes there comes
The young war-boy in war attire
And stands beside my midnight bed,
Pale and with a weary look;
So glad to see me, it would seem,
And yet so sad and yet so cold—
The dream does chill me to the heart!

He rests; but where? O, who may say?
He rests, but more we might not know.
They saw him lead the gallant Eighth;
They saw him in the fiercest fight!
They saw him strike for a noble cause—
And we shall see him after while.

Few are the joys without a pain,
Yet, truly, pain may bring us joy;
We may not know it as it is;
But, all things, surely, work aright,
And time does conquer every wrong,
And love can soothe our every grief,
And while the old earth still does smile
And while we live and yet may hope,
O, let us cling to that sweet rest
That's found within our own pure love.

In looking back o'er many years,
To summer days of long ago,
There sweetly smile the golden rod,
And myrtle bed rimmed with the rose,
And trellis cloyed with many a vine,
And ivy plat and jasmine—
Ah, still a sweeter flower was there,
I knew it then; I know it now.

And love sprang up and summer lent
A finish to the lovely flower,
And with an eager grasp I clung
To all its mild and winning bloom,
To all its lovely, strange, sweet moods,
Till I had plucked it all mine own.
And when the marriage bells rang clear
I clasped you to my breast, I knew
We lived in heart a man and wife,
And all our being shaped to one.

Come, let us read of old-time love—
Those sweet love letters, brown with age.
Untie the ribbon that has grown,
Like your pure lips, a trifle pale.
Yes, darling, read, that we may live
Anew those sweet, thrice sweet old days—
Love was the savor of our lives,
Love was the action of our souls.

TO EDNA, NEW YEAR'S EVE, 1827.

Edna, love is full and free,
Love is life for thee and me.
Thy pure heart this New Year's eve
Casts a hope that can not deceive:
  Though the wind is wild
  In the old pine trees,
  And sings a sad song
  Of the dying year,
  Yet a heart full of love
  Never agrees
  With things that are sad,
  And things that are drear.
  I send thee my love
  This New Year's eve;
  Wilt thou accept it?
  It shall not deceive.

Edna, thou my heart's sweet boon,
Treasured like some sweet love tune;
But above all earthly choice—
Love eyes, harmonized with voice
  Though the wind is wild,
  In the old pine trees
  And sings a sad song
  Of the dying year;
  It moves not the heart
  That love doth ease;
  It moves not the heart,
  For naught doth it fear.
  I send thee my love,
  It shall not deceive,
  Wilt thou accept it
  This New Year's eve?

Edna, there is that gives us joy;
Maxims and theories but annoy.
True love sprang from a germ of love,
False love cloyed whene'er it strove—
  And the wind is wild
  In the old pine trees.
  May the false love die,

With the dying year;
But, O, for a heart
That with heart agrees;
True love with a smile,
Perchance a tear—
I send thee my love;
It can not deceive;
Wilt thou accept it
This New Year's eve?

"Ah, young heart foolish in its love!"
I'd say if it were not mine own;
But have I cause for chiding it,
Now in the mellow days of age?
No, sweetest love! If I again
Were placed back in those old love haunts,
Matured heart and thought as now,
I'd but repeat it all again!

Come read the one I sent to you
When I was sad—you said, love sick!
The day when the young, gallant West,
Just home from college, called on you.

TO EDNA—AFTER COMMENCEMENT.

I'll seek the solitude,
Pathetic solitude, be free
From all this bickering world,
  Rest quietly.
Peace! peace! thou hast a wrinkle
  On thy brow;
Stay, ceaseless stars, to twinkle
  Ever now
For what is life
When love is fled?
What was before
  Alas! is dead.

Come, give me a smile,
  My Edna;
My sadness beguile,
  My Edna;
I am weary and sick;
As dumb as a brick;
But as straight as a stick
  In dignity—
And full as a tick
Is full of blood,
Of love that is pure
  And constant and good.
Edna, mysterious, sweet and mild,
Give me thy heart for mine is wild,
  And I shall be true
  Ever, ever be true,
Till my hair is gray and my days are few!

I see the smile on your fair cheek,
Which seems as fair as in those days
When, wayward, you would play some prank
On my poor heart!
Come, it is sweet to hear those rhymes,
So simple, silly too, and soft;
But, O, my old heart loves them so,
Much over her who gave them birth.
Now, Edna, read the one I sent
By Stafford's boy—the valentine.
I carry its echo in my heart
And there it shall for aye abide.

THE VALENTINE.

This token I sent to thee, true love,
  Edna, sweet Edna of Willow Grove,
  For aye I'll love with purest love,
Edna, sweet Edna, of Willow Grove;
And my life's sweetest duty,
Is the care of one of beauty.
And I shall be thine for aye
For true love comes to stay.

This token I send to thee, true love—
  I shall be thine for aye.
Sorrow will visit us many a day,
Sorrow will come but love shall not rove.
And when thy locks are hoary
I'll sing thee love's sweet story,
And I shall be thine for aye
For true love comes to stay.

I love those little glints of love;
Like you, age only makes more dear;
I cannot think them folly's quips,
And yet may call them little less.
We've lived and loved so long, forsooth,
One long, uninterrupted day
Of love and loving, loved, beloved!
I scarce can reckon when 't began.

So many things to reckon out—
It all has been a joyous feast!
The shade that came upon the shine
Did only sweeten more our bliss—
The bliss of living, you and I,
Together thro' these sad, sweet years.
But shine and shade are grief and joy;
And love is fortress over all.

Yet one more kiss, my dear, sweet wife;
The old church clock chimes twelve;
The fierce wind cuts the midnight vast,
And cries among the eaves.
Let me take your hand in mine;
Let me hold you to my breast.
My tears are not of sadness—no;
They come of joy from the heart!
Ah, ours, in truth, is love most pure;
Let us kneel in prayer—let us thank our God.

BATTER CAKES.

There's better cakes 'n batter cakes
  An' air a thousan' miles from here,
An', yit, a man can eat 'em

When he's hungry, don't you fear!
Take 'em when there's maple lasses—
They're away ahead o' sasses—
An' they eat first-rate fer breakfus
 'Long about that time o' year.

People in the city likes 'em
 Better 'n us people that's fret
With 'em through a natural lifetime
 'Way out here on Willer Creek.
Folks that's been brung up on baker's
Bread an' knick-knacks, if pertakers,
Thinks that they air 'bout the nicest
 Things, I guess, they ever et.

Many a time at J. P. Waddy's
 Resturant, I've seen before now,
When I've been to town an' dropped in
 Fer a little snack, you know,
Fellers jest a-goin' fer em';
Thunder an' lightnin' wouldn't skeer 'em
From their batter cakes an' lasses,
 Ner hardly nothin' else, I 'low.

There they set, an' shore as glory,
Some was that tarnation full they
Jest set there an' licked their knives
 An' laughed a perfect roar—
'Peared to sort o' dread to leave 'em;
An' I hardly could believe 'em
Raily so infatuated
 Till they said, they'd take some more!

HOME.

Home, that dear old resting place;
 The brightest spot on earth to all;
Sweet comfort 's there in all its grace;
 And joys we ever do recall.

There, too, and sweet, is mother's smile;
 How oft in after years we see
That same sweet, tender look the while
 We're lost in fondest memory.

The golden hours slipt swiftly by—
 The days of childhood's pure delight;
"Too soon, too soon they passed," we sigh,
 Those transient, halcyon days so bright.

We wander on through life, but can
 We ever gain so bright a goal?
O, is there offered unto man,
 Else dearer to his weary soul?

"That little home, may it be blessed,"
 We sigh when evening time draws near;
"I would, sweet home, within thee rest,
 To-night, old home, to me so dear."

A THEME SUPREME.

We reckon all our hopes for years
 And find but few were naught but vain:
Still was their transient solace sweet—
 A balm that soothed our fear and pain.
And thus we say: sweet hope, sweet hope,
 Though blindly after thee we grope,
Though seldom know thee as thou art,
 Still thou hast comfort for the heart.

True; joys may come to lift the cloud
 That hovers o'er the burdened soul;
And gifts may providence bestow,
 And fortune smile on us, and dole
Give way to peace and goodly things;
 But not to these the spirit clings,
But hope! that they may ne'er depart;
 Thus hope is dearer to the heart.

'Tis but the hope of that sweet rest
 That's promised to the soul of man
That lifts him from the viler walks
 And purifies as naught else can.
Oh, is there that in weary life,
 Of all the things to mortal rife,
Which, should sweet hope for aye depart,
 Could bring such comfort to the heart?

QUINTESSENCE.

When weary days have gone forever by
And all the goodness of the heart is known,
Then shall the virtue of the viler soul
Cast out the dregs, the bitterness, the sins—
Be penitent for all; the ruthful eye
Brimful of tears. O, heart, free from thy woe,
With not a trouble o'er the breast to roll,
But pure and like a child's, the soul begins
To know peace comes through pain; the other
 things
That sweeten life, alone are love and truth—
They go to make man humble, strong and good;
Yet goodly things are his who sweetly sings
His heart within the sacred home of youth,
And worships at the shrine of motherhood.

MISDIRECTED.

There's little in the happy eye
 By which may seem a blessing sure;
There's little in the trusting heart
 By which may seem it does endure;
There's little in the toiling soul
 That counts for anything of praise;
Too common, common are its plaints;
 Too common, common are its ways.

Strife seizes the unwary one—
  Youth in the subtle path of life;
And sordid motives lead the heart
  And weary days yet double strife.
I pity hapless, unwise youth
  That lives for great things ne'er to be—
E'er hoping for a haven fair
  Yet drifting farther out at sea.

A BIG RICH MAN.

When I was a boy I was poor without alloy,
And our little Hoosier home was always needy;
I worked hard every day without a thought o'
    pay,
And the clothes I wore were very, very seedy;
But one day, with mirth and song, a big rich
    man came along
And said, "My boy, you're doing all you can;
Here's a little purse for you and a dollar in it,
    too,
Now go and be a big rich man!"

  So you see I am a big rich man;
  Yes, indeed; just you beat me if you can!
  I have property and lands;
  Lots o' business on my hands,
  For you see I am a big rich man!

Just a dollar, nothing more, but I turned it
    o'er and o'er,
Till I had enough to buy a little farm;
Then I bought a spotted calf for two dollars
    and a half,
And built a little barn to keep it warm.
I also bought a pig, and a little two wheeled
    rig,
And all I did was work and work and plan,
And I loaded all my cares on a donkey with
    long ears,
Till I grew to be a big rich man!

THE ICY VINES O' WINTER.

The icy vines o' winter rasp
  The trellis with a sigh,
An' moanin' bows the old oak by the door.
The snow birds, discontented, twit
  Around the gable high,
As sharp the wind comes blowin' more an'
    more.

An' hangin' long an' dagger-like
  From last night's drippy eaves,
The clear icicles tempt the jolly bud,
An', whiz! a frisky current blows
  The fine snow up his sleeves,
An' makes him halloo an' his fingers rub!

With wistful eye an' easy ear,
  Stands at the frosty pane,
A maid, whose heart for her fond lover swells,
I see a blush suffuse her cheek,
  As, far across the plain,
She sees him come an' hears his merry bells.

But, O, adown the snow drift lane,
  Pale, hungry, pinched with cold,
Sits poor old Aunty Gray o'er scanty fire,
An' twixt her shiverin' an' her sighs,
  She murmurs, "I am old—
My sufferin' to rest but draws me nigher."

I WOULD THAT WE HAD PARTED.

I would that we had parted
  Ere to me you proved untrue;
Now, instead of broken-hearted,
  I'd have sweet thoughts of you—
Sweet thoughts of you would lighten,
  When heavy grew my heart,
Your smiles thro' fancy brighten,
  Tho' we were miles apart.
Oh, I'd give the hopes of heaven,
  Had you only proven true;
Tho' the sin be ne'er forgiven;
  I'd give them ne'er to rue.

Oft I'd hear your words so tender,
  When the twilight's mellow hush,
Wrapped the old wood over yonder,
  In the mantle of a blush.
And I'd thrill when blissful fancy,
  Joined our lips in sweetest kiss,
And you called me dearest Nancy;
  But the bitter truth is this—
Oh, I would that we had parted,
  Ere to me you proved untrue,
Now, instead of broken-hearted,
  I'd have sweet thoughts of you.

YOU CHOOSE THE HEART.

You choose the heart that never yet
  Did aught for love but it to spurn,
And yet you love with no regret—
  Content if there be no return.

You ask, at least, there be somewhat
  Of kindly feeling for your love.
Oh, ask, I pray you, even not
  That little you are dreaming of.

You choose the heart that never yet
  Did aught for love but it to spurn;
But, oh, it loved in deep regret,
  A love that never shall return.

YOU AND I TOGETHER.

Let us, dear one, walk together,
  On life's brief tho' weary journey;
Clasping hands, that naught may sever
  Our affections till the end.
Not to be as others want us;
  That their chidings may prevail,
'Gainst our pledge o' faith to daunt us,
  With the trials it may lend.

Let us, dear one, walk together;
  It is best for you and me.
Tho' our path may brighten never,
  We can help each other best—
Better than some strange hand, dear one,
  Tho' it seem more fair than ours;
While together we shall fear none,
  Lie together down to rest.

LITTLE THINK YOU O' THE DAY.

Little think you o' the day,
  That has passed forever by;
Little heed you when they say,
  Broken-hearted she did die.

I can see in fancy yet,
  Her false lover proud an' grand;
Round her eyes I read regret,
  As she holds him by the hand.

I can hear her pleadin' an'
  See him spurn her—hear his curse!
To her heart, the awful ban,
  Was a thousand times the worse!

Justice only was her wrath;
  Blighted love an' ruined name!
All along her dreary path,
  There were only grief an' shame.

Lo! they found him by the stream,
  With a dagger in his breast.
Cold her heart, they said, did seem,
  When they laid him to his rest.

But I mind me o' the day
  That has passed forever by;
Well I know they need not say—
  Broken-hearted she did die.

GONE.

Gone are the happy days
  Of boyhood fun and frolic;
Gone are the happy days,
  The stone bruise and the colic.

And through sad years I sail,
  Never, never more to hail
The rattle of the tin can
  On our yaller dog's tail.

Gone is the swimming hole
  In which we boys did wallow,
And gone, alas! the old school-house,
  That set adown the hollow.
And gone the crooked pin,
  And the old school-teacher thin,
With his look of deep dejection,
  When the point went in.

MANY A DAY.

Many a day we've gone a wandering
  O'er these gay, green fields;
Now, alas, I'm sadly pondering
  O'er what time reveals.
Mary, ah, there was a time,
When our hearts like some sweet rhyme,
Were united in their bliss;
Did you dream 'twould end like this?

Many a day we've gone a wandering
  O'er these gay, green fields,
Little thinking we were squandering
  All that true love yields.
Mary, tho' the marriage vow,
Binds you to another now,
Can you, can you quite forget,
With no feeling of regret?

I KNOW A MAID WITH DREAMY EYES.

I know a maid with dreamy eyes,
  Whose drooping lashes touch her cheeks,
Cheeks, ever blushing when she speaks,
And speaking ever through her sighs.

But oh, believe me, for in truth
  I know none other quite so vain;
  Her greatest joy is causing pain
To the unwary heart of youth.

When sweet May days of yesteryear
  Blew fragrant over blossoming hill,
  She led me at her own sweet will,
With sacred vow sealed with a tear.

But when had bleak November come,
  And all the windy hill was sear,
  Her vow was broken with a jeer
The day she was to bless my home.

Oh, trust not thou her dreamy eyes,
  Whose drooping lashes touch her cheeks,
  Their subtle dreaminess but seeks
To fill the trusting heart with sighs.

THE BLIND BEGGAR.

Tired of the long day's road,
  I fain would seek repose ;
I fain would rest my burning eyes,
  Forgetting all my woes.

I try to smile at pleasant thoughts,
  I try to have them stay;
I try to be as once I was,
  To drive my grief away.

But, oh, 'tis vain; the woe is mine;
  I'm traveling o'er its road;
If for a moment it is gone,
  It brings a greater load—

Greater, it seems, than I can bear,
  And yet I bear, I'll bear far more ;
The woe is mine; ah, let it come ;
  Hard storms are soonest o'er.

Grief circled, with unceasing pain,
  My weary eyes have sought the way;
Far up and down is life a blank,
  My vision is dismay !

Home of my youth were cool and sweet;
  The lofty maples nod to thee;
Oh, could I know thee as of old,
  What peace and joy for me.

I have a woe thou canst not heal,
  I love thee, but there's no release.
O, had I stayed, old home, with thee,
  I might now rest in peace.

NAN.

Nan Gant, the can-can't,
  Which ever way her notion bent,
Deared me an' jeered me,
  An' to me many a dollar lent.

Then here's a glass with Charlie Bright,
  With little care, if any;
An' here's good luck to every one
  An' long life to my Nanny.

Nan Gant, the can-can't,
  Is like a kitten with a ball ;
She baits me an' hates me,
  An' says she loves me best o' all.

O, SORROW DEEP WITHIN MY HEART.

O, sorrow deep within my heart,
  And O, regret, so vast in pain,
Desist a little till again
  I man me for my bitter part.

A little now ! thy branding fire
  Consumeth all my wasting life ;
O, free me from the wrong-waged strife;
  That robs me of all life's desire.

Hold thou ! if pity thou hast known,
  I struggling pray thee, pale and weak ;
Lo ! thou the hollow in my cheek
  Hath sunken to the aching bone !

Where hope doth end there wisdom dies;
  Where sin is rife there virtue falls ;
Tho' ever loud-voiced justice calls,
  It heedeth not the heart that cries.

O, sorrow deep within my breast,
  And O, regret, so vast in pain,
Ere I take up my load again,
  I pray thee for a little rest.

MARION.

O, tender beauty, sweet little Marion ;
  Jewel of purity and divine love ;
Woman whom man doth plant in the soul,
  And seal in the heart, ne'er forget ;
But on, on forever, where'er he may rove,
  O'er rose paths of summer, or where dark seas roll,
Thy sweet image ever is dear to the heart ;
  Tho' no more to see thee shall never depart.

LOVE'S REVENGE.

He used to say he loved me
  And spoke of future bliss ;
But O, to-night, before my eyes,
  His loving bride did kiss.
She was so pale and beautiful,
  And he kissed her so tenderly,
And smiled and spoke, in a way that woke,
  Sweet rapture once in me.

And yet I should not yearn for him,
  Tho' deep within my breast
There bide regrets the bitterest
  That e'er robbed heart of rest.
Tho' my soul weeps o'er the ashes
  Of the hopes that so early died,
I must wear the smile of yore the while
  I gaze on his lovely bride.

Oh, I wonder if he had forgot,
  As he passed so gallantly,
With his new-made bride upon his arm,
  The vows he made to me ?
And yet I cannot chide him now,
  Tho' my life no joy does see ;
Perhaps to-night, it's no more than right,
  I should weep as he wept for me.

THE GIRL HE LEFT BEHIND.

There's a light in the parlor window,
  And a fire in the parlor grate ;
There's a happy heart at the oaken door,
  That longingly does wait ;
There are hurried steps on the pathway,
  And loving arms entwined,
For the sailor boy returns again
  To the girl he left behind.

Then here's to the girl, the sweet, true girl,
  So loving and so kind ;
We'll sing of her yet, for who can forget
  The girl that was left behind?

Oh, the parting was sad and bitter,
  For duty and love were at stake ;
But love must wait when duty calls,
  Tho' hearts in their sadness break.
Oh, long were the days and weary ;
  But a blessing at last we find,
When we think of the sailor boy's return
  To the girl he left behind.

DEAR ROCK-A-BYE.

Go to sleep, my sweet little baby,
  While mamma rocks you gently, little dear,
And sings to you the sweet little song,
  That you always love to hear,
About the little mother bird,
  Way up in the greenwood tree ;
And all about her nice little home,
  And her babies one, two, three.

Dear, rock-a-bye—
Rock-a-bye, my baby ;
Rock-a-bye, my baby, don't you weep ;
  Papa's gone to town
To buy you such a pretty gown;
Oh, go to sleep, my baby, go to sleep.

The little mother bird named her babies :
  Itty, Mitty, Bitty, and she said,
"You must be very careful, my sweet little dears,
  And keep in your cozy little bed,
And I'll sing you a sweet little song
  Every morning, at break o' day,
And swing you in the cool, green boughs,
  Till with mamma you can fly away."

So, you, my sweet little baby,
  Like the little birds, must have mamma's care,
And mamma's arms are your cozy little nest,
  And she'll rock you in the old rocking chair
    And sing to you a sweet little song,
Like the little mother bird at early day,
  And when your little limbs grow strong
You may run and jump and play.

MISFORTUNE'S QUEEN.

Sweet little maid,
  With flowers in her hair
  And old ragged dress ;
  Begging in happiness ;
Heedless of care.

All patience and smiles ;
So fair and so pure.
  Ah, heaven is kind
  That joy she may find
In the life she does endure.

Sweet little queen
  Of misfortune ! yet
  Happy in song,
  All the day long,
With no regret.

CHARLIE'S WOMEN.

Where have all your women gone Charlie, Charlie;
  Where have all your women gone and left you here to sigh ?
They have gone to seek a lover lady, lady ;
  They have gone to seek a lover handsomer than I.

Your brow is white as cotton Charlie, Charlie;
  Your cheeks are like the roses, your eyes the deepest blue.
Like you, they called me handsome lady, lady;
  Like you, they called me handsome, but not one did prove true.

Did they tell you that they loved you Charlie, Charlie;
  Did they tell you that they loved you oh, will you tell me now ?
Yes, they told me that they loved me lady, lady;
  They told me that they loved me, and made me many a vow !

What did you give them Charlie, Charlie;
  What did you give them, what did you give them fine ?
I gave them precious jewels lady, lady;
  I gave them silks and satins and I gave them rosy wine.

When did they leave you Charlie, Charlie;
  When did they leave you, oh Charlie, tell me true?
When they had all my money lady, lady ;
  When they had all my money, 'twas then from me they flew !

Do not grieve for your women Charlie, Charlie;
But fly with me, Charlie, from women false
    and vain.
Oh, leave me in my sorrow lady, lady;
Oh, leave me in my sorrow; I can never love
    again.
I will take you to my palace Charlie, Charlie;
I will take you to my palace on yonder moun-
    tain high.
I can never, never trust you lady, lady;
But on your snowy bosom, O, lady, let me die!

THE CHANGE.

O, happy soul, your light did burn
    In vanity for many years;
Love of the powers of earth enthralled
    And led you thro' a vale of tears.
When tender friend reproved you mild,
    Fears of the outward change prevailed,
And thus the swelling tide of woe
    Had borne you till your strength had failed.
But came an hour of hallowed peace—
    A sweet and pleasant hour of rest;
No more to weep o'er doleful thought,
    Nor drown the sigh in stupid jest,
Nor battle with the dread of death,
    Nor long for good things but with fear;
Yes, came a sweetest, calmest hour—
    The voice of mercy lingered near,
And said, "Away, ye earthly joys;
    Away, ye tempters of the mind,
False as the smooth, deceitful sea
    And empty as the whistling wind!"

OH, CHIDE ME NOT DARLIN'.

Oh, chide me not darlin' tho' weary o' lovin';
    Tho' ties once so fond may be broken to-day.
Oh, think o' the time when your sweet smiles
    were provin',
Your love for me darlin'; they'll haunt me
    alway.

You take back the tokens o' love that I've
    cherished;
You gave them with blessin'; I return them
    with rue;
And, oh, when I think o' the sweet hopes that
    perished,
Too bitter the tears I go weepin' for you.

Last night, in my dreams, with you I went
    rovin',
Thro' dear scenes so often love led us before,
And oh, as we stood by the mill wheel slow
    movin',
You leapt from my arms and I saw you no
    more.
Some said that another you'd loved that ne'er
    wooed you,
And some said a secret you held in your
    breast;
But, oh, when at last from the dark wave they
    showed you,
They found for my love you had sadly sought
    rest.

Oh, darlin', lest fate should for aye our hearts
    sever,
Let's cling to the sweet love o' yore that we
    knew,
An' of your sweet smiles I'll tire, darlin', never;
I'll be happy with lovin' an' livin' for you.

WHAT CAN I WANT BESIDE?

What can I want beside,
    Nor gold, nor jewels rare,
Since thou art mine own bride,
    So tender, pure and fair?

Perennial flower o' love
    That wooes to blissful dream;
Thine eyes as stars above,
    Thy voice as sweet-toned stream.

But, oh, thy greatest worth
    Is true and loving heart;
What else on this whole earth
    Compares with what thou art?

What can I want beside,
    Nor gold, nor jewels rare,
Since thou art mine own bride,
    So loving, true and fair?

WOMAN'S HEART.
FIRST VOICE.

Oh, who can trust a woman's heart?
    Though fond and gentle words beguile,
Though kind and loving beam her eyes,
    Though sweet and tender is her smile—
Oh, who can trust a woman's heart?

Oh, who can trust a woman's heart?
    Though she be purity's bequest,
Though she all loveliness and grace,
    Though she with holiness is blest—
Oh, who can trust a woman's heart?

Oh, who can trust a woman's heart?
    Though she should kneel at sacred shrine,
Though she should lift her voice to God,
    Though she should with immortals shine—
Oh, who can trust a woman's heart?

SECOND VOICE.

Oh, who can trust a woman's heart!
 Thank heaven, legions trust and love:
Leave, foul misogynist, nor look
 Where thine own mother dwells above,
Till thou canst trust a woman's heart.

Oh, who can trust a woman's heart!
 May all the mercy of our God
Be turned to soul-consuming fire,
 And burn man to a lifeless clod!
When none shall trust a woman's heart.

A PROEM.

I give to you whate'er I've wrote;
 You read me right, you read me well;
You read me wrong, time sure will tell
When praise shall chide that's rightly sought.

THE SINGERS.

The mother sang a baby song
 Of sweet and pleasing little words—
"Oh, precious jewel of my heart;
 Fair brother of the flowers and birds;
Oh, go to sleep on mamma's breast;
 So tired of your broken toy,
A little bit to sleep and rest
 In mamma's arms, my baby boy.

"Sweet eyes that look so fondly up
 And smile at mamma while she sings,
Have tired, truly, mamma knows
 Of looking at their dull playthings.
But baby, baby when the day
 Is folded in the arms of night
There comes the sweetest, sweetest joy—
 'Tis papa's kiss, our hearts' delight!"

Another young in motherhood,
 A babe held to her sunken breast,
And with a joyless heart she tried
 To sing the little one to rest.
She brushed away a trickling tear—
 "Oh, go to sleep, my boy," she said,
And looking in her face it smiled;
 She sighed, "I would that we were dead."

Long at a picture on the wall
 She gazed, then kissed the child forlorn.
"You never saw your father's face,
 Sweet boy; he died ere you were born."
And sobbing held her aching heart—
 "Oh, go to sleep, sweet babe," she said,
And looking in her face it smiled;
 She sighed, "I would that we were dead."

OH, CHIDE ME NOT THO' WEARY HOURS.

Oh, chide me not tho' weary hours
 Weigh heavy on your restless heart,
For once I strewed your path with flowers;
 You prayed that we should never part;
But now you smile in other eyes,
 And teach the lesson you taught me;
But mine did end in saddest sighs
 And hopes, alas! to never be.

The little words you used to like—
 The little nothings, sweet and kind,
Now seem in cruelness to strike—
 No welcome in your heart they find.
And little acts that used to please,
 And brought the blush of maiden love,
Now only, darling, seem to tease
 And vex you when my love they prove.

And all my pleasing ways of yore
 Are faults you chide me for to-day;
And "the undying love is o'er"
 With you, you coldly to me say.
You chide me many a weary hour;
 I weep as you have wept for me;
You hate me with a secret power
 From which I never shall be free.

IT'S NOT THE WORK.

It's not the work but it's the worry
 That leads us tottering to the grave,
And thitherward care makes us hurry
 And few indeed does mercy save.
And those whose hearts are full of kindness,
 So often are the first to fall,
And those who love so often find less
 Of the sweetness than the gall.

How few of the sweet hopes we cherished,
 In the blissful dream of youth,
Live to-day; the sweeter perished,
 Leaving us the bitter truth.
Even old friends lose the cheery
 Words that used to thrill the heart,
And of sorrowing grown aweary—
 Spirits longing to depart.

And the old home and the beauty
 Of the old-time scenes so dear,
Lose their charms when sordid duty
 Drives away affection's tear.
And the old songs lose there sweetness;
 Tho' we love them—love them best—
Love them for their sweet completeness
 And the hearts they soothed to rest.

Oh, the swift-winged hours grow dreary
 When the hair begins to turn;

Happy youth and time so merry,
  Deign but our gray hair to spurn.
What, in this wide world of ours,
  Changes not within a day?
Liken we not to the flowers—
  Joy more brief, by far, than they?

You would chide me, and by chiding,
  But reveal the selfsame theme,
That your heart from you is hiding—
  "Life is but a troubled dream."
Smiling thro' the woes that gall us—
  Cheerful with a heavy breast—
Comforting, whate'er befall us—
  Tired—aweary—fain would rest.

DESTINY.

Though on the pages of the past
  Shines all that feeble man has wrought,
'Tis but the prologue to the play—
  The play of eternal thought.
True, wonders rise on wonders;
  Time, O, mighty teacher, Time!
O, when will you have done your course
  And comment cease in petty rhyme?

Bright thoughts arise from day to day
  To prompt the heart to better deed;
But, O, the mighty power of time
  Does level all. Some sow their seed
In fertile soil; some by the wayside—all
  Sow that time may sometime bring
A reward—great or small.

Thus unto time we cast our thoughts,
  And tho' years on years may grind,
Wait with brightest hopes, at last
  To find we sowed the wind.
But look! yon tottering hoary head,
  Who lived in want; in hovel rude;
Has reaped a harvest rich and rare—
  Has lived to know his God.

CHEERFULNESS.

As the springtime cheers the heart,
    Cheerfulness does cheer;
As a smile bids care depart,
    Cheerfulness does bid;
Tho' the mourner lowly kneels,
Keenly bitter anguish feels,
Aching heart and burning eye
May be soothed from tear and sigh
    Cheerfulness does soothe.

As the soft winds sweetest song
    Cheerfulness does sing
As the day tho' e'er so long
    Cheerfulness does stay
As the sweetness of the flowers
Brewed in mellow summer bowers
Where the cricket's melody
Thrills with mistic ecstasy
    Cheerfulness is sweet.

SONNETS OF PASSION.

I

O, why has time destroyed the magic spell,
That love did kindle with her dreamy eyes?
O, why vain hope, that time would sometime
    tell
The truth that love so many times denies?
Most to my heart, I can not beg it stay;
Most to my best of dearest prizes lost;
Locked in my breast with hope but for a day—
Grief's comfort for love's pleasure and its cost.
Light, as from heaven in the lonely night,
So gently 'cross the dreary grange that fell
To lead the fainting wanderer on aright,
So, I was led, love, by love's magic spell.
I weep to lose it now with parting kiss,
Since it all grief and sorrow turned to bliss.

II

Why try to paint those shifting scenes of love?
Tho' passion, greatest master of the art,
Creation never wrought that did less prove,
Than mighty *He*, shall know not love's own
    heart.
To paint the gentle face, the dreamy eye,
That holds the blue of heaven captive there;
To paint the pure brow that sacredly,
In silken tresses, o'er it hangs the hair;
To paint sweet beauty's inspiration when
Heavenly touches seem the efforts prove—
This can the master painter called of men;
But can not paint those shifting scenes of love.
Why try to paint those mingling griefs and
    joys,
That to retain, the painter but destroys?

III

O, think not strange, tho' blandly argument,
Does prove me false, that I should not deny,
Since I, those fondest tokens do relent,
For love's own sake, and since for love I sigh.
"Peruse these worthy motives," you relate,
"And then gainsay that you are justified!"
You say, and ask no more than this; then
    wait
No longer; but adieu, why linger at my side?
Love has no argument or caveling word;
It only speaks when inspiration proves
Its presence thrilling with love for reward:
He's surest false by argument who loves.
Why should I argue love to lose its charm?
Love holds poor argument that does no harm.

IV

To whom is love a convert humbly bowed?
Ah, not to him beseeching most her love;
And not to him who handsome is and proud;
Nor yet to him whose wealth immense does prove;
Nor yet again to him who victory gains;
Nor him who heaven makes good and worthiest;
Nor him who in the highest station reigns;
And least to humble spirit tho' the best.
All these know love in many a mood and dress,
And choose their lots as love and fancy fit;
But love bows but to one in humbleness,
And that is unto him of brain and wit.
For love looks up to strength of greatest worth;
And wisdom unto truest love gives birth.

V

O, sadly I confess the fated hour,
That severs us, draws nearer with its pain;
Seems nature sighing; bows the summer flower,
Like to some troubled mourner to complain.
'Tis not enough, that we in grief express,
The pangs that suffer love to parting hands;
But seem deep sympathy and tenderness
To laden everything with sorrow's bans.
Loving, parting, wailing needs must come;
Yet, O, how vile abuse it is to bear:
Fate-forced into the mighty wave and foam,
Of that grim ocean which is called despair.
O, why did fate a parting hour decree,
That hope can not engage nor grief can flee?

VI

I so far prove that better those delights,
Which active are with kindness honor yields;
That while the poet sings fierce battles fights,
Thus authorizing praise's loud appeals.
So love, do I delight the joy suffice,
That gently love does rhyme my being to;
Such pure delight; the soul's rejoicing price
Is reckoned only by the worth of you.
I give my suffering for offended sake
Of gentle love, whose honor is her name—
Poor woman, who forbears, tho' heart would break;
Or keeps a love that does embrace her shame.
Lest grief her happy treasure should invite,
Love should not trust to less than honor bright.

VII

What is there in a promise that delays,
Till gracious patience deigns to envy time,
That like a subject whose purport conveys
An argument against its own true theme?
For love, so is your own; do you deny
Inconstancy your promise has construed
Till changefulness and smiles my heart defy?
How can I make you make your promise good?
Come, love, have done with this forlorn degree
To which poor patience has been dragged for you,
I do beseech; come, will you hear my plea?
Your promise now is full twelve months past due.
Why promise go for nothing that is fair,
That you delight that lover should despair?

VII

Tho' glorious over summer's bloomy glades,
Does mighty Sol course onward with the day;
Tho' mighty be his light it quickly fades,
And with the twilight fainter dies away;
But in my heart the love-light of your eye
Ne'er wanes but brighter grows forever there;
What matter tho' the weary day goes by,
At night it brightness sheds beyond compare.
By hap that I complain of cloud and rain,
Of lowery tempest, time of harvest moon,
One tear, ten thousand times, would cause more pain,
That tender love's bright light should cloud so soon.
'Tis from the eye reflects love's purest ray,
Increasing in its might to endless day.

IX

Do I recall the words that I have spoke
That I too cruel being prove for love?
Flattery many a trusting heart has broke,
And truest love of fewest words does prove,
Else heart speaks from its fullness unawares.
I've been so quiet, since, by chance, we met;
Before my moods were gay, not given to fears;
Nor bitter tears for years these eyes have wet;
Now, when you say you are to leave me soon,
My anguish burst confessing from my heart—
How much I love my love of happy June—
My grief confessing love since we must part.
And, so 'tis faulty heart again at bay,
'Tis best to never love than to delay.

X

Lest you should think that fortune's golden horn,
Does every rack and thorn of life destroy—
The clouds dissolve before the happy morn,
That forth, with smiling face, you fly with joy,
That wealth heals every wound, no matter what,
Unknowing one, know that this glitter is
The fever of deceit, disparaged not,
Behind its mask, the region of love's bliss.
Roses and fountains know of adverse hours
Of storm, and thorns oft dainty fingers prick;
That love survives the death of autumn flowers,
Trust love to only love, love's pleaful pick.
Tho' wealth is good and speaks, forsooth, its need,
'Tis best that love have none than widow-weed.

XI

Ah, what is this commotion of the heart,
Since rapture has enveigled loneliness,
This thief of every gift it does impart,
This donor of a myriad thrills of bliss?
If it be love then I am blest for aye;
If it be it, then it, it surely is:
O, how can I rebuke the fate I weigh
In such a scale, e'er tipping to me bliss?
Should I deny this wage against my heart,
Because I cannot name it certain, sure?
Not I, for why should I from bliss depart,
If but in guessing happiness secure?
I'll coin a word, by love allowing me,
And call such case as this, *itisity*.

XII

That I'm reproved unjustly I deny,
Tho' cause, perhaps, would witness that I am;
But when I see those sad tears in your eye,
I know that love thus would her right reclaim.
Borne on by garish fashion, derelict,
I did forget you once, so still and plain,
Till tired of vain formality's respect,
I turned with longing heart to you again.
Sweet country girl reproving with your tears.
Ah, heaven's way to win love is your own;
Yet mine were truly won for all life's years,
Ere sadly tears reproving had I known.
Love needs reproving ofttimes to be true,
And true love ofttimes gets more than is due.

XIII

How can I say that I have hapless been,
Tho' fortune has rejected plea on plea—
Hiding her face, that 'midst her kindness seen,
So oft of yore, gifts smiling unto me?
For, where the darkest lingering shadows lay,
Rare blessings proved, as if 'twere heaven's gate;
I, groping in the dark, in brightest day,
And, longing and forlorn, inviolate.
How can I say that I have cause for grief,
And I acknowledge you earth's richest gift,
That, unawares, I held against belief,
'Till your one word those darkest clouds did rift?
Ah, truly, we too oft court discontent
To wonder how it proves but blandishment.

XIV

To toil from bed to bed, day after day,
Confronting thus a war so desolate,
Offended sorrow can but little stay,
The fault and folly that's decreed by fate.
Fierce in the battle till at night oppressed,
I pay my trust to heaven and seek repose,
Yet, how from me, of tender love confessed,
Can fate take back both love and sacred vows?
Like weary journey winds to finished end,
A pilgrimage of love shall meet reward,
For love does triumph in the hopes that lend
Strength to the heart and arm to yield its sword.
So, love, lest I ambiguous may prate,
Come, trust your love to me and not to fate.

XV

Why should delay these moments ere they fly
If better hours do mourn your absence now,
When weighted by the sadness of a sigh,
Or cherished for the token of a vow?
What is the right to waive reproachful tear?
That heart despair, oh, should you hope dethrone?
The ready lapse to which has sped the year,
Sad love, relenting, buries all alone.
Yet, let the hours fly from day to week,
And on till dumb oblivion knows nor does;
Too full, the hope deferred, of grief to speak,
Since grief has killed the happiness that was.
Sad heart, that's been deceived by time's deceit,
Whose enemy is love, whose friend is hate.

XVI

Poor diffidence whose rights are her despair
That fortune, unawares, yields choicest gifts,
Sits oft alone and braids her silken hair,
And plans brave exploits while her fancy drifts.
Ah, very brave she is thus snugly hid,
And muses, plans and sings, and laughs at fear,
Till 'neath the window sounds a step not bid,
When all her thoughts of bravery disappear.
Poor diffidence! incur not her disdain
By showing in yourself her greatest fault,
Or rather greatest charm, if her you'd gain,
For, strange to say, she only stops for *halt!*
And, true it is, to capture timid love,
Deal like a soldier and not like a dove.

XVII

'Tis beauty's part to yield those graces rare,
That so befit her rarest legacy.
No art suffice those gifts beyond compare;
O, may her bosom be of purity.
Delights she bears that ravish painter's eye;
But far too often given to heart that's vain.
Lest she should weary 'come and haply sigh,
Who could deny a wish to beauty's reign?
Her favor does eclipse the rack of wrong,
And wisdom beauty's witching smile destroys;
But in the heavenly sweetness of her song
Do live ten-thousand griefs, ten-thousand joys.
That beauty may have done with vanity,
That beauty thereby more divine may be.

XVIII

Pray, ask me not, tho' youth has scarcely fled,
That sorrow has besieged my brow so sore;
I sicken at the heart tho' it be dead,
To answer would but wreak of sorrow more.
Suffice, dear friend, some less in youthful years,

Than I, to sorrow, am defenseless heir,
That faith inspired by beauty's sighs and tears,
Knows yet a sadder valley than despair.
Your brow is smooth and fortune on you smiles,
And sound you sleep and dream so pleasantly;
Could I but foster you from beauty's wiles,
You'd live to haply weep, nor long to die.
But now I've made you take a serious mood,
Go fall in love and trust your luck be good.

XIX

To deal with such law as isonomy,
(If it may be allowed to be love's word,)
O tenderest affection, consort be,
Lest she despair for love that is deferred.
I being but a novice in the maze—
This co-existence of twain love and truth,
I sigh through many long and weary days,
And waste my profit as I waste my youth,
And, longing, waste my profit all on love,
My profit which is patience that hope cheers.
But shall I reckon all love's profits prove,
That time pays not with pleasure but with tears?
If so, love, let us reckon love and truth,
One crabbed age, the other sighing youth.

XX

Ah, truly I should write the muse I feel
Ere does decline the impulse of its power,
Which, sudden born, is keener than all steel,
But tempers with its age like to the flower;
And, of itself, is like to purest love,
Which, first no flame is fiercer in its rage;
But intermingling love with love does prove,
Emolliating, as my pen to page.
For who possesses soul of purity,
As love and poet, purest themes impart,
Tho' pointed as the flame as gentle be,
As song of love or gentle woman's heart.
For these, of all life gives to weary man,
Do more of heaven yield than all else can.

XXI

Like to the clouds, the thirsty earth appeals,
Tho' far divided, lend a willing aid,
Ere summer's beauty fades to barren fields,
And golden harvest perish in the blade;
So, love, am I appealing unto you,
For your kind word and smile ere hope shall die,
That, fainting heart, thus nurtured by love's dew,
May bloom to love's perfection 'neath your eye.
Lest willful wrong shall entertain desire,
Temptation's fear in absent love disproves,
I kindly bear your fault in honor higher,
Than love whose ear is deaf to heart that loves.
May my appeals distasteful ne'er become,
Else, haply, love has flown and hope is dumb.

XXII

I can not chide time for the hours of day,
Tho' long they drag in weariness, they give
An eagerness that quickens all delay
When wrapt in thoughts of love that in them thrive.
Wide world deny me place to lay my head,
Should I deny possession unto love
The twelve long hours of light between my bed
And happy night that all too brief does prove.
Too soon, at night, does ring the hour of ten,
When I, indeed, must go, tho' slow to move;
I linger yet for the last kiss and then
Go home to dream and yet again of love.
Thus love consumes each hour or slow or fast,
And most of love is fear it will not last.

XXIII

Now summer unto earth her beauty lends,
And mating-time has passed to chirping brood;
Now fairest are the flowers of the glens,
And love bewitching in romantic mood.
Her rights are stretched to all the points of view,
A braveness now pervades her snowy breast;
She shouts disdain to formal retinue,
And nature's large and legal chances test.
Brave is the heart that follow her does dare,
And braver yet the heart that her can stay.
Fair, daring love, with breast and arms abare,
Whose presence far eclipse the smile of day.
Thus, youth goes wild, but chide him not for this,
Love leads this merry way all for a kiss.

XXIV

If, ere yourself, I shall have passed away,
Should these endearments linger in degree,
That proffers recollection to a day,
Whose happiness love's sacrifice should be?
The destiny of love were best forgot,
Or why a tear be shed for by-gone hours?
Sweet love, the heart of homage knoweth not
The mouldering heart beneath fair summer's flowers.
'Tis little asks he who has loved for love;
Why, e'en tho' death-defied, would not complain.
To live and to be loved, to him does prove,
Not death, but recollection is the pain.
That, as to now, life may no sorrow shed,
Think of the living love—forget the dead.

XXV

Could I define wherefore you often sigh,
Thus fortified by beauty's vastest wealth;
Why languish in the wastes of sweets the eye,
The hands clasped o'er the heart tho' fearing stealth;
Could I your secret guess and stand amain,
'Gainst fate's vehement tide, in self-defense,

What happier fortune could I yielding, gain,
Than that for which you sigh in preference?
What selfish increase does decrease your peace,
What subtle motive does the sad heart move?
That tyrant, you would say, has dared release
His legion warring forces, who is love.
Ah, this is love, of all love, loved the best,
That makes us guess when we are surest.

XXVI

O, that love well considered her deserts,
And folly bred its quality alone,
Whose inconsistency so oft reverts
To many a weary day love would disown—
O, could love cast blind passion to its fire,
'Twould better be than unwise heart within,
That craves and clings unto its vain desire,
Whose dazzling bribes end where grief does
   begin.
Its richest prize the heart bestows on love,
And love in turn to her posterity.
Sad breach for love, that unwise would disprove
Her royal worth to serve disparity.
Yet, love like this, tho' so unwise, allures,
That above all other, unto death endures.

XXVII

Tho' from the sky, there streams a mellow
   light
Upon the lovers' path as they would stroll,
Yet, fortune has decreed that such a night,
Shall hide, by beauty's arts, a cunning soul.
"Let's count the stars," a fool would say, perchance,
Or, haply, start his plague with wildest vow,
When love, thus fortified by fool, her lance
Strikes deeper till poor fool at length does
   bow!
Then love would sigh, "time is so brief, sad
   luck;"
In fright predict a storm, this wily dove,
When fourth he hies, disgraced for lack of
   pluck,
And love in effigy to other love.
Sure, prattling fool with love is sorry game:
To fight love's battle right fool is too tame.

XXVIII

Why, that yourself, not given to kindly deal
Unto yourself the justice that is due?
Such happy turn the heart must needs would
   feel,
That to your worthy self you do prove true.
Why feel your drooping lashes indicate,
The lesser of yourself for modesty,
And that the depths of dreamy eyes relate,
Disparagement 'gainst beauty reigning free?
Your lips, possessed of accents all divine,
Your judgement sets to falter, and your cheek,
Wrapt in a milder crimson of the wine,
Does deepen to the rose when you would
   speak.
And yet, I can not chide these faults so rare;
That time may keep you so shall be my prayer.

XXIX

When weary of the light, day's eye does close,
And summer's earth rejoice, that dew appears;
The early moon glance thro' the trellised rose
Where love sighs in her languishment and
   tears,
Then I would go and list unto love's voice,
If I would catch the sweetest tones of all;
'Tis love, in sorrow's voice, that makes my
   choice;
Sure, heaven could not resist it not to fall.
When low the sob, the tender bosom pained,
The broken accents, tearful, pleading eye—
Who could withstand her wish should not be
   gained,
And who to gain would even fear to die?
Yet, tears and grief are oft in sad discord,
And silence oft speaks more of grief than
   word.

XXX

Love dreads those saddest days of all to come,
When she shall reach her dotage feeble-eyed;
When beauty shall have fled and left her home
So desolate 'tis painful there to bide.
Ere beauty leaves joy nor wit nor wealth do
   lack,
And gay the throng and music sweet and
   praise;
The monster plague called time, the charm
   takes back,
And poor, sad love is left to weary days.
She sits and sighs in retrospective dream;
Her wrinkles deeper grow while runs the sand.
Thus love floats down life's ever-changing
   stream,
And blessed be he who holds her by the hand.
Young love, lest she despair and would complain,
At such an age would live not life again.

XXXI

Could shame deny youth's folly, and defend
Such accusation 'gainst the truth of time,
The purport would be crime with dividend,
Which, far exceeding folly, breed worse crime.
Consider not perfection god of joy,
'Tis folly's lion that youth does ensnare.
All qualities of fortune seek alloy,
And time does prove youth gets the lion's
   share.
Who of himself is so improvident,
That has no dividend of this dread beast,
This tyrant of decay and punishment,
That beauty on us all has made to feast?
O, could we drive this monster beast away,
Perhaps that this were heaven wherein we
   stay.

XXXII

Love, in her widowhood, wails of a grief
Born of despair and to death nearest kin;
No tearful semblance, stormy and as brief,
Does hold shameful countenance her heart
  within.
Grief, that converts all the soul, does despise
Succor's kind word, and hope does dethrone;
Truly, the tears of widowed love's eyes,
Speak of an auguish relief ne'er has known.
Mention not duty that's due, nor condole;
Nothing does profit the promise of weal;
The widow's weed give her whose weary soul
Is lost in a sorrow time ne'er can heal.
But, by such grief, who can such love divine,
That lives to die of grief it would confine?

XXXIII

Then saddest fall the strains from 'Pollo's
  harp,
To die in weary wandering of grief,
When timed to count of new-made love whose
  sharp
Lance pierce the willing heart to vain relief.
Those hours o'er-laden with successive smiles,
So proving happy heritage to love,
How weak, strong youth despairing, sadly
  whiles,
And treasures all the sadness that they prove.
Love, in her dotage, weepeth in dismay,
Poor youth thus burning wild with love's sharp
  flame,
And honest nature, shrinking, turns away,
Recording trouble yet another name.
But this is love, the saddest lesson yet;
To haven't learned, 'tis sad, and yet to have,
  regret.

XXXIV

Lo, breaks the morning's splendor o'er the
  hills,
The night mist risen and the birds rejoice;
Attuned by kindly nature sing the rills,
And I inspired of love, my love do voice.
Yet, profitless it out-pours to the air,
And o'er the long glens wafts a weary way;
In song, or notes of pipe, to failure share,
While on in saddest pleasure drags the day,
For she disdains the hand of husbandry,
Beguiled by praise deserved from worthier.
The tide of fate 'tis folly to decree,
Or precious love not his who loveth her.
I thus to morning's splendor make refrain,
With pipe in cadence of a love in vain.

XXXV

A grewsome feast is that, does love declare,
When Bacchus fills the cup and care has flown,
As round the board, with song and goodly
  cheer,
Where blush, suffusing, claims youth for its
  own.
There, where the gallant, fired of hope the
  while,
Whose joy belies his sadder turn of life,
Lets nothing but youth, love and wine beguile,
The three in one, the one of love most rife.
Ah, then let all the muse attend on me,
That I may catch each accent's blissful tone,
I being as a pagan on love's sea,
To drift in blinding bliss to sink alone!
For that fair witch that's seen with wine-lit
  eye,
Of all love's witches, first for her we'd die.

XXXVI

O, eyes, or should I call you by such name?
For you the tyrant of my heart have been
E'er since we met—an e'er-increasing flame
That saps me of the courage man may win:
Yet, eyes of love, and dreamy witchery;
Kind, yes, and shed your warm light unto me,
That thither strayed, my heart sinks with a
  sigh,
Again returned, is lost in regency.
Your valance has but sparkled with the gem,
Your liquid depths, responsively, have shed,
Now, I returning, kiss the diadem
Of broidery that rests upon the head.
O, eyes of love, responding thus with tear,
Sure, such a tyrant I should gladly bear.

XXXVII

Ah, sweet the hour that young love, dreaming,
  strays,
Bedecked in all the finery of spring.
The breeze, enamored, with her tresses plays,
The birds, inspired by voice, songs sweeter
  sing,
The brook reflects her form, entranced the
  while,
Its sprays, in rapture, leap to kiss her feet,
And in the wood, the dove moans for her
  smile,
And in the glen, the bee sighs for her sweet;
But on the hill the shepherd-boy looks deep
Within her eyes, and dreams and pipes all day,
"Love do not stray that you my heart may
  keep;
Bide on the hill with the shepherd-boy for
  aye."
Young love, thus roving in her happiness,
Once reckon she the hearts she does possess?

XXXVIII

Beauty strayed within her musky bower,
And in the rare sweets, reveling, did entwine.
The fairest flowers to 'deck her for the hour
When ardent lover kneels to call divine.
Tho' beauty, truly worthy of her name,
Perfection fain would spoil with lesser worth;
How thoughtless, sightless, heedless of her
  fame,
Her bounteous legacy, her envied birth.
By chance, she sees, that from her reach does
  blow,

A flower, yet, by chance, a commonest,
That she would pluck or else the hour forego;
But failing, sighs, refusing all the rest.
Ah, why should beauty suffer this dispraise,
Is it in possessing that her charms lose grace?

XXXIX

Tho' hand-made beauty with her garish show,
May hold dominion o'er the heart awhile;
But, fraught with vain presumption, does forego
The cunning of her art in every smile.
Real beauty sadly turns from flattery;
False beauty joys in flattering compliments;
This sinful being in her battery,
With smiles, does war poor love for recompense.
But, love is strength, but purity can own,
Who, readily, conflicting farces reads,
Tho' quite replete, the counterfeit soon known,
Makes hand-made beauty worse off for her deeds.
Yet, beauty can hold value not above,
The value of the tender heart of love.

XL

What's the reflection in your glass you view?
Ah, it is beauty at her faded forty.
How changed she is, her wrinkles are not few;
How dull her eye, her figure grown so portly.
O, is this beauty I to gallant played;
The coy, sweet creature, fairest of the fair,
Who lived on love, beloved, nor e'er gainsaid
Aught that beguiled, or wealth or jewels rare?
Is it the fay, the lithe, the willowy
Queen of the ball, the captor of all hearts,
Whose snowy breast to roses pillowy,
Heaved ne'er a sigh or knew of wily arts?
I can not gaze on her to thus regret,
Lest th' reflection her gallant too beset.

XLI

O, fairest creature, sad with that disease
Which love, contagious, wars upon the heart,
Till thereby beauty knows but little peace,
Besieged by all the wiles of Cupid's art.
Your dreamy eyes are traitors unto you;
Their cunning to your heart brings many a woe,
And what your tempting lips have spoken true,
Your witching voice denies in accents low.
How can you this dread malady forbear,
And not vouchsafe your heart unto your cure?
Your sickness I would gladly with you share,
Thus making for us both, less to endure.
My patient be, the secret I will tell,
Love is the potion that can make you well.

XLII

I know not wherefore pleasure should achieve
So great a presence of disparity,
Tight-griping sorrow, lest she should not live
Out half her days in such vain rarity.
I know not wherefore that her rose-tint cheek.
Is only ruse, when once we know it true;
I think, poor thing, if she would dare to speak
Would tell us weeping of its sadder hue.
I know not wherefore trouble she denies,
Since constant trouble her companion is;
And yet, we love her, and with longing eyes,
Oft seek her far and wide, alas, amiss.
But, love, lest I be faulty and you sigh,
Come, let us fly with pleasure till we die.

XLIII

Pray, let my love be called as it should be,
Not merely reckoned kindness with a smile.
Hypocrisy yields only misery!
Vex not my heart with this, your idle wile.
As is my love for you, to-night be kind—
Constant, yet, throughout this kindly hour
That fate has given us and love defined,
Sad, longing for your smile of witching power.
Dissemble not, is all my argument,
From innate theme that woman's heart affords:
Your varying moods and languishment be spent;
Come, say or yes or no the fated words.
O, tell me true, lest feigning you should fall,
That well you know I love you all in all.

XLIV

I cannot think those hours were idly spent,
That love did lade with all her dainty joys,
Tho' at my conscience window I relent
On gazing, as a child, on broken toys:
Yet, sweetly love's transitions rhyme with me,
Unworthy wight, whose foibles are a score;
Those gay, forlorn and sweetest hours that we,
Dear love, lost love, shall see again no more;
Tho' undivided we confess and steal
With hope back to that shrine exceeding bliss,
And there, as sinful spirits, humbly kneel
To seal the broken vows again with kiss.
O, why should love's sweet hours be stole by time,
That he be vilest thief of vilest crime?

XLV

'Tis with delight I meditate and praise,
Your many things of interest merit gives;
Who, kind abettor, is in many ways,
Oft at a loss to know if justice lives;
For so entitled he has reckoned you,
That famous you have grown in consequence—
An every-day acknowledgment o'er due,
With yet a surplus left for love's defense.
Your graces of abundance innovate
In all the pretty charms that heart invent,
And civil war do wage with happy fate,
Who, lacking self-defense, yields you content.
Yet, I myself, need chiding, for the while
I meditate and praise, I lose your smile.

XLVI

As unto me is atticism strange,
When I dare court the ethnic page of clime,
As dull-wit, guessing in my narrow range,
And, failing, sadly turn from buried time;
So, too, is this disease of heart called, love,
That makes one sick when he is surest well,
And e'en vice versa does this ailment prove,
That diagnosis juggles that would tell;
Whose symptoms are made up of smiles and sighs
And rarest joys and hopes and doubts and tears
And that lorn look of happiness of eyes;
But for a day it may affect or years.
If there were skill this baffling plague to cure.
Such doctor's fortune would be made for sure.

XLVII

O, I would fain o'er Afric's deserts roam,
Unseen, in shame, to justice fugitive—
Thence, in my sorrow, far from friend and home,
Lord of the desolation doomed to live.
Ah, I would deem this happier lot by far,
Than that these ties prove traitors to their plea.
Like to the heathen, in a savage war,
To die on barren desert, meant to flee;
So, I, such limits, far remote, would pray,
Wrapt up in grief, my heart as marble dead,
Than live to see you but a single day,
Should you have proven false these vows I wed.
As lessens time the morrow's coming dawn,
So, may my fears confessing, loving on.

XLVIII

I strayed to bower where wood-bines sweetly blow
And shade and shine do revel in delight,
Where time does linger, over-loath to go,
And locks his arms to muse—foregoes his might.
But who, to this bewitched, sequestered spot,
Would think had strayed poor love with saddest heart,
To weep unseen to envy her sad lot,
That envy should delight and hope depart?
Art, worthy comforter she did displease,
Set me to paint the picture in the bower;
But love starts up, attendant mine agrees,
And art turns from us twain to weep the hour.
Strange that this thing be true, love cannot hide,
Nor plaint, nor plea, nor prey, nor foe confide.

XLIX

Whence in the vale does sleep the placid lake,
I trace the silvery streamlet to the hights.
My spirit as an angel's flight does take,
Drawn by a sweetest voice to its delights.
Lo! on yon happy hill, where humble cot
Sets 'midst the brakes, beside the singing stream,
There, sure, is beauty—there I cast my lot,
And there is love in young and blissful dream.
Ah, there, instinctively, my step does bend,
Drawn by some power that I cannot define,
New-found and strange and little hope does lend,
And yet so full of happiness divine.
O, that those hours of life love's charge does bear,
Were merit's to recite, and hope's to share.

L

Like to despised calumny in her thrall,
Whose life is saddest of deploring lot,
Where adverse fortune ever casts her pall,
To thus immure her, till at length, the spot
Grows sinful as a curse and its disgrace,
Whose canker robs the soul and stings the heart!
Ah, so is this sad lot that I embrace,
Since from the hour that you bid me depart.
Cruel disgrace that lovers' quarrel bestows!
Saddest despair for comment's anxious ear!
Why that you taint poor character who knows
Nothing of this, that hasty judgments bear?
A lovers' quarrel, whose petty griefs and sorrow,
Turn to regrets thrice sadder on the morrow.

LI

O, think not of those griefs that love has taught,
And hope has cherished with a paining heart,
Till poor contentment with dejection fraught,
Seeks every way to digress in her part.
That nothing common deigns her royalty,
Sad, self-respect, perforce, checks deeds for shame,
And leaves the sequel, timely, in degree
That saves poor love, at least, her own good name.
Wayfaring hope goes on nor glances back,
Spending her conquest in a mournful song,
And heart possessed of promise does but lack,
The happiness that doubt denies love's wrong.
Thus, love possessing all—a miser born,
Wastes all at length, in doubt, to sadly mourn.

LII

That I have come where pride aweary sits,
To pitifully beg oblation's smile,
Where hope to please, as best she can, the wits
Of providence, song sweetest sings the while;
That I have come to this, ah, me, blind fool!
To not have known love languished long before.
Whereto my curse does bend and ardor cool,
'Tis all too sad, too sad, for happy yore.
Justly, ah, yes, I cannot truth deny;

Love led, and I have followed her to this.
Far better none the glory than the lie,
Far better love denying than her kiss.
Ah, poor the concord fickle love retains,
That sweet in beauty suffers saddest stains.

LIII

O, how shall I confess these proofs of love
Ere, self-despised, thro' fear, I shall become—
Love's convict; thither, hapless, I be drove
Into a baffling world of woe from home,
To count, and bitterly, each filching hour,
Too base to dare look in an honest face?
Were I that less the coward, with the power
To be the man, my manliness does grace,
O, I would, love, confess to you my heart;
But I am cowed too much by your sweet voice
I cannot speak; in silence we must part,
Else, haply, you discern my waisted choice.
Love's conquest is too awful and complete!
The lip denies the heart, the heart does lip defeat.

LIV

What is this rare insight love does possess
Into man's motives that do actuate?
How came she by this baffling acuteness?
Sure, she had not possessed it but by fate.
A cunning that is covered up by mild
Degrees, and proofs accentuating lack:
Simplicity, with credit for a child;
With many a thing vouchsafed she would take back;
A keenness underlying all that shows;
A veritable deception of self's own;
A shrewd conception hiding what it knows;
A subtle strength that riddles facts unknown..
Yet, we may laugh this down as silly boast:
Love little knows, indeed, that knows the most.

LV

How can I dare thus to presume since he,
O, mighty Shakespeare, feasted all the world,
To be denied, with proof perhaps for me;
To be belied: calumny at him hurled
E'en this far day, to rob him of his due?
Ah, sinful jealousy this does confess,
Whose rankness does disgrace his grave anew
Each little while, with each time greater stress.
Wherefore, can such as I presume to speak,
Whose littleness is less than little's own?
Confessing but to you what I do seek,
Love, I can but appeal to you alone.
O, bear with me, I pray you, since you know
That everything to you, love, do I owe.

LVI

Words are too few love's meanings to relate.
When I would court the muse to your degree,
I fail to yield desert to your estate,
And failing, ask you but to pity me.

Ah, love unnamed, tho' Alta is your name,
So far away, nor knows my reflex here,
Written in my longing, all for my blame,
For undue hope I would confer in fear.
Ah, that my words could bear my thoughts to you,
In vain I strive to find words to express.
Truth, there is none that can such love construe;
I can but ask you, love, my love to guess.
O, that I could to you my heart portray;
But failing, fearing, sadly turn away.

LVII

I often weep for one who loved me well,
My fault reverting in eclipse of pain,
When, of the wasted time, sad thought does tell,
Excelling constancy for poor love's gain.
Ah, often do I weep, foregoing all
The pity rendered of forgiveness kind.
Having possessed self-all-despised of soul;
Unlearned, and my belief was dull and blind,
Yet, pity was her tender word of love;
Still trusting she the heart at least did own.
Bitter, O, stinging bitter do they prove,
Those tears for love the truest that is gone.
To weep, and, yet, to know we weep in vain,
Is of all weeping bitterest of pain.

LVIII

When age against my youth shall be complete,
And, I, with rounded back and trembling hand,
Bow at, with snowy locks, my captor's feet,
Where no resistance deigns his stern command;
When shall decline these days of youthfulness,
To rougher days of age's winter's chill;
When all these leases end that youth compass,
My heart's reflection says, I'll love you still.
'Tis love, of all, inconstant time no power
Has that can take perforce or steal or stay;
Love needs no guard, but like unto the flower,
Unchanging lives till death does take away.
As age the vine binds closer to the tree,
So, age shall bind you closer, love, to me.

LIX

When winter casts her gloom athwart the glen,
And those sweet flowers that 'deck your tresses gone,
Housed in with meditation's sadness then,
Responsive to the spirit thus alone,
Will echo in the heart the last farewell
In doleful accent as some specter there;
Tho' treasured for the love that it would tell,
Yet, saddest for the blameful heart to bear.
Farewell; farewell; yourself were happier
That I go hence to-day, perhaps, for years—
Forever! yet, farewell; a long good cheer;
The conquest is to you, to me the tears.

My heart rebels that heaven should cast the
    spell ;
Ah, sad—too sad it is to say farewell.

LX

Now that remembrance brings back by-gone
    scene,
I weep to gaze upon it, for too sad
Those haunts so beautiful, of waving green,
Since love has wandered forth with heart so
    glad.
When love was young, with golden hair hung
    down,
And sweet her song, and hope had cloudless
    sky,
Those dear old banks above the dear old town,
What true devotion bloomed there 'neath my
    eye:
I even hear her sing the songs I knew,
And it is morning, love with smiling face
Comes down the long glen with her lover true,
To gather wild-flowers for the Sunday vase.
Ah, this is love remembered—always best ;
A living presence that's forever past.

OLD AND POOR.
—

Sad, as the hours dragged slowly by,
    Oft sighing sat she by the door
And speaking to herself she said,
    "I am so poor, so very poor
And age has made me frail, so frail
    I scarce have strength wherewith to rise ;
My only solace is in that
    Sweet rest for me in yonder skies.

"This holy book—my staff and guide—
    This dear old bible brown and trite—
I love to hold, tho' my old eyes
    Long since have passed their second-sight ;
But, oh, I see it, read it all
    From that great page that memory gives ;
Blot out the tears, the grief, the pain,
    But His sweet word forever lives.

"John gave it me, kind husband John ;
    That makes it doubly dear to me ;
And memory slipping back, 'way back,
    A blithesome youth and maid I see ;
She in a silken lilac gown
    With sunny face that knows no pain.
Oh, liken her not now to me
    With trembling hand of swollen vein.

"Those days were bright and life was sweet
    Not then was fortune fickle—no ;
And circled round with dearest friends
    Oh, could my dream be that of woe ?
Yes, days were bright, those happy days,
    When John was here—those days long-gone.

Kind husband, looking from above,
    Rejoice for soon shall life be done.

"And tho' I love to think about
    My kindred and my dear old home,
Yet there's a sadness in the thought
    I've striven hard to overcome ;
For those I counted dearest, aye,
    And love no less to-day in dole,
Were they who drew the mantle grim
    Of poverty round my sad soul.

"And every friend has wandered far;
    The old-time, truest friends, all sleep
That silent, never-waking sleep
    That I'll soon sleep, with none to weep;
For who shall miss me ? None ; without,
    Perhaps, some ask, 'Old Betsey dead ?'
But should I grieve ? Cold charity
    Is naught compared to Him who bled.

"I know that every grief shall end
    With those who watch and pray and trust ;
Tho' I be poor, so very poor,
    My soul is rich and not of dust ;
Tho' age has made me frail, so frail
    I scarce have strength wherewith to rise,
Yet, O, my soul, more fair than day,
    Has strength to fly to yonder skies."

THE REVELERS.
—

I

Ah, yet I see their wine-lit eyes
    As round, repeating, went the cup ;
Seem even clearer now than then
    The songs of mirth that they took up.
And there was one so strangely fair
    Who kissed the wine for him she loved ;
Bright as the diamonds on her breast
    Her eyes but with his being moved.
And she would kiss him oftentimes
    And twine her white arms round him, say,
With her low bosom pressed to his
    Full manly breast,—"I'll love thee aye."
Then round would go the merry laugh
    And round would go the sparkling wine.
"Wine-lit," I said a thousand times,
    "Sweet eyes, oh, laughing eyes divine."
And when the low, sweet music came
    Stealing softly o'er the throng
Some love-clasped in the dreamy waltz
    Sang to their lovers this sweet song :
"Flow on soft strains from passion's harp,
    For music lifts the heart to bliss ;
Look deep within my soul and see,
    Sweet one, if there is proof of this.

"Oh, keep the sun behind the hills
And keep the midnight moon above;
Oh, let the mild night's revelry
Be sweet as love, be sweet as love."

II

And there was one of fairy form
And 'mid the laces on her breast
There clung a tear, I saw it drop
And trembling sparkle at the rest.
And once I passed her as she stood
Against a pillar near a youth,
And heard her say, "Oh, let me die,
Dear one, if they must know the truth!"
And then I saw her smile and quaff
A glass of wine another kissed,
And cling against another's breast,
And when he kissed her not resist.

III

And there the youth who first had touched
The subtle cup smiled in his sin;
And there old age and hoary locks
With foolish jest and wonted grin.
"Pass round the cup! pass round the cup!
Oh! let our joy be ever whole.
Drink deep, drink cheerily to-night—
Here's to long life and merry soul!"
And then a merry, rippling laugh
Told of some maiden's sinful bliss;
Or yielding to the tempter's snare
That stung her virtue with a kiss.

IV

Then softly a fair maiden sang
Juanita, that sweet song of songs,
My soul drank in each tender note;
I sighed for heart that loving wrongs.
I touched her fair hand with a kiss;
A faint smile played o'er her sweet lips;
A tear fell from her dreamy eye;
A rose fell from her finger tips.
I spoke a pleasant word to her,
Sad memory passed, she took my hand
And thro' the waltz with merry laugh
We gaily glided to the band.
But once she said, "Dark eyes are mine,"
In mine long gazing said, "Tho' vain,"
And deep within her soul I looked,
I read her heart, I knew her pain.
And when the waltz was o'er I pressed
Her hand and wished her pleasant dreams;
She smiled; I saw her nevermore,
And, yet, I see her oft, it seems.

V

"Thou art the balm that soothes our woes!"
Sang loud an old man to his wine.
"In thou the life, in thou the soul;
I'll drink thee till thy joy is mine!

"I'll pour thee on my inward woe—
My secret woe—and smile like those
Whose spirits gay, if likened to
A fault, are pure as yonder rose!"
Thro' saying which he plucked a rose—
Snow-white, the choice of nature's mart,
He kissed it thrice and strewed its leaves
And found a canker at its heart!
"O, cursed whorl! O, guile, O, guile!
Fling life to fortune—man to man:
What glory in us moulded urns;
Bereft of virtue—weak in ban?"
And with a sordid laugh he drank,
Drank, drank nor ever ceasing save
While babbling with one less in sin,
Held back the glory from the grave!

VI

Without the window, where the musk
Of roses cloyed the midnight air,
I saw a maiden in a swoon,
So pale, so lovely lying there.
One waxen hand across her breast;
Her golden curls half hid her face;
As silent as the pale moonlight
That wrapped her in its kind embrace.
I stood long gazing at the form;
I took her hand; I touched her brow;
So cold, so cold, I shuddered lest
Her struggling spirit fain should go.
At length I bore her forth where leapt
A cooling fountain from the sward,
And bathed her brow and gave her drink
And spoke to her a kindly word.
But when her eyes looked into mine
She paid my kindly deed with woe—
Yes, heaven be kind! the same sweet face
I loved so fondly long ago!
She knew me, grasped my arm and sobbed,
"Forgive me if I caused you pain!"
She kissed my hand; I turned from her;
I could not take her back again.

VII

Thence thro' the shadows of the park,
Past plat and urn I took my way,
Into the long and silent street,
Across the bridge above the quay.
Faint flushed the morning in the east,
And low the moon hung in the west,
The waters lapped the cold gray stones,
A sea-bird started from its rest.
And far toward the virgin light,
Swift as an arrow, on it flew,
Till lost within the misty robes
Of morning—blending red and blue.
And so, I thought, is not less swift
The flight of hope, of love, of life;
They who are surest of their peace

Are they who surest meet with strife.
I pressed my pillow with a sigh
 For yet a little peaceful sleep;
But oh, the pleasure's after pain,
 I could but weep! I could but weep!

AMARANTH.

Pale hung the moon in fleecy drapery,
And fevered August panted for the dew,
And in the dusty vines the cricket chirped,
The bat from out the musty cellar flew;—
"No more forever in the empty hall
Shall song be heard or shall his footstep fall."

She gazed athwart the dreary, barren waste,
And far into the sweltering summer night;
The thicket roundabout the deadly swamp
Seemed cloyed with weird forms attired in white;
Then turned she toward the cypress o'er the dead
And weeping said, "Oh, dreary is his bed."

And when at length dark frowned the midnight sky
And all the palsied forest swooned away
The cricket's chirps grew fainter, fewer, ceased,
And sank the leathern bat, exhausted lay,
She drew the shutters closer, and the air
Died on her bosom; sighing, dropt she there!

'Round rolled the morning and the southern sun
Rose up and singed the panting, dewless earth;
The midnight clouds rolled far into the north,
But not unto a drop of rain gave birth,
And passing by an old man to the town
Peeked o'er the lattice that was fallen down.

But not a sound; the old house seemed a tomb.
He, silent, creeping to the window-blind,
And, cautious, pulling off a broken slat,
Peered in the darkness, saw the dead and whined—
"Ay! ay! alack! pale death is on her there—
She loved—I saw them once—he dark, she fair."

A SONG.

Oh, drop a truth within a song
 Its glory truly shall be long—
Shall stand as steadfast as the hill
Tho' it be fought with sternest will;
Tho' simple song, tho' simple word,
It shall not perish from the Lord.
Oh, drop a truth within a song
And sing it trusting all day long.

Sing you an humble sort o' song,
For truth is humble as 'tis strong;
Sing of the hope there is for man
And joy awaiting him,—not ban;
Sing of the comfort set apart
For those that hunger at the heart—
Its glory, truly, shall be long,
Oh, drop a truth within a song.

SONG OF LOVE.

Oh, love is a blessing and life is a span,
So love while you may and love all you can;
Your burdens grow lighter in love's magic spell
And sweeter and brighter your life grows as well.
But there's much to forgive and much to forget
And there's much to remember and much to regret;
But love while you may and love all you can,
Since love is a blessing and life is a span.

Oh, love is the fountain of sweetest delights;
It leaps with the soul on its bosom to hights
Beyond the grim shadows of things commonplace
Till angels of beauty smile down in the face.
But hope wanes and dies and sorrow steals in
And at length beauty fading may haply breed sin;
But love all you can and love while you may,
For living is loving if but for a day.

OLD AUGUST.

Old August in his yellow gown
 Has drunk the river shallow,
An' as he breathes the dust flies high an' thick
To settle on the silent town
 Askirt with land which fallow,
Afforded many a mess o' greens for pick.

We see him in the withered wood
 An' valley sadly faded,
An' on the hill with bleatin' flock apant,
A-reapin' all in silent mood
 In open land an' shaded
An' hangs to dry the goodly mullen plant.

An' from her tawny, wrinkled brow
 The honest sweat is fallin',
As many a load he bears o' summer's good;
While from the bendin' apple bough
 The blackbird is a-callin'
His mate to feast with plenty for the brood.

But, as he passes by we sigh,
  For soon the melancholy
Days will come, no matter what's the cost,
  When we the light o' his kind eye
    Shall miss an' days so jolly
That passed away with him an' left us frost.

CUNNIN'HAM'S HILL.

I'd love to go rovin' o'er Cunnin'ham's Hill,
  Thro' the dear scenes that linger in memory
    still.
I'd love to go back where the moan o' the dove
Set my young heart to dreamin' its first dream
  o' love.
Oh, here in the soft, wavy grass I'd repose
Whose fragrance was blent with the musk o'
  the rose,
A-drinkin' the beauty that summer revealed
Lookin' far o'er the bloom o' the sweet-scented
  field.

I'd love to go rovin' o'er Cunnin'ham's Hill,
Where hopes that are fondest are lingerin'
  still,
And there with my love in the old grape-vine
  swing,
Sweep the long fern that shaded the cool,
  crystal spring.
'Tis there, only there that my heart e'er shall
  feel
The blessin' o' love an' the blessin' o' weal,
Tho' the world comes a-courtin' in robes rich
  an' rare
It can ne'er win my heart, for I left my heart
  there.

I'd love to go rovin' o'er Cunnin'ham's Hill,
Where the song o' the robin did chorus the
  rill;
I long for the rest 'neath the cool shady beech,
Where fancies the sweetest fore'er did beseech.
Tempt me not with the beauty that's passin'
  to-day;
If my smile is with you, my heart's far away—
Away gaily rovin' o'er Cunnin'ham's Hill
Thro' the dear scenes that linger in memory
  still.

OLD-TIME ROMANCE.

Oh, give to me old-time romance
  With all its dazzling splendor,
Of fair Bagdad, with mysteries hung
  On many a thread so slender;
Of palmy days of that wise king
  And goodly king and clever,
And kindly king and loyal king—
  I'll scarce forget him ever·

Oh, king Alraschid, how I wish
  You were alive in my day,
For many a canny jaunt we'd take
  Thro' darkest night and by-way;
And many a maid o' beauty rare
  We'd find right hereabout, sir,
All wrapt up head and heels in some
  Dark mystery, no doubt, sir.

Or thus about perhaps we should
  Run on to genii too, sir;
Or strike a cave chuck-full o' gold
  And diamonds, not a few, sir;
Or o'er the bloomy Hoosier hills
  Go roving light and airy,
And find a singing tree, good king,
  Or pretty Hoosier fairy.

We Hoosier folk would make a shrine
  For you and quite as fine, sir,
As that you graced in old Bagdad,
  With jewels it should shine, sir;
Nor like myself address you, "Sir,"
  Tho' rhyme permits it now, sir;
But true as ever mussulman,
  Full low to you would bow, sir.

And may be such a man as I
  Should grand vizier to you be,
And were I with such honor blessed
  I certainly should true be.
And dancers with their harps o' gold
  Should give you jolly life, sir,
Only—times have changed, you know—
  We'd allow you but one wife, sir.

But, you no less a just good king,
  Withal as happy yet, sir,
Should in your royal palace be
  On throne the richest set, sir,
To listen to strange stories and
  Deal equity nor rue, sir,
Your happy, happy lot, but proud
  To call yourself a Hoosier.

OH, SYMPATHY HAS RUINED ME.

Oh, let me be if friend to me,
  I've nothin' worth your wishin',
An' every charm has turned to harm
  An' luck has gone a-fishin'.
With little shame you spoke my name
  Linked with, "My dear, dear brother,
Lend me a five, we always strive,
  You know, to help each other."

Your pleadin' face drawn out o' place
  By many a mark o' trouble;
I reasoned thus,—Unlucky cuss,
  I'll give him five or double.
Here, take the five. Why, man alive,

The favor's small I'm sure.
From you I part with pityin' heart—
Also with dollars fewer.

Oh, shame on you! who would eschew
Your mellow-hearted neighbor.
If it be just, take my last crust;
But spare me strength to labor.
I never poor turned from my door;
They've shared my milk an' honey;
Oh, sympathy has ruined me,
An' taken all my money.

HOMEWARD.

White sails that wing the troubled main
  Oh, bear me onward swiftly flying,
Oh, bear me, bear me home again,
  Sweet home, where hearts for me are sighing;
Oh, bear me, bear me home again,
  Sweet home, sweet home where hearts are
    sighing.

Fly toward yon bright star in the north
  That's hanging o'er my babies sleeping;
Speed on to all on earth I'm worth—
  The loving hearts within my keeping;
Speed on to all in all I'm worth—
  The loving hearts within my keeping.

GOD BLESS THE HONEST GERMAN.

An honest German was my friend
  When I was poor, ah, very;
He gave to me five dollars to spend
  When Christmas-time was merry;
When Christmas-time was blowin' cold
  And my clothes were rather seedy,
He gave to me five dollars in gold
  Because I was so needy.

I never thought once of myself,
  But quickly home I started;
'Twas long since I'd possessed such pelf;
  From my old self I parted,
And left the past all covered up
  And jumped into a new life,
Just thinkin' of the temptin' cup
  Of joy I had for you, wife.

We just three years were married then,
  And it was merry Christmas;
We bought a goose for a dollar-ten
  And settled down to business.
And, oh, the dinner that we had
  With sagey gravy steamin'
And, oh, we felt so very glad
  It seemed that we were dreamin'.

For you I bought a new plaid shawl,
  Myself a pair of breeches;
You said that they were surely all
  Consistent with our riches.
And, oh, we felt so very warm
  And full of goose that we did
Laugh and joke a perfect storm
  Enjoyin' what we needed.

But that was many years ago
  When we were poor, ah, very,
And many a winter and many a snow
  And many a Christmas merry
Has come to us and passed away
  And preached us many a sermon;
But when Christmas comes we always say,
  "God bless the honest German."

SLEEP.—A SONG.

To sleep and dream the hours away
  And rest from care the tired heart,
Is sweeter, dearer to the soul
  Than all that other joys impart.

Under the silent moon alone
  I count the forms o' departed ones.
Sweet repose, only to dream
  And rest while the sand-glass runs.

Deep in the breast there is a shrine
  On which the soul doth sit;
Sleep, sweetly sleep while the world flies
    round
  And the eye from sin is unlit.

Thou like a babe dost smile in thy sleep,
  Rest thy soul from the barbs o' woe.
Sweetly sleep, sweetly sleep,
  Sleep, for there's trouble enough we know.

WHEN SWEET SMILES.

When sweet smiles lead me otherwhere
And sweet songs thrill from voice so clear,
I say, I say tho' sweet it is,
I say, tho' it be perfect bliss—
My love bides ever in my heart
And keepeth me from thee apart;
Oh, tempt me not with smiles and songs
I'm happy where my heart belongs.

When dreamy eyes with me would stray
Thro' scents of mellow afterday
I say, I say tho' sweet it is,
I say, tho' it be perfect bliss—
My love bides ever in my heart
And keepeth me from thee apart;
The joy, I say, is all divine,
But tempt me not, I am not thine.

A CHARACTER.

I'd give the very hope I dread
  'Bove all to lose to taste of youth,
And losing all when hope is fled,
  With bitter chidings of the truth
I'd lead my tottering form along
  As in the days when wise you spoke,
With some sweet, soft, old-fashioned song
  That rapture in my heart awoke.

Man, wider in his views than else
  And stronger in his love likewise,
But like the early frost soon melts
  The moulded thought in deeper eyes.
And heart, a thing of doleful use
  That wrings the bitter with the sweet,
Transcendent till its songs seduce
  Or lowly as the mercy-seat.

But looking at the rise of some,
  At others' ever downward way—
Predestined things that take the form
  Of grief or glory for a day;
Or fame held up to ardent youth,
  The poet's laurels at his grasp—
As wind-blown vines in deed, in truth,
  That with no rue the gnarled oak rasp.

Yet welcome to the trusting heart
  The fated years come flying in;
O, soon enough all shall depart;
  O, woe! for whom is cloyed with sin;
Yet while we have a pleasant sea
  And full of sweet expectant joy,
A surplus is for you and me
  Of hope and peace naught can destroy.

SWEET LABOR, O, I LONG FOR THEE.

Sweet labor, O, I long for thee,
  These idle hands of mine
From sordid burdens would be free,
  To gladly welcome thine.

I long to wipe the honest sweat
  From my once sunburnt brow,
And face the world with no regret
  To follow up the plow.

But O, thou idle hands so soft,
  I look on thee with shame!
From old-time friend I hide thee oft
  And blush to speak thy name.

Nor once tho' horny overmuch,
  Was shame the lot of thine;
Nor circled thou with dainty touch
  The cursed glass of wine.

Not then didst languish thou in sighs
  With sad heart otherwhere;
Not then in dreary moments rise
  To dry a bitter tear.

Sweet labor, O, I long for thee,
  These idle hands of mine
From sordid burdens would be free,
  To gladly welcome thine.

OLD JOE BOSS.

I try to be truthful an' honest
  An' stick to the old golden rule—
Give my neighbor, you know, as myself the
    same show,
  Heed the wise an' consider the fool;
But with all my good told time oft does unfold
  Some miserable, backbitin' son-of-a-gun,
Whom I've helped when in need with a dime
    or good deed,
  An' with whisper does blister me under the
    sun.

But that is the way o' the world, the world;
  We get many a buffet an' jam;
But when I consider my heart is all right,
  Why, I don't give a Billy be damn!
Yes, when I consider, consider,
  Why, I don't give a Billy be damn!

I don't say my dimensions are greater
  Than others that live hereabout;
But the poor many a time has got my last
    dime,
  While I went with my toes stickin' out.
This for praise I don't say, 'tis charity's way,
  You'll find it the world o'er an' o'er;
But the wickedest ban was the curse from a
    man
  When thro' feelin' I's stealin' for his starvin'
    poor.

THE OLD HOME-HILL.

Oh, the old home-hill with its spring an' rill,
  An' the musk o' the wild rose blowin',
An' the shady beech an' oak that reach
  Far out o'er the daisies growin'.
Oh, let me rest on its soft green breast,
  Lookin' far o'er the purple heather,
There let me rest for I love it best,
  So sweet were our days together.

Dear, dear old hill, how my bosom does thrill
  With love for you nothin' can sever;
Tho' fleetin' the years in joy an' in tears,
  My heart wanders back to you ever.

Oh, the old home-hill where the robin's trill

An' the dove's moan set me dreamin',
An' the swingin' mist that the river kissed,
Hung o'er in the morn's bright gleamin';
Ah, beauty's there beyond compare
An' scenes I shall e'er be lovin';
In song an' prayer my heart is there,
Tho' truant feet go rovin'.

THANKFUL.

I'm thankful for the perfect peace
    That falleth on my breast;
I'm thankful for the perfect light
    That leadeth me to rest.

And thro' the toil of the weary day,
    Ay, thro' the stretch of month and year,
The burdens laid on me have not
    Brought one regret nor caused a fear.

I know, tho' I have wept for friends,
    Wept tears as bitter as e'er wept,
I know, tho' you would doubt it true,
    No woe can brook my heart's precept.

And yet I meet it—deepest woe;
    But on my soul does lightly fall
As snow e'er fell on yonder hills,
    And peace remaineth—peace withal.

I saw a mother pale in death—
    My last and only mortal friend,
And yet, I kissed her lips and smiled—
    I knew her troubles there had end.

Some frowned on me in deep contempt,
    Not reasoning with me as you might—
Leave me to buffet life alone—
    Give to her weary soul the light.

I see so many goodly things—
    The sun, the moon, the stars, the sea,
The earth and man, next to his God,
    And stores of rich prosperity.

Oh, what could, added to my life,
    Afford me yet more perfect bliss?
A thousand things contribute joy,
    And love does cover all of this.

I say, I'm thankful for the peace
    That falleth on my breast;
So thankful for the perfect light
    That leadeth me to rest.

MY JOHNNY BOY.

Oh, my dapper Johnny boy,
    I've known you but to fear
It's most too soon to marry yet,
    My Johnny boy, my dear.
You say you love me, Johnny boy,
    An' ever will prove true
An' that a month o' courtin'
    Is quite enough for you.

But oh, my dapper Johnny boy,
    I know you little yet,
So ask me not to marry now,
    Lest we may both regret.
Oh, let us wait, my Johnny boy,
    Till we wear the first love out
An' then see if we know enough
    To know what we're about.

BETTY.

Oh, yonder on the peaky hill
    Lives Betty's aged father,
A man with long an' curly hair
    An' kind an' handsome rather;
He tells me many a queer old tale
    Of early times so "fretty,"
But I ne'er catch the pith o' them
    Wrapt in the charms o' Betty.

I often sit with mouth agape
    While story long he spins me;
With mouth agape, but look askance
    At Betty, she who wins me;
'Tis not the story, yet I laugh
    Like him or sigh forlorner,
While pit-a-pat does go my heart
    For Betty in the corner.

Oh, Betty has a laughin' eye,
    A kindly eye an' lovin';
So deep I cannot fathom it,
    As every 'tempt has proven.
In dreams I see her downward glance
    An' cherry lips so pretty;
I pray the old man's tales hold out
    Till I have won my Betty.

IN EACH LIFE.

In each life there is a season
    All too full of happiness,
Coming to us without reason
    Other than it comes to bless;
But it lingers with us only
    Till the trusting heart's secure,
When it leaves us sad and lonely
    With the pain that we endure.

You, perhaps, have sipt its sweetness,
    And your heart thrilled with the bliss;

Was it love in its completeness—
Sweetest vow and sweetest kiss?
And to-day you count them over—
Would you call them back again?
Heaven pity the true lover
Who in silence loves in vain.

If we murmur, who that heeds us
Has a healer for our grief?
We can do but as fate leads us—
Duty, only, gains relief.
Ours, alone, is vision clearest,
Gazing far into the past,
Where the things that were the dearest
Are the saddest at the last.

WHEN SWEET-BREATH JUNE.

When sweet-breath June comes blowin' mild
O'er thorny wood an' bloomy glade,
An' o'er the hill an' sweet-brier wild
An' ferny brake an' pleasant shade,
When sweet-breath June comes blowin' mild
Oh, then, oh, then I'd be a child.

Way up on the hill a-lookin' o'er
The tops o' the forest trees below,
That gently wave an' faintly roar
Like a summer sea when the south winds blow,
Softly, an' gently drawin' me
Far away o'er its tide o' witchery.

Or down where the water lilies grow
An' lean way out o'er the frisky creek,
An' the sunbeams thro' the branches low
Weave us a garland an' kiss the cheek—
I'd be a boy a-dreamin' then;
But not o' the glory o' frettin' men.

I'd dream o' the sparkle o' the gems
That at early morn are on the flower,
An' the golden-tinted sky that hems
At eve full many a summer bower;
An' the dear old friends who passed away,
An' the hopes that lingered for a day.

An' I'd dream o' boyhood days whose grief
Was joy compared to the bitter tears,
That come to us with no relief,
To mingle with pain in after years—
An' one I remember who loved me well—
An' thus I'd be dreamin' away the spell.

IF MEN WOULD WALK AS MEN WOULD TALK.

If men would walk as men would talk,
Alas, 'twould be for Trouble,
To walk each day the narrow way
Would mean our joys to double:
But oh, the woes o' Sunday clothes,
They're idols that we marry;
I'm, too, afraid, I oft have said,
Scant piety I carry.

O' style in search some sit at church
Meek in the amen corner;
Their voices raise in songs o' praise
High o'er the choir an' horner;
But he who blows with measures chose
The music agitator,
An' she who "vocs" an' nearly chokes
Than Christ are somewhat greater.

Lo, in does plod, spare-haired to nod,
The staid an' honored deacon,
Who sits an' dreams o' stock that seems
To grow strong or to weaken;
While he who stands with lifted hands
The sacred Word revealin',
Seeks more for praise for polished ways
Than contrite heart an' feelin'.

AS THRO' THE WOOD.

As thro' the brooky wood I rove,
By reedy pools asleep,
I dream the dream o' old-time love
An' dreamin' can but weep.

For, here beneath the thorny boughs,
An' shimmerin' sky above,
I learned the sweetest, sweetest vows
In the first dream o' love.

An' here I learned the lover's sigh
An' here with fate I strove;
The warm light of a glintful eye
Here lit my heart to love.

An' here I spent the honeymoon
O' my young heart's first bliss;
But here, alas, I learned too soon
How sad a world this is.

THE OLD TUNES.

Oh, Anna hang the fiddle up
For I cannot play to-night;
I've played you many, many a tune
And played it with delight;
I've played you many a tune, Anna,
And I know you love them well;
But ask me not to-night, sweet child,
Just leave me alone a spell.

You love the old-time tunes I know,
Your mother loved them too;

The selfsame tunes I played for her
  Are the ones I've played for you;
But they were all new in those days
  And sounded as sweet to the ear
As the ones you often play for me
  And I like so much to hear.

Your mother always used to like
  To hear me play at night,
Just as you do, Anna, my child,
  When the moon and stars are bright,
And we'd sit out on the porch here,
  In the soft light of the moon,
While our happy hearts together
  Kept time to some sweet tune.

But there's something in the old tunes now
  That I can't quite understand;
It may be fancy, Anna,
  Or the trembling of my hand
As I draw the bow across the strings,
  Or, may be, as you said—
I played them for your mother—
  They remind me of the dead.

Anyhow, there's something about them
  That is soothing and sweet, it appears,
And, yet, at times when I play them
  My joy breaks into tears;
For it seems to me the music
  Sounds so mournful-like and low,
That I have to stop a-playing,
  My old heart pains me so.

It never sounded that way when
  I played for your mother dear,
Tho', sometimes I'd play a tender strain
  To mingle with joy a tear;
But my old heart never ached like now,
  Tho' the tune was mournful and low,
And tho' a tear dropped now and then,
  There was never a tear of woe.

But your mother—there, never mind me,
  I'm getting old and weak,
And it's hard to keep back the tears, Anna,
  Sometimes when I want to speak—
Your mother, I was going to say, Anna,
  And I were married to-night
Just twenty years ago, dear child,
  Right here in the sweet moonlight.

I was young and strong and happy then
  And she was my star and queen;
The loveliest girl I ever knew
  And many I had seen.
She had no fault but one, Anna,
  And that a too tender heart;
But she died—'twas hard to bear, Anna—
  Death only could us part.

You were hardly a day old then, my child;
  But you thrived and grew apace,
And the good nurse said your mother left
  Her picture in your face,
And I'd come and stand and look at you
  And weep for your mother and you,
While you would coo and smile at me,
  You know, as babies do.

But when you were old enough to walk
  And talk a little and think,
We would go to the graveyard yonder,
  Beyond where the cattle drink,
And plant flowers on your mother's grave
  And talk about her and pray,
Till you loved her so much you often
  Cried to go over there and play.

But when the weather got bad I took
  The fiddle down from the door
Just to amuse you, and played for you
  The old-time tunes once more;
You listened till you dropped asleep,
  And each night you'd teased me till
I'd take down the fiddle and play for you
  After supper when all was still.

That's why you love the old-time tunes—
  Your mother loved them too;
I played them for her long years ago
  And I will play them again for you;
But ask me not to-night, sweet child,
  For my old heart is not right;
Yes, Anna, hang the fiddle up
  For I cannot play to-night.

THE OLD MAN'S SOLILOQUY.

Few pleasures are there as of yore,
  Few things inspire me with delight;
My heart seems wandering in the night
Far from the joys that are no more.

My brightest, sweetest hopes could last
  Scarce till my hair was tinged with gray.
  It seems the kindest hearts were they
Who loved and blessed me in the past.

Yet, I may count my blessings o'er
  With many a gladsome heart whose love
  Fills my life's measure far above
The marks of hope, by many score.

And fortune has been kind to me;
  I scarce can grumble at my lot;
  I chide me oft when trickle hot
Tears as a homesick child for thee—

Thee, Past, my honeymoon of life;
  Oh, fairest, sweetest, fondest, best;
  I faint, oh, fold me to thy breast,
With thee I knew not any strife.

But oh, I see thee speed away;
  Grow dimmer, dimmer, dimmer still,

While trembling comes old age and chill
To bow me lower day by day.

What is there left? what joy can last?
My palsied hand is loath to bless;
My only little happiness
Is in the memory of the past.

THE ELOPEMENT.

At twilight tide the leathern bat
Sailed thro' the dreary room,
But seeming fearful of the place
Flashed forth into the gloom.
And when the wan moon threw its rays
Within the window on the floor,
The cricket ceased its hearth-home song
And sang not any more.

So still, so still the whole world seemed
As wrapt in silent, deep repose;
But when at length the sleeper woke
The musk was wafted of a rose,
And fell upon her lovely brow,
She faintly smiled as in regret;
But when the breeze the wild rice stirred
She trembled 'neath the coverlet.

And then the moon took on a shroud
Of inky black, and on the hill
Across the pool the thick pines moaned
To doleful song of whip-poor-will;
But when she heard the bandog bay,
And wan again the moonlight fell,
Her lover 'neath the window came
And sang the song she loved so well.

At length her light foot pressed the pile
Of homely carpet by her bed,
She, gliding to the window, sighed,
And kist her lover's forehead—
Descended in his arms and touched
With dainty slippered foot the sward;
He said: "I love you, oh, too much
For me to tell in deed or word."

A moment 'neath the spreading elm
He clasped her in his longing arms,
His restless horse neighed by the pool
And champed his bit at vain alarms
And pawed the turf. The lover turned—
"Come," whispered he, "'tis time to flee!"
And swiftly to the uplands sped
His noble steed so gallantly.

Away they flew far to the south,
Their path lit by the moon above,
Far on they sped till early dawn
Broke at the moaning of the dove.
She sighed: "Oh, can you love me well
Since I am as I am?" she wept
The balance that was yet unsaid
For him too coldly to accept.

But when at last they stood without
The high-post gateway to the lawn,
The sun was bright, the roses gay
And from the hedgerow leapt a fawn,
And laid its head upon her arm;
She smiled; while thro' the elm tree boughs
Her lover pointed—"There," said he,
"Stands high the palace of my vows."

In palace walls the fountain leaps
With perfume wafted thro' the halls;
In palace walls the white rose blows
And to its breath the song bird calls;
But, oh, in all the splendor there
The heart may pain beneath a woe,
And paining, sigh for homely home,
And sighing, break, alas! to go.

I SIGH AT NIGHTFALL.

O, wing me weary moments back again
Beneath the maple-shaded cottage roof,
Where I was given every, every proof
Of that pure love whose joy was turned to pain.
O, let me gaze once more within the bower
Where she and I have loved and pure and gay;
Where never came within the livelong day
A grief to mar one joyous, sunny hour.
O, moments of the weary, weary Now,
Tho' memory twines 'round thee a smiling past,
I know thy subtle pleasure cannot last—
Count thou, O, Time, the wrinkles on my brow.
There, there way back, thro' that strange mist was love—
I lift mine eyes—a face smiles from above.

WHO BIDES HIS TIME.

Who bides his time does win the prize;
And justice surely finds its own:
Tho' weary, struggling on alone,
Truth never dies, truth never dies.

O, little profit weeping eyes
And paining heart and vain desires
Tho' weary, struggling truth aspires
To hope's eternal paradise.

Who bides his time all things are his—
Who bides nor weakens but is strong,
And being strong has not so long
To bide, for will the victory is.

GENT FROM THE OLD HOOSIER STATE.

I'm a gent from the old Hoosier State—
The home of the good and the great;
Where poet and minstrel tho' young
Thrill the world with the sweetest of song.
I'm a gent with a heart true and proud,
May my voice ring with praises full loud
Of my birth-place, dear old Hoosier State,
The home of the good and the great.

I'm a gent from the old Hoosier State
Where poet and minstrel tho' young,
Thrill the world with the sweetest of song,
And the home of the good and the great.

I'm a gent from the old Hoosier State
Whose name does the nation elate;
Whose valleys and hills richly bloom
With wild-flowers in sweetest perfume;
Their picture I hold in my heart,
No artist can win it by art,
Naught else can my heart satiate
Like my birth-place, dear old Hoosier State.

I'm a gent from the old Hoosier State,
Where loving hearts for me await;
Tho' others to me you'd commend,
There is none like a true Hoosier friend,
I'm a gent that's gone roving at will
From my roof-tree and own native hill;
But my heart's there and inviolate,
In my birth-place, dear old Hoosier State.

I LONG FOR THE PLACE WHERE MY HEART IS ABIDIN'.

Oh, I long for the place where my heart is abidin',
Far off where the gay hills reflect in the stream,
That ever, an' ever as onward it's glidin',
Is singin' the song that's so sweet in my dream.

You would teach me to love the fair hills you are lovin';
You would pluck me a rose with its musk rare an' sweet,
An' beside your cool streams you entice me go rovin',
But never a joy in their beauty I meet.

I see the warm light in your eye soft an' glintful;
Your sweet kisses thrill an' your fond hands delay;
Should I yield to your love it would be oversinful,
An' sweet hopes I waken can only betray.

Forget me, I pray you, my heart is abidin'
Far off where the gay hills reflect in the stream,
That ever, an' ever as onward it's glidin',
Is singin' the song that's so sweet in my dream.

DISAPPOINTMENTS.

When disappointments make us hard and cold,
And fleeting pleasure wings us into woe,
And happy hearts and faces that we know,
Their old-time mirth and smiles from us withhold,
'Tis then within the soul the sunshine of
The long-passed hours we sigh for oh, so much,
Brings us in saddest pleasure unto such
Dear scenes in days agone when all was love.
O, for one hour of childhood purity,
To hear at mother's knee some sweet old song,
Than all these years more joy 'twould give to me—
These years that have so sadly dragged along.
When disappointments make us hard and cold
'Tis then that love is sacrificed for gold.

SELF.

There is a bitter truth which lieth deep
In many a soul who ne'er will own the fact
To his weak self e'en in the midnight hour;
And, yet, no greater blessing hath he lacked,
In store is greater happiness for none,
And that grave truth is Self, and nothing more.
It maketh life miserable and the soul
Cryeth woe, woe, woe! and that repeated o'er
And o'er; while blindly he goes on and on,
Aye, knowing all the while the cause of grief,
Yet sighing,—"Oh, what is this in my soul
From which I cannot find one hour's relief?"
Bow thou confessing 'neath the chastening rod
And trust thou not to Self; but to thy God.

PURITY.

If thou, dear brother, find in purity
The image of thyself and nothing more,
O, I beseech thee look not on before;
But shut thine eyes to thy small selfhood—be
Thou a lean and withered frame of self,
And look not to the world expecting dole;
But turn, O, turn thee from the whole—
Thy soul shut in its mustiness and pelf.
But if in it thou find the precious seed
That angels prize above all other worth,
O, then, dear brother, I would lead thee north
South, east and west proclaiming thy good deed.
Forsooth, no sacred thing deserves more praise
Than virtuous man, in humble, righteous ways.

NIGHT.

Deep night that brings us deepest, lasting thought—
Thought of the underlying part we sought
Thro' all the weary day so anxiously—
That part of truth our blinded eyes ne'er see
Save in the vastness of the midnight hour.
Deep night, hast thou some charm, some subtle power
Which gives us clearer vision as we gaze
At pictures on the midnight wall where plays
The shadow of the soul of mystery,
Or turning to the star-lit vault we pierce
The endless space where dart the comets fierce—
Where swing a million worlds ; and read as we
A book the workings of the Infinite—
Lendest, O, night, this subtle power to sight?

AFTER YEARS.

Sweet scents and scenes of yesternight
 Tho' twenty years I date them back :
O eyes— soft, laughter stirred and black,
 Dazed emblems now of perfect light.

 But let us sing this chorus, dear,
 The happy years before us, dear,
 Smile thro' the dark clouds o'er us, dear,
 And bid us have good cheer.

O hopes and joys that early died,
 O smiles that smiled me into woe—
 Sweet words of love I once did know
When I were happy by thy side.

O'er-joyed I hold thee to my heart
 In this tranced issue of delight—
 In coming from the dark to light
And never—nevermore to part.

WHILE OTHER HEARTS ARE GROWING FAT.

While other hearts are growing fat
And weary wails the widow,
Poor, weary wails the widow.
 Would Hoosiers bear a shame like that,
 While other hearts are growing fat
And wails the weary widow ?

Never, never, never while our green hills stand,
Never, for our help is the Lord's right hand,
Never, for each Hoosier to his dear free land
Is faithful, ever faithful.

While other hearts are growing fat
And friendless weeps the orphan,
Poor, hungry weeps the orphan.
 Would Hoosiers bear a shame like that,
 While other hearts are growing fat
And weeps the friendless orphan ?

While other hearts are growing fat
And soldiers' bones are bleaching,
On Southern fields are bleaching.
 Can we forget a woe like that,
 While other hearts are growing fat
And soldiers' bones are bleaching ?

COME, SHAKE A FAREWELL.

I'll away on the morrow, I'll away to my sorrow,
 I'll away from my love to go rovin' afar,
For the hopes that I cherished alas, now have perished—
 Come, shake a farewell to your friend, Andre Mar.

I'll away from my duty an' green hills o' beauty,
 Since the light has gone out in my bright guidin' star ;
Oh, I would we had parted ere I's broken-hearted—
 Come, shake a farewell to your friend, Andre Mar.

I'll go rovin' to-morrow o'er hills that but borrow
 A breath o' the sweetness my gay hills unbar ;
I may see valley rarer but never that's fairer—
 Come, shake a farewell to your friend, Andre Mar.

Oh, the vows sealed with kisses an' sweet hopes an' blisses
 That fed my soft heart now wage fiercest war,
An' love lies a dyin' oh, I long to be flyin'—
 Come, shake a farewell to your friend, Andre Mar.

I'll away on the morrow, I'll away to my sorrow,
 I'll away from my love to go rovin' afar,
For the hopes that I cherished alas, now have perished—
 Come, shake a farewell to your friend, Andre Mar.

THE CRICKET'S SONG.

The hollyhocks in the mellow wind
 Bow to the young moon long,
And thro' the musk of the early dusk

Floats the cricket's old-time song.
Chirr, chirr, till the midnight drear;
But its song is not of sorrow;
Chirr, chirr, these the words we hear—
"Pleasant dreams and a kind to-morrow."

And in the lilacs by the wall
The firefly faints and gleams,
And the humming-bird catches every word
As the burden of its dreams.
Chirr, chirr, till the midnight drear;
But its song is not of sorrow;
Chirr, chirr, these the words we hear—
"Pleasant dreams and a kind to-morrow."

From out the hive the old drone bee
Calmly rests in the damask rose,
And his joy's complete in his safe retreat
Away from his thrifty foes.
Chirr, chirr, sings the cricket near;
But its song is not of sorrow;
Chirr, chirr, these the words we hear—
"Pleasant dreams and a kind to-morrow."

WIDOW BROWN.

The brumal birds fret in the wood,
An' moanin' fly December gales;
But little grief o' theirs I heed
Lost in yon lowly widow's wails.

I passed her cabin on yon hill
Where broad the oak groans in the blast;
"Oh, God!" I heard her humbly pray,
"How long shall want an' hunger last?"

Her little children huddled close
Around her frail an' slender form;
She weepin' held their little hands
An' prayin' sought in vain to warm.

My tears fell streamin' to the ground,
I went a-sighin' to the town;
I sold my coat an' yearlin' calf
An' gave it all to widow Brown.

The brumal birds fret in the wood,
An' moanin' fly December gales;
But little grief o' theirs I heed,
Lost in yon lowly widow's wails.

ALICE.

From yonder weepin'-willowed bank
Where droops the blighted lily,
A misgone qua-bird upward shot
To yonder fallow hilly.
It had no prey, the stream was dead,
It winged alone, forsaken;
I saw it drop beside the cot
Where fondest hearts are breakin'.

Sweet Alice loved a wooin' Jake
O' wily manners fancy,
Whose silver jingled in his purse
An' dapple grays were prancy;
He g'lanted her thro' autumn's glint,
With tender word did flatter;
But when at last her heart was broke,
It was a winkin' matter.

Alas, on yonder dreary bank
Where fortune has belied her;
Alas, on yonder downy bed
That cruel fate denied her;
But curses! on the slinkin' Jake,
Nor stinted grief befall him;
I hear the dove moan o'er her grave
An' vengeance loudly call him.

WILDIN' ON THE BLOOMY HILL.

Oh, mother take the riddin'-comb
An' comb my locks so wavy,
An' tie a ribbon at my crown
To please my gallant Davy,
For Davy is a dapper boy
An' lettered, gay an' reignin';
Oh, on my breast a lilac rest
That he may know its meanin'.

The wizen thing he courted last
Had little van or valor;
No wavy locks nor comely brow,
But lips an' cheeks o' pallor.
She had a purse that measured long
An' it was full o' money;
The trollop trite did Davy fright,
An' he calls me his honey.

Oh, mother where the river winds
Around the sedge a-sighin',
There Davy met me when the wild,
Gray clouds in March were flyin'.
He helped me up the braky hill
To yonder gate o' wicker;
'Twas there our hearts by wheedlin' arts,
With love began to dicker.

Oh, wildin' on the bloomy hill,
An' wildin' in the valley,
A maiden has a right to kiss
No matter what's the tally!
Oh, mother take the riddin'-comb
An' comb my locks so wavy;
Tho' maid or bride whate'er betide,
I'll love my darlin' Davy.

DADDY SOLD A BAG O' GRAIN.

Daddy sold a bag o' grain
An' gave its worth to Fanny,
An' Fanny bought a yard o' silk
An' made a cap for granny;
Granny wore it to the fair
Its beauty little summin';
But every one she greeted there
Said it was so becomin'.

Some did praise its comely shape
An' some the frill around it,
An' some did praise its spreadin' bows
An' ribbon that adorned it;
Some did praise its neat design,
Its beauty made them hunger,
An' all that saw it said it made
Her look full ten years younger.

An' there young Newby rich an' gay
With merry crowd did gather;
Full many a maid with glintful eye
Had sought his love to weather;
But Fanny, modest, blushin' turned
When he said with rapture risen,
"Who made that cap shall be my wife,
If she be young or wizen."

Then, every eye on Fanny turned,
Her flutterin' heart sank in her;
The deacon wiped his glasses off
An' gazed as at a sinner,
He wiped his glasses off again
An' gazed awry an' gapey,
"Why, on my soul!" the deacon cried,
"She fairer than the cap be."

Young Newby touched her soft white hand
O' dimpled fingers slender;
A tear fell from her bendin' eye
That e'en a charm did lend her;
Young Newby touched her soft white hand
An' told his love to Fanny;
The deacon cried—"God bless the maid!
That made the cap for granny."

THE GHOST LOVERS.

The faun and satyr play within
The midnight forest wide;
Beneath the wan moon o'er the hill
The lynx doth slink and hide,
And thro' the shadows o'er the lake
The leathern bat doth glide,
And deep within the covert nook
A sweet voice sang and died.

I heard the curbed steed's low neigh
Beneath the gnarled oak stayed;
I saw the lover slowly pass
Athwart the dewy glade;
I heard the maid weep bitterly
Half hid within the shade;
I moaned beside the still dark lake
And wept for vows they made.

"Never again," the lover said,
"Beneath these thorny boughs,
Shall I hold thee to my heart, love,
And whisper sweetest vows.
Never again," the lover said,
"Shall linger on our brows
The kisses that love-passion yields,
With blessings hope allows.

"Seal in thy heart thy lover's vows;
None other shall inspire
With feelings such as these, my love,
This heart, nor quench love's fire;
But I must ride the old world round
Till I'm great to thy desire."
And she floated o'er the silent lake,
And he rode thro' wood and brier.

The faun and satyr play within
The midnight forest wide;
Beneath the wan moon o'er the hill
The lynx doth slink and hide,
And thro' the shadows o'er the lake,
The leathern bat doth glide,
And meet the lovers' ghosts and part
By their low graves side by side.

THOU, HAPPY MOON.

With thy far-reaching rays of mellow light,
Oh, moon, oh, kindly, smiling, happy moon,
Light thou the face that thro' the window-pane
Looks up to thee this happy night of June,
This blissful night when all serene my heart
Beats 'gainst the heart I know in truth is mine.
I spurn the thoughts of love I knew before
When at fair woman's feet I kist her wine.
With thy far-reaching rays of mellow light,
Oh, moon, oh, kindly, smiling, happy moon,
Kiss thou, the lips that speak from soul as white
As is the snow that caps yon mount to-night.
Thou, happy moon, naught else that's less divine,
Shall touch the lips alone to-night are mine.

WILD-A-WITCH.

Wild-a-witch, wild-a-witch over the hill,
Over the hill where the barley grows,
Over the hill by the old windmill—
Wild-a-witch, wild-a-witch nobody knows.

Wild-a-witch, wild-a-witch thro' the green
    grove,
  Thro' the green grove with its musky rose,
  Thro' the green grove with a song of love—
    Wild-a-witch, wild-a-witch somebody knows.

Wild-a-witch, wild-a-witch down in the vale,
  Down in the vale where the river flows,
  Down in the vale with the lilies pale—
    Wild-a-witch, wild-a-witch nobody knows.

Wild-a-witch, wild-a-witch what can it be?
  What can it be that so gaily roves?
  What can it be?—a sweetheart for me;
    Wild-a-witch, wild-a-witch somebody loves.

TWILIGHT.

Come, favored transport, to the longing soul,
Calm twilight, with thy mellowness and hush;
Give to the tired soul thy freshening breath
To lift the heart in thankfulness and song.
Far more than other time our joy is whole,
When all the western sky's a waning blush,
And magic shadow-forms the forest throng
To soothe the fevered day to silent death.
So dear unto the weary, worn and weak
Art thou, oh, gentle twilight, calm and mild
How sweet it is to fold thy bosom meek
And rest as in the mother's arms the child;
While all the work and worry of the day
Has passed with it forever far away.

I MET YOU, OLD HOPE.

I met you, old Hope, by the river side
  When the tide was high and the wind was
    strong,
  And you soothed my heart for my heart was
    sad,
    You soothed my heart with a sweet, sweet
      song.

And you carried me over the dancing waves,
  And our boat sped on to the yellow seas,
  And we sailed away 'neath the young moon's
    smile
  Far into the South with its balmy breeze.

But, oh, you were fickle and you were false,
  And the tide ran down and the moon grew
    old,
  And the love I left by the river side,
  I never again to my heart shall hold.

I met you, old Hope, by the river side,
  When the wind was strong and the tide was
    high,
  And you bore me away to the balmy South,
    But, alas, you bore me away to die.

FLOW SEAWARD, GENTLE RIVER, FLOW.

Flow seaward, gentle river, flow
  And bear me with thy happy drift,
  While soft the southern moonbeams sift
Thro' thy bank-willows as we go.
'Mid trembling rushes on thy shore
  The pale moon-lilies smile and dream;
  Oh, bear me onward happy stream
Where one true heart of me doth dream.

Flow seaward, gentle river, flow;
  In blissful cadence from above
  The nightingale tells of a love—
A perfect love without a woe.
Where slant the shadows from the tower
  I see the midnight fountain gleam;
  Oh, bear me onward happy stream
Where one true heart of me doth dream.

THE GOLDEN PRIME.

The sky is blue, the field is green
  And balmily the southwind blows,
  And falls a shimmer o'er the scene
Where blooms the yellow rose;
  And in the soft and wavy grass
  The dandelions smile at the sun;
In flower and tree the busy bee
  Its labor has begun.

Ah, such a time as this it is
  The poet's soul is thine and mine,
  And wrapt within themselves in bliss
Dream dreams that are divine.
The brooklet sings its sweetest now
  And rare's the wild-flower's musk that's
    blown,
While earth and sky, to heart and eye,
  Yield joys before unknown.

SHORT PENCIL.

'Tis easy enough to write poetry,
  Some can rattle it off like a song;
  But 'tis not very easy to write, friend,
  With a pencil a half an inch long.
Still poets are poets, remember,
  Not the long-penciled gilt-edged elite,
  Sort o' flavored, my friend, with December
  And the worse off the more they write.

Now don't think that I mean to speak pointed,
  That is not as a poet would speak,
  For a poet is a timorous creature
  Entirely void, friend, o' cheek.

I'm yours, yes, in June and December,
Not a link of our friendship I'll drop;
But—my pencil is short, you'll remember—
So short, friend, I really must stop.

BLITHE MARY.

Blithe Mary, ere the dew was dry
Came trippin' o'er the lea;
Blithe Mary sang a wooin' song
An' wooed my heart from me,
An' wooed my heart from me,
An' wooed my heart from me,
Blithe Mary sang a wooin' song
An' wooed my heart from me.

Oh, sweetly sang the happy stream,
An' sweetly cooed the dove;
But o'er them all in sweetness was
Blithe Mary's song o' love,
Blithe Mary's song o' love,
Blithe Mary's song o' love,
But o'er them all in sweetness was
Blithe Mary's song o' love,

She twined a wild-rose in her hair—
Oh, happy be her lot—
An' crossed the stile an' dropt to me
A sweet forget-me-not,
A sweet forget-me-not,
A sweet forget-me-not,
Oh, never shall within my heart
Sweet Mary be forgot.

THE SLUGGARD.

I love the honest, truthful man,
An' frank with conscience whole,
I'll do for him whate'er I can
An' thankful in my soul;
I love the open, upright man
With mercy for his foe,
That lookin' o'er the race he ran
We'd proudly o'er it go;
I love the the man that for his bread
Strives, tho' reverses roll,
Nor sits him down an' bows his head
In grief nor asketh dole;
I love the brave, the noble man;
But the sluggard—love who can.

WHEN HOPE WENT FLYIN'

When hope went flyin' away from me
On swift wing ne'er relentin',
A broken heart she left to me
An' long hours for repentin'.
Oh, was there e'er a viler thief
On all this earth abidin'?
She stole my name an' left me shame
An' a wide, cold world a chidin'.

When hope went flyin' away from me
With tear-dimmed eye an' sighin',
My heart an' I flew after her
An' at last we found her dyin';
She only spoke these words to us
When her quiverin', pale lips parted—
"I know, I know your deepest woe!
You're blessed tho' broken-hearted."

PLOWMAN.

Oh plowman in the low land
Where soil is dark an' rich,
Your work is full o' plenty;
Ne'er lack you flour nor flitch,
An' there the plover settles
In meadow thickly grassed,
An' there the waterlilies
Blow first an' longest last.

Oh, plowman in the low land,
I love to hear your song
As you the loamy furrows
Go ploughin' straight an' long;
Oh, you're as full o' gladness
As the robin flyin' by,
Or the swallow that goes scuddin'
Thro' the deep blue o' the sky.

Oh, plowman in the low land,
Oh, plowman in the low land,
Oh, truly there is no land
Blest as the Hoosier soil.

Oh, plowman in the high land
Where air is pure an' clean,
Oh, many a ripened summit
Your horny hand does glean,
An' there the clear spring gushes,
An' there's the musky rose
In ferny brake, an' swingin'
O'er head the wild grape grows.

Oh, plowman in the high land,
I hear your windin' horn;
I pass the gate an' see the maid
With rosy cheeks at morn,
An' dotted are the rollin' hills
With many a bleatin' flock;
Your home is full o' plenty,
An' built upon a rock.

Oh, plowman in the high land,
Oh, plowman in the high land,
There ne'er was wet or dry land
Blest as the Hoosier soil.

WORD CHARACTERS.

Word characters are truest of us all.
Some low and mean, and others great and good.
Their love is best ; their friendship never small,
And when they hate, their hate is understood.
Far better characters words make than we,
Ourselves, who so imperfect ever are.
Our seven stages so defective be
We call ourselves old fools we would ignore ;
But when we paint a character with words,
Or good or bad, it e'er unchanging lives,
And on the author many attack affords,
And many a word of praise for what he gives.
Why chide for bad if good imperfect would ?
Best praise for both if perfect bad or good.

TURN TO ME.

Turn to me then, when deep regret
Hath settled in thy weary soul,
And subtle images do toll
The midnight bell of conscience yet ;
Turn, tho' the painter, gaunt and grim,
With burning pen of fire hath wrought
The midnight-pictured wall of thought
And gloateth o'er his pampered whim :
Turn if, beneath the chastening rod
Poor love's last spark flies to the void ;
Turn to me, turn tho' sin-alloyed,
I'll take thee, love thee, thanking God.

JOE JOHN SMITH.

Oh, let's not hang the fiddle up
  With all its old-time measures ;
But fill again the temptin' cup
  O' joy with all its treasures ;
Let's spur our laggin' spirits with
  Some pleasin' variations—
The tunes, you know, that Joe John Smith
  Played on the old plantations.

Oh, Joe John Smith could use the bow,
  As we can well remember,
An' always ready, rain or snow,
  In June or in December.
An' he could make a fellow's feet
  Fly off with all religion,
An' saw the Rye Straw hard to beat,
  Or gayly wing the pigeon.

I see him yet with eyes tight shut
  A-yellin' out the changes,
An' sawin' hard the tuneful gut
  Thro' quaint an' pleasin' ranges ;
But when he started up the tune
  Called, "Willie Was a Rover,"
He nearly went off in a swoon,
  He felt so good all over.

An' many a time we've danced the night
  Far into the next mornin',
With pretty Polly in delight,
  An' Betty's smiles adornin';
An' many a step did Joe John teach,
  An' many a caper frisky,
An' fiddled long as was in reach
  The old brown jug o' whisky.

He fiddled roses to the cheeks
  O' many a merry party ;
He fiddled tunes the lover seeks
  An' meeker ones an' hearty ;
He fiddled low, he fiddled slow,
  He fiddled high an' flyin',
He fiddled till the tears did flow
  An' painin' heart went sighin'.

I took the fiddle from the wall
  An' kissed it for old Joe John ;
I could but weep for it is all
  That's left o' him to go on.
Come, let's not hang the fiddle up
  With all its old-time measures ;
But fill again the temptin' cup
  O' joy with all its treasures.

STEEL TWIST.

'Tis seldom I am quite at ease
  Tho' fortune has been kind to me ;
Few dark days of adversity
  Have come to rob me of my peace.

Yet, there is somewhat in my life—
  A deeper, vaster discontent—
The passion of a youth misspent,
  That cuts as does a two-edged knife.

Tho' covered o'er with many years,
  Deep scars are on my troubled soul.
O, were the shame but mine the fall
  Had saved me many bitter tears.

The child smiled down its mother's scorn,
  While yet it clung unto her breast,
She looked upon it as the best—
  Begot in honor, in honor born.

But loving which pollutes the name,
  Tho' guiltless as a lifeless clod,
There bides and from the face of God
  That ever chastening fire of shame.

And yet I wandered to the lane
  To look upon her dreary cot ;
Viewed dear old scenes thro' tears so hot
  That coursing down my cheek did pain.

Pale, weakened with the weight of dole,
  They said, those passing, she always
  Sat with her Bible pleasant days,
Against the casement: friendless soul.

And strifeful passers-by would look.
  "Hers is a storied life," they said;
  "I knew the boy; thro' shame he fled;
She may find comfort in her book."

Once 'neath a road-tree she reclined,
  Returning from the town was faint,
  A former *friend* laid in complaint,
Declaring her of unsound mind.

And, I—Ah, well, 'tis best unsaid.
  The puppet's ill-starred lot is passed,
  And, yet, I chid me when at last
I saw his mother begging bread.

Young barristers must needs be known—
  Suppose a foe one should hoodwink—
  And thus behooved perhaps some think
They do somewhat they scarce would own.

But oh, our foibles point us out:
  Revenge to-day, to-morrow sigh.
  O, thro' my soul steals trancedly
The strange quintessence of self-doubt.

Doubt rules the things that truth disowns.
  Doubt—doubt is man—what's in his soul?
  Is joy the greater part or dole?
I would truth laid our stepping-stones.

Crumbling ruins gilded o'er
  Hint of old fame and royal blood;
  But, oh, the little perfect good
Abiding with us evermore.

But you would say, "life's full of hope,
  And let us sing of coming joys;
  Take grief as do the gay school boys
And laugh it down, not o'er it grope.

"And take the issue, 'tis for you,
  And they who suffer let them know
  That comes with every good thing woe,
To woe is every good thing due.

"And fortune has been kind to me,
  And you may count your blessings o'er;
  The sinless have not any more,
The sinful share as equally."

Yes, fortune has been kind to me;
  But idle twaddle makes us lean;
  Are maxims to us what they mean—
Does truth deceive the eyes that see?

Ah, dealing with the human heart
  Is dealing with a grave affair;
  Go, leave your proverbs otherwhere
To guide the meek and foster art.

But, oh, confessing to the wrongs
  That are the echoes of the heart,
  The soul stamps out the better part
That leaves it where the woe belongs.

And, yet, oh, let my heart's desire,
  To You, who would avenge, reach out.
  O, fill the vacant vault that doubt
Has graven with a pen of fire.

And, tho' a groan may ease a pain,
  And, tho' a tear may soothe a grief,
  O, heart of mine, where is relief,
If yet our ailments do remain?

When I were young they told me then
  There was a blessing for us all,
  From which all sin would tottering fall
And leave us pure and perfect men.

But, woe to him whose trusting heart
  Knows only this in simple word.
  Cry 'gainst the hills—the echo heard,
And vacancy's the larger part.

But, man—oh, leave him as he is.
  He's frail and foolish, vain and kind;
  The woe about him you may find
Is what he thought would be his bliss.

O, hard heart softened with regret;
  O, eyes o'er-steeped in bitter tears;
  In gazing thro' the stretch of years
Her sweet face smiles a blessing yet.

She was so kind—too kind—too good;
  I loved her well—she loved too well.
  (A certain love does lead to hell—
Beware of it! if peace you would.)

But over there, just over there,
  O, Elsie she is sleeping now,
  Where is the love—the sacred vow?
Is grief e'er more than we can bear?

Go, leave me in my tears and sin
  And let stern justice read me out.
  Whose heart is softest never doubt
May seem as hard as e'er has been.

But let me lay, ere I shall go,
  Upon the grave that I would fill,
  This flower, and pray His gracious will
Shall make her sin my double woe.

TO A DUDE.

Go thou, oh, mild lapwing, go hence—
  Thou with the marks of the sweet tit
  On thy wise lips that never yet
Have done save smile a little bit.
Go bask supinely with thy set,
  And, ragged rearward, smiling thus—
"O, aint I great!" Thou flimsy cuss!

SALLY'S BIG LORD.

Sally's pap was rich and he took her off to England
Where she fell in love and married some big lord
Who wasn't worth a cent, but had a great long title
That o'er the door hung with his gran'pap's sword.
Now, Sally's pap got mad when he viewed the situation ;
But he only said, "There's one more to be fed."
So he started up a little retail business for the couple ;
But her lord to make a bigger pull he said :

"I can't be contented with a retail business
A-dealing out the crackers and the cheese ;
'Tis a little bit too small for a man so great as I am
Who's been always used to living at his ease."

Now, Sally saw his drift and she thought she'd use her temper,
So she did and turned her big lord from her home,
And he hung around the depot with a dollar and a quarter,
To make believe he'd ever from her roam ;
But Sally held the fort while his cash it dwindled smaller,
Till at last the fellow didn't have a red,
So one frosty morning early he came tapping at the door,
And in a tearful voice to her he said :

"I guess I'll be contented with a retail business ;
Just take me back and see if I will, please ;
I love you so, my darling, won't you give me a few crackers
And cut me off a little piece of cheese ?

MY LOST SHIP.

On an enchanted sea did sail
  A gallant ship—I saw it oft—
With sail aspread and white and soft,
And there the captain calm and pale.

It came from siren-haunted isles,
  And from Arcadia's blissful vales,
  And where Youth's Fountain never fails,
And golden Eldorado smiles.

Its swift keel grazed that far, strange shore,
  Unknown to man, unmapped, unread :

Oft to the Happy Isles it sped,
And haven of Content, for o'er.

O gallant ship, that cleft the main—
  O sweet, fond fancies idly fed ;
  Beyond the hopes my spirit wed,
And never to return again.

I CANNOT SING AS I WOULD SING.

I cannot sing as I would sing,
  My lips refuse to utter
The songs I hear my still soul sing,
  So softly, clearly, echoing
In simple sweetness, yet, too great,
Too subtile for these lips to mate ;
I cannot sing as I would sing ;
  My lips can only mutter.

I cannot sing as I would sing :
  The tribute I would bring to you
Is ever far beyond my reach,
And, yet, I grasp it and beseech,
And try to sing the songs I know ;
But fail—I know not wherefore though ;
  I know not why I cannot sing
The songs that I would sing to you.

GOOSE AND ROBIN.

GOOSE—
Come, tarry Robin, in these boughs
Where blushed the fruit of mellowness
That burdened air with sweet perfume
To tempt you and your kin.
Here on velvety sward I've listened
To your early-morning sweet song
O'er and o'er for weeks ; but now you
Sing a song of grief to me.

Come, tarry in the autumn boughs
And sing the sweet song o'er again
That charmed the plowman in the field,
The merry maid and me.
Tho' green has turned to golden hue,
And chilly winds frisk thro' the leaves
I know you can as sweetly sing
As once you did if you but will.

ROBIN—
My breast is red, oh, sorrow !
I must leave you ere to-morrow,
I'll fly away, away to the south
And hush from your ear my noisome mouth,
For often frost does nip the bud,
Thus summer birds had better scud ;
But what will become of the linnet
And the bull-finch ? wait a minute,

I'll call them now, that I may talk
With them, the blue jay and the hawk,
The wren, the martin, swallow and quail
And the turtledove with its wonted wail.

Come hither, come hither, my feathery kin,
The farmer is stowing his grain,
If we linger yet longer on this autumn scene
We shall roost in cold dew and fall rain,

Away let us fly to the bright, sunny south
And besport in the soft, balmy breeze,
And chant to our matelets a much sweeter song
From the boughs of the green pine trees.

Or down by the brooklet where minnows are shy,
Where the southern sunbeams on the shallows of sand
Dance to our notes in familiar glee
And the bright cope of heaven does gladden the land.

Oh, who would not go from the frost and the snow
From a place cold and drear to one bright and clear,
From hard frozen ground till spring comes around.
Away to the south there's food for each mouth
And a home bright and gay; come, let's fly away
Or else we shall roost in cold dew and fall rain.

Come, feathery kin, the autumn wind's din
Is heard in the trees ere long wintry breeze
Will catch us I trow, oh, pray let us go.
Come plover and wren, from thicket and glen,
Come, ere it's too late—come, let us migrate,
Or else we shall roost in cold dew and fall rain.

Away let us fly full high in the sky
To seek the south sun for summer is done.
For the gay south I yearn with its flower and fern,
With its berry and brook, with its sweet-scented nook;
Not here, hardly yes, for you must confess,
Ere long we shall roost in cold dew and fall rain.

GOOSE—

Stay, my prettily-feathered cousin,
We shall share in joy together
Stored-grain which, in great abundance,
Fills the farmer's granary.
We shall watch the fall together
Furthering on to winter weather,
Housed—domesticated wholly,
With no thought of else but weal.

And on days that are bright and sunny
Wander thro' the fall wood gayly,
Watch the wanton gray squirrel busy
Gathering in from mast his store,
And, at length, when clouds grow lowery,
Threatening us with stormy season,
Then repair we to the garner
Where a shelter 'waits us sure.

I'll be loyal, feathery cousin,
Share with you my every comfort,
Give you place as warm and pleasant
As the farmer's barn affords;
You shall warm in lucent sunbeams
Peeping thro' the spacious barn door
Falling on the goodly hay-beds
In a golden flood of light.
And I think, tho' winter weather,
You will gladden at its beauty
As you watch the flying snowflakes
Wrapping field and grove in white.
What more pleasant, cousin Robin,
Could there be than merry winter?
I think it, you will think it, likely,
Happy as the summer time.

ROBIN—

My breast is red—come up, come up!
My mate is fled—come up, come up!
Come rest in the boughs of the apple tree,
Far the days are growing short, ah, me!

My heart is sad—come up, come up!
For things grow bad—come up, come up!
My home is not here tho' pleasant and fair
The winter may seem with its chilling air.

O, sorrow all—come up, come up!
Sorrowful fall—come up, come up!
I'll dip my wing in a brook more clear
Than the dark and chilly streams of here.

O, light and free—come up, come up!
My heart will be—come up, come up!
When the southland sunny and bright I see,
With its myrtle and fern and orange tree.

ENVOY—

Comes the lark from meadow nigh.
Blue jay, wood-dove, goldfinch shy,
From forest all, from meadow all.
Alas, farewell! alas, 'tis fall.

Comes a note, comes a cry,
Comes back Robin's glad reply,
And the apple tree boughs bend low
With happy birds before they go.

Glad are their hearts, glad their cry,
Lo! the goose that standeth by,
Speaks: alas, comes back the scoff:
"Well for you; but we are off!"

IN THE CHAMBER.

She closed her blue eyes gently to her sleep,
And within the dreary chamber death did creep,
And within the lonely chamber all was still
Just the sob and the moan; that was all.
  Her life had gone away;
  Flesh resume the silent clay.
And the silent shadows on the dead did fall,
Ane hope had dropped her last tear on the pall.

There's a heart without hope; without light:
There's a life without joy—all is night,
And within the silent chamber lonely, sad,
Sits a weary form that happiness once had—
  Had, but sped thro' fear away,
  Leaving it to selfish sway
Thro' the dreary, silent chamber—there to sigh,
To weep, to sicken, writhe in pain and die.

DOZY BLINKS THE LADY-BIRD.

Dozy blinks the lady-bird
  When day is wanin' red,
An' dozy blinks my lady love
  When time to go to bed—
When the hours are creepin' small
  To the cricket's fitful song,
She, yawnin' on my bosom sighs,
  Now, you must jog along—
  The light has flickered out, love,
  An' you must jog along.

When rosy blinks the mornin' sky
  O'er yonder peaky crest,
An' wanin' blinks the mornin' star
  A-hangin' in the west,
An' the rooster crows astir
  To the robin's early song,
I, breakin' off from wooin', sigh,
  Now I must jog along—
  The light has flickered in, love,
  Sure, I must jog along.

ABOUT ONE BROKEN-HEARTED.

A stone for a heart and a heart for a hand
And a sad, sad life and a lot o'er-drear,
For mine is the part of a broken heart
  With a smothered sob and a bitter tear.
I'll lock the chamber of a broken heart
  That flutters and pains like a strength-spent dove;
I'll bury the hopes with the curse of shame
  In the sands of a disappointed love.

But read not the truth in the laughing eyes
  Of the heart's deep woe in its miserable shell
That longs for the fetters to drop from it
  And free it from a life of hell.

DADDY'S HARD-GROWN NAG.

Daddy on his hard-grown nag
  With his gad an' frown.
Daddy on his hard-grown nag
  Startin' off to town.
Stiff o' joint an' short o' wind
Scant o' tail that bobs behind,
Measley hipped an' blinkin' blind—
  Daddy's hard-grown nag.

Then, heigh ho! heigh ho!
  Throw him the old saddle-bag.
Heigh ho! heigh ho!
  Daddy on his hard-grown nag.

Once upon a frisky nag
  Daddy rode to town.
Once upon a blooded nag
  He rode his neighbor down.
But he traded an' he swapped
An' from bad to worse he dropped,
Now on flea-bit Nance he's propped—
  Daddy's hard-grown nag.

OF FANCY I'D SING.

O of fancy I'd sing; but not of the heart
With its burden of grief and its tale of regret.
I'd not lead thee sighing far into the night
  With a song over-doleful thou'd strive to forget;
But of gay-crested fancy in her rapturous flight
As her pinions sweep wide thro' the vastness of joy—
Of her I would sing while the harp of delight
Mingles bliss with each word that time ne'er can destroy.

ABOUT CLOE REA MOORE.

With one press on her tight, hot lips,
  She winced and fainted in her bliss,
And then she sighed and bounding wild
  In ecstasy her love did kiss.
He drove the cruel dagger deep;
  At every thrust she blessed him o'er,
She held him to her snowy breast,
  In rapture dying—Cloe Rea Moore.

He raised her from the downy bed
  And kissed away regretful tears.
Love-passion drove him to the wrong,
  Injustice weighed him down with fears.
But when at length her waxen hand
  Touched his and pleading eyes of yore
Looked up, vile passion rose again
  To goad and gloat sweet Cloe Rea Moore.

When moons had waxed and moons had
    waned
  And time had passed and parent mourned,
There came a stranger in the night
  And weeping loudly to be scorned.
Forth rushed the servant with the light
  To heed the voice ne'er heard before;
The lover 'neath the window sighed,
  "Alas! alas! for Cloe Rea Moore."

And then when the coffin was lowered from
    sight
And the cold earth her body did fold—
Forever, forever shut out from the light—
Forever left silent and cold:

How then in my anguish I turned from the
    spot
With a heart hot and restless with pain
And returned to the lonesome, bereaved,
    dreary cot;
But my heart longed by her to have lain.

So now and forever my only solace
Is the thoughts of my Nancy so dear,
Thus lonely I sit by the old fire-place
Just waiting—the meeting is near.

WAITING.

Lonely I sit by the old fire-place
  And think of when Nancy and I
First met—just a look into each other's face
  And the old story read and passed by.

Then next when we met at the old country
    church
And sat on the same wooden seat
Without any back save a pole of white birch
Made fast with a peg to a cleat.

Then just how she looked and just how I felt
  When I asked her permission to call,
How she dangled the locket that hung at her
    belt
And blushed her consent, that was all.

And then of our courtship and also the ring
  I placed on her finger, while she,
With a look of devotion as pure as a spring,
  Dropt a tear in reciprocal plea.

And then of our marriage and union thro' life
  With its many of hardships and cares,
And that undying love which continually rife
  Kept our hearts in the sunshine for years.

And then when I watched with an anxious
    desire
O'er her bed in her sickness and pain,
How I bathed her hot temples to drive off the
    dire
Fever-specter that clung to her brain.

And then when she lay cold and pale in her
    shroud
And the hot tears of misery fell,
How my heart sank within me and cried out
    aloud
In a bitterness words ne'er can tell.

TAKE BACK THE VOWS.

Take back the vows that lightly fell
  From thy false lips of beauty;
What matter tho' they never dwell
  In hope or love or duty?
And turn from me those dreamy eyes
  That sadly have misled me
Into the dreary vale of sighs
  Where happiness hath fled me.

Oh, wouldst thou that the spell remain
  That hapless, led me dreaming
Thro' pleasures, oh, so sweet I fain
  Did worship their bright seeming?
Oh, wouldst thou that the spell rema
  To lead sad love a-sighing
While this o'er-burdened heart of pain in
  Sinks low where hope is dying?

Take back the vows I know too well
  The sin thy false lips smother;
But, oh, I pray the sin that fell
  On me shall curse no other.
But ask me not that I forget
  Tho' I forgive forever,
Fond memory shrouded in regret
  Is crying—never—never!

WILLIE.

Oh, Willie thou so erudite—
  Thou whom with hope my heart inspired;
Plump, round—two hundred pounds of joy,
  A good condition; much desired—
I see thee yet as long ago
  When gayly singing thou passed by
With dignity as high as heaven
  And heart as tender as the eye.

'Tis oft I turn with sweet delight
  The pages memory's keeping yet;
In fancy feel the old-time joy
  That's flown away and left regret—
No bitterness of unwise youth
  To haunt the margin of the past,
There's no regret that lingers there,
  Save for the joy that could not last.

So full of charity thy soul
  Gave over credit unto all.
No odds what one's dimensions were,
  So true his heart, were never small.
I say I see thee as of old,
  When gayly singing thou passed by,
With dignity as high as heaven
  And heart as tender as the eye.

SWEET MARY.

Sweet Mary with a face so mild
  And gentle it did seem divine,
And yet I knew that she was mine
And dared to kiss her, I defiled.

And when I took her on my knee,
  "Wherefore," she asked me with a sigh,
  "Are tears within your kindly eye,
O, will you tell the truth to me?"

I turned my head away from her.
  My heart was cloyed: I spoke no word.
  I only thought—Have mercy, Lord,
Grief is too hard, too hard to bear.

And then she coughed that hollow cough,
  And blood was on her pale, thin lips:
She touched it with her finger tips
And sadly turned and brushed it off.

And I would say, to ease her pain:
  Be of good cheer; your eye is bright;
  The rose is on your cheek to-night—
You'll soon be well and strong again.

O, stretch of years that memory fills
  'Twixt her and me, 'twixt love and love,
  I'd give for one brief hour to rove
With her again o'er these green hills.

These tears that wet your grave-sod now
  O, Mary, if you can but know,
  Bind closer, closer as they flow,
My heart to you with sacred vow.

AUTUMN.

The saddening sound of autumn winds
  Is heard among the old pine trees
And down the glen where the daisies grew
  And played the musky summer breeze.

The foliage wears a withered hue,
  The dew lies long on faded grass,
The honeysuckles on the wall
  Are retrospections sad to pass.

The whirlwind plays in dusty road;
  Its rings and pyramids are seen
To sparkle in the sun's bright rays
  As transient magicals convene.
The brook runs shallow o'er its sand,
  And strewn with dead leaves—red and gold;
The water-lilies droop and hide
  Their beauty in a lifeless fold.

The birds have left their summer home
  To seek the warmth of southern sun;
The gray squirrels thro' the branches leap,
  And autumn nutting has begun.
The withered flower left in the vase
  We'll use to mark a verse, perchance,
That in the golden summer time
  We read thro' blissful circumstance.

But, looking o'er the autumn fields
  We sigh, 'twere best some joys should pass.
Some hearts rejoice while others weep,
  Some with their dead hopes sleep, alas!
But while we gaze the thoughts arise
  Of life—youth, maturity and age.
We mark the glowing sun decline—
  We turn from what it does presage.

THE OLD HOME WITHOUT MOTHER.

O, shrine beneath my own roof-tree,
  Where mother, in her holy grace,
Smiled down in new-born eyes to see
  Her perfect likeness in my face,
O, yield me, yield me something yet
  Of all the varied scenes so dear;
O, wherefore is this sad, sad change
  That's made the old place all so drear?

The Hoosier hills are all abloom
  In beauty as I once did know,
The wild rose has not lost its musk
  And yet the sweet-breathed lilies blow,
And yet the orchard sends its mild
  Perfume o'er heatherly glen to me
As in the days of yore—but hush!
  For where is mother—O, where is she?

Is there a link that binds my heart
  To all the beauty of the scene?
No; not for me—not one for me!
  There's gone from it what once has been—
The tender heart, the perfect love,
  The hand that smoothed my pillow—cease!
O, let me hasten far from it—
  For me it has not any peace.

THE HERMIT'S SONG.

When shadows creep athwart the lawn
  And vesper light shines thro' the pane,
I hear the whir of unseen wings
  And voice of sweetest silvery strain.

When pictures on the midnight wall
  Stand out against the pitch-dark vast,
I feel a warm breath on my brow
  And soft-fold robes swayed gently past.

And when the cock ere daylight crows
  A myriad glories trance the skies.
I look within the golden gates
  Upon the blissful paradise.

O, perfect peace, O, perfect rest.
  Wherefore, O, eyes have you to weep?
There is no pain within my heart
  Since now His perfect love does keep.

O, perfect fullness of my joy;
  No slightest care within my breast;
My humble cottage is sublime—
  My sleep, the calmest, sweetest rest.

YOUTH.

In all this happy world I cannot see
Aught worth a sigh, if I not reckon love.
In fact, my heart's so light I often be
In doubt such organ as that mine would prove;
Yet, how my pulses thrill! My step so quick—
My limbs, as yet, have never deigned to tire;
My curves of beauty, and my muscles thick,
Heap praises on me from whom do admire;
And all my thought is joy from morn till night;
Save when I think of love I ne'er am sad;
My bright eye never sees the wrong or right,
So many happy fancies fill my head.
Too strange to think man wears out unto grief;
Seems this too silly notion for belief.

OLD AGE.

Sadly I regret this quavering voice.
My virile force all gone—decrepit—weak.
I saw these wrinkles grow against my choice;
And these stiff joints—I hate of them to speak.
Eh, long I with conflicting nature strove;
But must succumb to her at last—at length.
I've battled her past four-score years to prove,
At this late day, I'm robbed of all my strength.
I'm deaf; my sight is gone; my teeth; my hair;
My blood that thin I shiver in the sun;
I'm shriveled to a waste far past repair—
My work is done—my race is almost run.
Sometimes I feel to curse that time should spoil
Such perfect work—but, thinking, bless his toil.

LITTLE HAPPINESS IS HIS.

O, little happiness is his
  Who casts his virtue to the wind
  And adds a wail to humankind
While sin recordeth who he is.
But perfect happiness is his,
  With power e'en in his garment hem,
  Whose virtue is his diadem;
Ah, heaven recordeth who *he* is.

WILLIE BOWERS.

When Willie came a-courtin' me
  My heart went in a flutter,
I was so shy an', oh, my, my!
  So fat I shamed the butter.
An' I was in the garden-patch
  That was besprent with flowers
When rovin' Willie clinked the latch—
  Gay, rovin' Willie Bowers.

Oh, Willie was a rover,
He roamed the wide world over,
There was ne'er as gallant lover
  As my rovin' Willie boy.

He tipped his hat in gallant style
  An' asked to pull a blossom,
An' for me chose a milky rose
  An' pinned it in my bosom.
An', oh, I blushed an' felt so queer
  As fleetin' went the hours
I chippered with my Willie dear—
  My rovin' Willie Bowers.

Said he, when bloomy summer past
  An' sharp the wind came blowin',
"If there be shame an' I'm to blame,
  'Tis best that I be goin'."
I said a weepin', If there be
  It is no fault o' ours;
But shame 'twould be a leavin' me,
  My lover—Willie Bowers.

So Willie stayed at home with me
  An' no more went a rovin';
But bein' dead in love we wed
  An' just kept on a lovin';
An' Willie minded well the farm
  An' I the house an' flowers:
May never to him fall a harm—
  My own dear Willie Bowers.

YOU SLATTERN, YOU SLATTERN.

You slattern, you slattern, you set me a pattern,
You set me a pattern an' ruined my name.
You led me astray with your lyin' an' flatterin';
You led me an' left me a-weepin' in shame.

Oh, gay are the hills that rise o'er the wady
An' dear is the cot tho' humble withal,
An' bloomy the paths a-windin' an' shady,
An' happy my heart ere I list to your call.

But, oh, you would meet me an' kindly would treat me
An' smile when I smiled an' weep when I wept,
Till if for a day you should fail to greet me,
I sighed it to darkness when little I slept.

An' away to your cot I'd steal from my mother
To list to the false tales you poured in my ear,
An' away to the town in quest o' the lover
You said that would love me an' call me his dear.

But, alas! for my heart, for it found only sorrow.
No lover it found when, alas! 'twas too late.
You gave me to drink a vile potion o' horror!
An' God only pitied my miserable fate.

An' from the big house I gazed on the people
An' saw my old mother a-weepin' for me,
She gazed on the street an' she gazed on the steeple
An' prayed for her child that she never shall see.

Oh, gay are the hills that rise o'er the wady,
An' dear is the cot tho' humble withal,
An' bloomy the paths a-windin' an' shady
An' happy my heart ere I list to your call.

But now it is breakin'! oh, now it is breakin'!
Dear mother, dear mother, I love you the same;
But, oh, I am lost an' forever forsaken—
Too bitter the tears that I weep in my shame.

YOU LITTLE KNOW THE GALLIN' YOKE.

You little know the gallin' yoke
A-lookin' in the smilin' eye;
You do not see the heart that's broke,
Nor feel the pain, nor hear the sigh.

For you there is a tender word,
A smile, a kiss, before you go;
But oh, the sorrow never heard
An' you, I pray, may never know.

Behind the eye is vain regret,
An' withered hope, an' blighted peace,
An' there, forever too deep-set,
A woe from which there's no release.

You little know the gallin' yoke
A-lookin' in the smilin' eye;
You do not see the heart that's broke,
Nor feel the pain, nor hear the sigh.

McCRACKINS'S MILL.

O, McCrackins's Mill at the foot of the hill
And the dusty old miller a-singing,
I remember so well and the picture does dwell
In my mind and sweet thoughts ever bringing.
Oft I fancy I am by the old mill-dam
That the water poured over so madly,
And the fish dart and gleam in the clear, deep stream
And the mill grinds on as gladly

Round went the wheel from morning till night
Grinding the flour so pure and so white.
O, McCrackins's Mill I remember it still
And the dusty old miller a-singing,
And the dusty old miller a-singing.

O, McCrackins's Mill at the foot of the hill,
With its chaff flying over the heather,
Oft all the day long I hear its sweet song
Tho' years have flown since we're together.
Yet gayly I rove with my first sweet love
To the mill o'er the old hill-path winding,
Tho' sleeps my heart's bride on the windy hillside,
And the mill long ago has stopped grinding.

AMERICA.

Oh, land of happiness! oh, land of liberty!
We lift our hearts in thankfulness
For blessings full and free.
Oh, hearts so pure and true, and strong and brave and good,
What tho' they boast in other lands
None hath more royal blood.

All hail! America, where poor are not oppressed,
No pompous king or lord to gall;
But with sweet freedom blest.
Shake hands across the void, the North and South invite.
More perfect peace no nation hath
Than that where hearts unite.

Trust not to those who seek to mar our time
    of peace;
From schemes and theories wrapt in doubt
All thy support release.
The brawler countenance not, he leads thee to
    his gain.
Two people struggling for a cause,
The right, at length, shall reign.

Fair is our land of peace abloom with all that's
    good,
The sweet hearthstone of millions souls,
Nor want doth e'er intrude.
Keep from our happy homes, oh, Lord, the
    tyrant's hand;
Give unto him whose heart is pure
The keeping of our land.

FORSAKEN.

Dark o'er the midnight hill
    Wild clouds are flyin',
And hopes o' yesterday
    Sadly are dyin';
Ne'er in the breakin' heart
    Shall song awaken;
There but an echo bides
    Cryin', "forsaken!"

Hearts that are truest e'er
    Find surest trouble;
Hopes that are brightest oft
    Our sorrow double;
But, O, for the maiden's heart
    Regret is breakin';
Peace leaves it all alone—
    It is forsaken!

OH, SHOULD I WRITE A SIMPLE RHYME?

Oh, should I write a simple rhyme,
    Or should I strive with juggled words
To please the weaker of mankind—
    That kind that smile—the empty gourds
That point the finger at the mind
    That in a simple, homely way,
Brings some sweet truth to light of day?

If a sweet truth, tho' in the least
    And simplest words, be told to man,
Is it less sweet since told that way?
    I hold, 'less vision feigns its plan,
The soul in the bright light of day
    Is nobler, purer, oftener right
Than that in sordid shades of night.

Who writes a simple rhyme is less
    Than he who writes a subtile verse,
Yet, he who writes the mazy lines
    Is often young, may be perverse.
"Dig in my sonnets as in mines
    To find the treasures that they hold."
When but pedantry they unfold.

CLARA.

Why, little Clara, do the days
    Go speeding by so merrily?
I riddle thus the reason why:
    At me you smile so cheerily—
    At me you smile so cheerily.

Ah, merry days go speeding by
    Adorned with smiles of ecstasy,
And tho' content and happy quite,
    Yet, there's somewhat that vexes me.
    Yet, there's somewhat that vexes me.

Where, little Clara, is your heart
    For which I sue unceasingly?
You make me happy with your smiles
    And make me sigh increasingly,
    And make me sigh increasingly.

Yet, juggled 'tween my joy and grief,
    The days slip by so merrily.
Anon your smiles dispel my grief,
    And grief my joy—aye, verily,
    And joy my grief as merrily.

A PSALM.

If you are doing the best you can, brother,
    Your reward will surely be great;
Care not what the world may say, brother,
    Its love you'll find oftener hate.
There are many to trample you down, brother;
    But few that would you elevate.
If you are doing the best you can, brother,
    Trouble not, your reward will be great.

Tho' you sink till you see no hope, brother,
    Tho' the last crust you take from the plate,
Tho' the ones that are dearest to you, brother,
    Turn in coldness away from your gate,
Tho' you see in this wide, wide world, brother,
    Nothing but the advance of sad fate,
Keep on doing the best you can, brother,
    For in truth your reward will be great.

There will come a bright day to you, brother,
    A bright day if you only wait,
And the ones that trampled you down, brother,
    May raise you to the highest state,

And the ones that laughed at your works, brother,
  And discouraged you in their hate,
May call you exceeding wise, brother,
  And give you reward that is great.

Then, bide for the day will come, brother,
  Come surely, brother, as fate,
You're to do but the best you can, brother—
  Just patiently labor and wait.
Tho' the world may not bow at your feet brother
  Nor your words not the nation elate ;
But by doing the best you can, brother,
  Trouble not ; your reward will be great.

THE OLD FOREST TREE.

When grandpa was young he bought himself a farm
And built a house and married Alice Moor,
And his Alice dear to please, while cutting down some trees,
He left a big oak standing by the door.
"This," he said to dear grandma, "when the winter winds are raw,
Will be a shelter for our home, you see,
And in summer dry and hot we can find a resting spot
'Neath the shady boughs of this old forest tree."

There rested grandpa when aged and hoary,
There played the children in innocent glee,
There's where the lovers at eve told their story—
There, 'neath that wide-spreading, old forest tree.

When grandpa at morn woke at the robin's call,
As on the topmost bough it was a-singing,
He sought the old oak tree and in fancy I can see
Him smiling while the breakfast bell he's ringing ;
For there the old bell hung and there the children swung,
And there the farm-hands chatted merrily,
And many a summer night strolled lovers in delight,
To the shady boughs of that old forest tree.

Oft in fancy I drift back to dear old grandpa's time,
And memory brings me many a queer old story,
That, 'neath the old oak tree, he used to tell to me,
Of early days and old-time hero's glory.
But years have passed away and the tree is in decay,
And grandpa from the cares of life is free;
Yet I look back o'er the years mingling sweetest joys with tears,
To the shady boughs of that old forest tree.

THE RAIN.

The moon tipt over in the middle of the night
  And it began to rain,
And the mud grew deep and the roads grew bad
  Ere daylight came again ;
And the drift did cloy the old mill stream
  And it groaned and splashed and roared,
And the clouds hung low and the wind did blow
  While it poured, and poured, and poured.
"But what's the use," the farmer said,
  "For a man to fret and scold ?
I'm satisfied if it's wet or dry
  Or if it's hot or cold.
These folks that are complaining always,
  Every time it's raining, always
Find that, though complaining always,
  It's not always dry."

A townsman coming down the road
  Was wrapped in his rubber coat,
And his big black horse was covered with mud
  When he got to the ferry-boat ;
But the ferryman was a mile away
  And the boat swung to and fro,
And the rain just poured while the townsman roared—
  "Halloo ! halloo ! halloo !"
"There's quite enough to worry one,"
  Said the townsman's wife, at home,
"My good man is two miles away,
  And through all this rain must come.
These folks that are contented ever,
  Never aught relented, ever
Seem, I have consented ever,
  To ever little gain."

Next Sunday morn the sun shot up
  And set all the windows ablaze,
And the mud dried up and blew away
  And clouds o' dust did raise.
And the preacher took this for his text—
  "None should the poor oppress ;
That wealth can't buy, though hard we try,
  Our peace and happiness."
But the townsman's wife in her dusty silk
  Just sat and fussed and fussed ;
But the farmer satisfied with rain
  Was satisfied with dust.

And the preacher said that "leisure only
Vexed the heart. Life's measure only
Filled with peace and pleasure, only,
When content was in the heart."

OLD FASHIONED FRIENDS.

Give me the old-fashioned friends
　That sweetly in memory dwell ;
Give me the old-fashioned ways
　An' old-fashioned whiskey as well.
I'll drink for the sake o' the friends,
　The old-fashioned friends tried an' true,
An' a glass for the old-fashioned hearts
　That have grown very few, very few.

Yes, give me the old-fashioned friends
　That sweetly in memory dwell,
And give me the old-fashioned ways
　An' old-fashioned whiskey as well.

My hair has grown frosty with age,
　And my step has grown feeble an' slow ;
My heart only clings to the joys
　That I knew in the long, long ago.
One drink for the sake o' the days
　When my young pulses thrilled with delight ;
One glass for the old-fashioned friends
　That forever have gone from my sight.

AN EVERYDAY SONG.

Strive to be cheerful, strive to be happy ;
　Put trouble aside for a song.
For few have relented of being contented
　As thro' life they journeyed along.
There certainly is nothing more amiss,
　Than to let trouble our peace destroy,
And as days pass away grow wrinkled and gray,
　Being robbed of life's pleasure and joy.

Then strive to be cheerful, strive to be happy ;
　Always drive trouble away ;
You are sure to live longer, grow wiser and
　　stronger
　By just being happy each day.
By wearing a smile you'll find afterwhile,
　This old world is not hard to endure,
And as days pass away, now mind what I say,
　Your cares will grow fewer and fewer.

POGUE'S RUN.

With dirty face you creep along,
　You wily, little crooked stream ;
You fret your pebbles with no song
　O' sweetness, nor is limpid dream

A gift o' yours, nor pleasin' rhyme
　A-jingle in your stenchy bed.
A-strollin' by you many a time,
　I've seen your murky bottom dead.

But, lo ! withal, a frisky spell
　Comes o'er you scarce an hour hence,
An' how you'd roar an' dash an' swell,
　Till you were great in consequence ;
An, all along your cavin' banks
　The folks would watch you in great fear
Or chinnin' o'er your rifty pranks
　That cost the old town overdear.

Yet, you deceitful little spurt,
　With banks chuck-level I've discerned
You threatenin' the whole town to hurt ;
　But scarce to you my back was turned,
When down you dropt as would a rock ;
　An' when at morn I've gone apace
To see your ruin in many a block,
　You'd only washed your dirty face !

MARY ALLIE.

October winds come blowin' sharp
　O'er hill an' sheeny valley,
An' o'er the wood an' o'er the grave
　O' darlin' Mary Allie,
An' o'er the last rose on her grave
　The hoary frost comes stealin',
An' bows it as is bowed my heart
　That's deepest anguish feelin'.

Thro' all the bloomy summer time,
　My darlin', darlin' Mary,
Was full o' mirth an' full o' life
　With lips an' cheeks o' cherry.
We vowed our vows o' love so sweet—
　Vowed naught should part us ever ;
Ah, little thinkin' that cold death,
　The fondest ties could sever.

But now beneath the cold, gray sod,
　Sleeps all in life I cherished,
An' there, alas, the last fond hope,
　Like the last rose, has perished.
An' moanin' fly the autumn winds
　O'er hill an' wood an' valley,
I would to God my dead heart lay
　With darlin' Mary Allie.

OLD NEGLIGENCE.

I can't shake off Old Negligence
　He sticks to me so closely ;
With laugh and joke, an' talk an' smoke,
　He takes my time up mostly.

He's with me at the mornin'
  An' at the twilight mellow;
I can't shake off Old Negligence,
  He's such a clever fellow.

I can't shake off Old Negligence,
I can't shake off Old Negligence,
I can't shake off Old Negligence,
  He's such a clever fellow.

He leads me 'neath the coolin' shade
  That summer is a-wooin';
He courts me in my old arm chair
  When winter winds are blowin';
And many a task he takes from me,
  Tho' little to my credit,
I can't shake off Old Negligence;
  I'm always in his debit.

I SIGH FOR THE RIVER.

I sigh for the river that flows 'tween the hills,
An' the cot smilin' down on its bosom so bright.
I sigh for a picture that vacancy fills
An' hangs on the wall at the stilly midnight.

Whatever the fate o' the cot an' the stream,
Oh, why should it matter? I ask o'er and o'er.
Oh, could I forget them, never, never to dream
O' the birth-place o' Love an' the grave o' No
  More.

I WROTE A VERSE TO CHARLEY BOY.

I wrote a verse to Charley boy
  With passion runnin' high, sir,
An' put a drop o' harm in it
  To make it all the nicer,
An' tho' I'd wrote far better verse
  O' moral tone an' letter,
Than any verse I'd ever wrote,
  He said 'twas ten times better.

So in his classic undertone
  He praised the verse I wrote him;
He praised the verse with look askance
  Till scores o' friends did note him,
An' caught the whim, an' caught the rhyme,
  An' rhythm as the poet,
An' so the circle grew an' grew,
  Till many a one did know it.

An' many a man o' manner staid
  Did read it o'er an' o'er,
An' lay it down an' pick it up
  An' read the verse once more;
An' many a maid an' wizen wife
  With furtive wink did quote it,
Till many a word o' undue praise
  Fell on the one who wrote it.

An' friend an' stranger at me gazed
  An' wished that they could be me,
An' many traveled many a mile
  An' paid a price to see me.
"A genius, truly!" they remarked,
  With little stint to honor,
An' even old acquaintance sought
  To serve as glory's donor.

An' thus it ran—the drop o' harm
  Wrapped in the verse did make me;
That was the secret, golden key
  That unto fame should take me;
But now with feathered nest I sigh,
  Tho' praised for erudition,
An' lead old fortune by the nose,
  Low burdened with contrition.

PASSION'S SONG.

Transient are the joys of life,
  Constant are the sorrows;
Slowly drag the weary years
  Full of vain to-morrows.
I have said to one I knew
  In the spring time of her life,
Love doth conquer that is true—
  True love never borrows.

Better far the heart repose
  Than to mere endeavor—
Merely trust, and then regret
  What its trustings sever:
Comes a sweet voice to my ear—
  One I prized above all others,
Long years silent, now so clear—
  "Trust a heart, never."

Had I words to tell my thoughts—
  No, you would but chide me:
Ah, this world is vain and cold,
  It would but deride me.
Better far my weary heart
  Drown its grief in silence,
Tho' the poet fire may dart,
  Tho' the world belied me.

Man can only fill his sphere:
  Few live long in story;
Only vessels wrought of clay—
  Humbleness or glory.
I have hoped and know the pain
  Of the bitter sequel;
I have hoped and hoped in vain,
  Now my locks are hoary.

When the passion of the heart
  Every vital singes
And the heart has tired at last
  And in weakness cringes,
And the struggling passion cries—

Cries for love that's vanished—
Then true woe is come, nor dies,
Never hope infringes.

Let her rest, nor know of pain
In her shrine of beauty;
Gloating o'er her sordid wealth
And her love-gained booty;
I have sadly turned to life—
Sadly? aye—forever
Battling down an inward strife
For a nobler duty.

ALLOW ME, WHEN YOU SADLY MUSE.

Allow me, when you sadly muse,
My dear old friend, one stray regret,
For old-time sake we should forget,
But memory sternly does refuse.

I'd give to you the old-time song
The old-time joy an' laughin' eyes,
Were it not for the sighs, the sighs
That I have listened to so long.

I can not ask your pleasant dream;
I'll be content if thro' a sigh
You say, "O I regret!" but why?
Unfinished, dashed in silence' stream.

A HOME FOR EVERY MAN.

Oh, here's a home for every man
Who has an honest heart,
And Freedom stands to welcome you
Who come to take a part—
Come to share the blessings
That are waiting here for you;
But woe to him a thousand times
Whose heart is found untrue.

Then, if you come from England,
Or if you come from France,
Or if you come from Ireland,
Or Scotland, as you chance,
Just so you love the right, boys,
Just so your hearts are true,
You're welcome to America
And the old red, white and blue.

No king does sway his scepter here,
No lord does rob our lands;
But plenty fills our happy homes
Of peace and helping hands.
A thousand million acres broad
These rich lands stretch for you;
But woe to him a thousand times
Whose heart is found untrue.

JOANN THE SERVANT.

Yesterday, seventy years ago,
My eyes first saw the light.
Mother—oh, she passed away
Seventy years yesternight.
Old have waxed my bones and stiff,
Many a spleeny day rolls round,
Yet I know for a truth that rest
Lies not far beyond.

Well I remember and forsooth
Remember what I should not,
Remember the day I killed the love
He bore me! Love is what?
Eh, I've learnt the lesson of love.
Of all the sad, sad things
Is to kill the love you know is yours
While your heart to it desperately clings.

Hope to me is a shallow dream:
Never to hope is never to sigh.
Hope was the sunshine of my soul;
But as a shadow passed me by.
All of sorrow and all of joy
Lies 'neath yon rose-bush over the way;
Sad is my heart when fall is come
And weary wind and cloud so gray.

It was in the fall when he
Came to the village—fifty years,
Yes, just fifty years ago,
I was twenty—mind not my tears—
And we loved, but jealousy
Filled me with that awful hate
That's born of love in a woman's breast—
Only there—Ah! it was great.

And, alas! I killed his love,
Killed his love while loving him;
Hating him yet loving him more;
Often I weep till my old eyes are dim.
All of sorrow and all of joy
Lie 'neath yon rose-bush over the way;
Sad is my heart when fall is come
And weary wind and cloud so gray.

I WONDER.

If I or soon or late should know
My cherished hopes so very sweet,
Were come to the reality,
Oh, would my peace be then complete?

I wonder, should truth be their lot,
Nor any doubt, if there will be
In them the blissfulness of now
That mans my soul and leadeth me—

Aye, thro' derision and regrets,
And envy's ban, all for their sake.
I wonder will they be more sweet—
My soul to fuller peace awake.

I CAN'T BREAK OFF A-SIGHIN'.

I can't break off a-sighin' tho'
  I see you all so boon ;
Far more I feel like cryin' tho'
  I step some sweet old tune.
I'll drink with you for lastin' health ;
I'll hope with you for comin' wealth ;
But 'tween our glasses if I sigh,
  Oh, chide me not. If in my eye
You see a tear, an' wonder what ;
  Oh, question not, oh, question not.

I can't break off a-sighin';
  I can't break off a-sighin';
For many a hope is dyin';
  But I pray you question not.

Your kindness I will treasure, tho'
  My heart be otherwhere,
An' friendship deep in measure, tho'
  'T has cost me many a tear.
I'll shake with you for loyalty ;
I'll vow with you for constancy ;
But 'tween our pledges if I sigh,
  Oh, chide me not. If in my eye
You see a tear, an' wonder what ;
  Oh, question not, oh, question not.

JOHN.

What can I build my hope upon
  Since John is lowly sleepin'?
The black hearse bore my heart away
  With his an' left me weepin'.
I did not know the worth o' him,
  Nor the love he told so often ;
I did not know the worth o' him
  Till he was in his coffin.

What can I build my hope upon ?
What can I build my hope upon ?
There's little now, since John is gone,
  For me to build my hope upon.

I passed his grave on yonder hill
  Where bloomy summer 's dyin';
But, oh, the moanin' o' the dove
  An' weary wind a-sighin'.
I passed his grave on yonder hill,
  The moon was pale at even,
I raised my eyes thro' bitter tears
  An' saw him smile in heaven.

The cricket sings a song o' woe,
  O' midnight silence weary ;
The old dog whines beneath the hill,
  Where stands his cabin dreary;
The weepin'-willows sigh an' moan
  Beside my window swayin';
Oh, God, oh, God that I could die !
  I'm prayin', ever prayin'.

BOYHOOD DAYS.

When night has thrown her curtain
  O'er the last smile of the sun,
And I sit down in the old arm-chair
  To rest—my day's work done,
'Tis then my thoughts run back to where
  Youth's sparkling fountain plays,
And on its flood of blissful seeming,
  Drift thro' boyhood happy days.

There's mother's smile to greet me,
  And the old home o'er and o'er,
Looks the same—the yellow roses
  Hanging o'er the low-swung door ;
There the same pink morning glories
  Cluster 'round the window still,
And I tread the path that twisted
  To the stream beneath the hill.

And I drift in fancy further—
  Down beside the dear old stream
That in boyhood days has lulled me
  Into many a blissful dream ;
And I picture out the beauty
  That my youthful fancy wed,
When the sun was slowly sinking
  And the sky was growing red.

Still I drift along in fancy—
  Down the same old grassy lane
That has led me, oh, so often,
  To the golden fields of grain ;
And I hear the long-remembered,
  Dear old merry song again
That the harvest hands were singing,
  And the reaper's sweet refrain.

And in fancy from the old oak porch
  I watch the star-lit sky
At evening, while the crickets' songs
  Grow fainter till they die.
And I have again the feelings
  That so sweetly o'er me fell
When the wind was softly sighing
  Thro' the cedars by the well.

And again I hear at evening,
  When the candle-light is dim,
Mother's prayer ; and then I listen
  To some sweet, old-fashioned hymn ;
Feel her hand upon my pillow—
  But, alas, the spell is vain ;
Fancy takes me back to boyhood—
  Could I ever there remain.

YOU AND I.

You write for glory's empty wind,
  I write to elevate my kind ;
But if I fail nor can abide,
  I rest, God knowing I have tried.

SEPTEMBER.

September with her kindly eye,
  Is beamin' on the valley,
An' sets ablush the orchard hangin' low,
An' whistles o'er the forest dry
  With many a prankish sally,
An' hollyhocks that in the garden grow.

An' all about the faded land
  She wanders kindly soothin'
Nature as a mother soothes a child
That has, with tired foot an' hand,
  Returned from work behoovin',
To greet the blessin' that is undefiled.

The heart leaps gladly as her voice,
  That gently o'er the wavin',
Rustlin' corn comes balmily along
A-croonin' softly o'er her choice
  O' pleasant days, an' savin'
Every day for peace, an' mirth, an' song.

An' in her hand is plenty, too,
  For all the toilin' poor;
An' in her heart is charity and love;
Tho' riches only for the few
  That to the end endure;
Yet, hope for all that unavailin' strove.

MY PEOPLE.

I'll style them not with cant or jest,
  I'd every good o' them unbar;
Beholden not to vain behest,
  I'll write my people as they are.

Cursed be the man that would abuse
  The virtues of a heart or mind.
Of my dear people, you that choose,
  Hint not to me in word unkind.

Ah, theirs is a kindly heart,
  And theirs is a helping hand,
And ne'er from truth they stand apart—
  My people in their blessed land.

I'll style them not with any fear
  Of ethics' euphemistic scar,
Believe me, you of kindly ear,
  I'll write them shining as a star!

I KNOW A VALE.

I know a vale, a sheeny vale,
  With musky rose an' windin' stream
  An' on whose margin nod an' dream
The water-lilies, sweet an' pale.

An' somber hills rise high above,
  As sentinels, guard the lovely spot;
  I question not, I question not
It is a sacred spot o' love.

For there when once I wandered lone
  I pulled a rose beside the stream
An' with it in a spell did seem
Standin' claspin' loved Ione;
  An' sweetest music floated o'er,
  An' craggy hill with hangin' vine
  Re-echoed, "She is mine! is mine!"
She wept, "I love, O, never more!"

JOE WINDERING.

The dewdrops on the petals gleam,
  And wild-flower musk blows o'er the hills;
  On topmost bough the robin trills
To morning wakened from her dream.
And far across the valley-land
  Swings low a vapor o'er the stream
  Which frets its rocky banks where cream
Its shallows o'er the silvery sand.

But, roundabout the old brown cot,
  Blooms 'mid the weeds the marigold;
  Blent with the sweet-fern is that cold,
Strange, sickening scent from shade and rot.
And deep within the thicket nigh
  The serpent warns all from the spot,
  And thrice his rattle heeded not,
Darts, hissing, past with glassy eye.

Half round have warped the oaken boards
  That serve as pathway from the gate;
  And in the green-scum pool do mate,
And croak the hoarse-voiced frogs in hordes;
The old well, caving, ceased to yield—
  Its waters buried—but affords
  A home for bats, which void of words.
And reason, hapless, live concealed.

Low, leaning on the mouldering wall,
  He hid his care-worn face and wept:
  "I know, I know, tho' she has slept
Thro' all these weary years, that all
My hopes and prayers and memory's pain
  Have been for her—these tears that fall—
  These bitter tears—for her in vain.

"I call to mind the happy days—
  Call thro' the woe—call thro' the pain—
  Call back the vows, alas, so vain
And heart that strayed in vainer ways.
I turn again to thee, fond past,
  With vision veiled by some strange haze,
  Which hope consumes with passion's blaze,
Yet, knowing it shall ever last.

"That light-haired boy on yonder hill,
  Is all of life fate left to me.
Lo! standing o'er this grave I see
  His mother's sweet face smiling still—
The same sweet smile she used to greet
  Me with returning from the mill,
While at the gate our hearts did thrill
  With joy at baby's pattering feet.

"O, heart! O, unwise, foolish heart!
  What profit your repentance now?
You leave me but a broken vow,
  From happiness so far apart.
What profit doleful memory now,
  And its vague pictures strange to art?
That awful something makes me start,
  While cold beads trickle from my brow.

"But, O, sad memory, grant me yet
  That little peace o'er due my heart—
Grant me that little set apart
  For contrite heart and deep regret.
I murmur not that mine own head
  Shall wear the thorns so I may weep,
Forgiven where my dead hopes sleep,
With tender memories of the dead."

A DANCE SONG.

Trip lightly, volant dandy,
  And let your feet be handy—
Tra, la, la, la; tra, la, la!
    Gallantly to maiden bow;
    Ring and swing—tra, la, la!

Nimble-shanked and gaudy;
Do not be a boody—
Tra, la, la, la; tra, la, la!
    Strike the heel in proper time.
    Ring and swing—tra, la, la!

Sweet music in sweet metre
Makes maidens far more sweeter—
Tra, la, la, la; tra, la, la!
    Tho' the hours are growing small,
    Ring and swing—tra, la, la!

When the sun has come again
Peeking thro' the window pane—
Tra, la, la, la; tra, la, la!
    Only then we'll think o' time—
    Ring and swing—tra, la, la!

LET NOT THE DOUBTS.

Let not the doubts that round us gather
  Stay our onward march to right;
You and I, true hearts, may ever
  Hold our banners to the light.

In our path may lie deep sorrow;
  Some may taunt and some may hate;
But to-day lost in to-morrow,
  Leaves them fallen to their fate.

Our strength, the strength of right, is greater
  Than ten thousand in the wrong.
Led by the light of the Creator
  Where wrong cannot endure long.
Why should we fear or trouble borrow,
  Or heed who selfishly assails?
Tho' truth does have its days of sorrow,
  Yet, truth at last prevails.

I CAN BUT WEEP.

I can but weep in thoughts of thee,
  Tho' ties for aye are broken:
Tho' coldly we each other pass,
  And few the words are spoken.
I can but weep, I can but weep,
  When thoughts revert to other—
To other days so bright, so sweet,
  When we loved one another.

And yet I know, I know 'tis best
  That we should thus be severed;
But to forget the bright, sweet past,
  Oh, vainly I've endeavored.
I pass thee by to haply speak,
  Or smile, a sigh to smother;
But chide me not that I should weep,
  Since we have loved each other.

AUNT MARGARET.

Sweetest thoughts for days agone,
Sweetest hopes for mellow age:
All the beauty of thy soul
  In thy kindly eyes:
Ah, 'tis sweet thus looking on—
  On thy life's fair graven page;
Not a blot nor mar; the whole
  Pure and good and wise.

All the margin of past years
Shineth with thy kindly deeds;
Charity is thy sweet boon,
Love thy crowning grace;
    Thou hast dried the widow's tears,
    Given to the poor their needs—
    Soothing like some sweet old tune,
    Heart and care-worn face.

Aunt, to all thou seemest by right:
Freely flows thy sympathy
No less to the fallen than
Those of purer soul;

Yet I know for a truth that night,
Night of sorrow, thou didst see,
But thy soul seemed greater when
Peace had turned to dole.

Sweetly in thy humbleness,
Blessed with bounteous providence,
Thou hast reached a goodly age
Of thy useful life.
To live has been with thee to bless;
Thy heart in holy confidence
Rests, nor all life may presage,
Troubleth thee, good wife.

DO NOT RAISE THE WINDIN'-SHEET.

Do not raise the windin'-sheet;
Hush you: shudder only!
Hasten by nor even greet
You the watcher lonely.

Careful, through the awful hush,
Lest your breath betray you—
Careful, lest your garment brush
Aught an' death dismay you!

Leave the smoulderin' fire to die,
With its shadows liftin'
On the wall, where sings the fly
At their weird driftin'.

Slip you through the half-closed door,
Raise your hand to shield you,
Lest your eye, a-glancin' o'er
Death, to death does yield you!

Glance but at the windin'-sheet;
Hush you: shudder only!
Hasten by, nor even greet
You the watcher lonely.

A FRIEND INDEED.

I've a friend indeed, not a friend in need;
A gentleman and a scholar;
Always pleasing, yes; and I must confess,
He never borrows a dollar.
Just after my mind, and really the kind
I would introduce as perfection;
And, in truth he's sought much, for it's not
often such
With us share so agreeable connection.

It's not simply because, now mind you,
He's a gentleman and a scholar;
But don't think it amiss, when I say that it is,
Because he ne'er borrows a dollar.

I've a friend indeed, not a friend to feed,
And with him I feel quite secure;
And we often talk, and laugh and walk,
And he has not one fault to endure.
Just my ideal of man, and really I can
Grasp his hand with true friendship's confession;
No fear in my breast—true pleasure with zest;
To one's list quite a lucky digression.

O, BROTHER, YOUNG IN TROUBLED WAYS.

O, brother, young in troubled ways,
I would that I could lead you on;
But O, the hopes forever gone,
And weary days, and weary days.

I see you worn and pale with fears;
O, I would help you; I would soothe;
But for stern facts that do reprove,
And bitter tears. and bitter tears.

I grieve to see you stand apart
And long for things, in truth, are yours—
Unworthy his who but abhors
Your paining heart, your paining heart.

Were it my power, I'd place you nigher
The goal you long to worship at;
I long to do for you but that;
But vain desire, O, vain desire.

'Tis not for such as I. Truth takes
The heart to bless it at the last,
When weary of the night, so vast,
It faints and lo! the morning breaks.

SHE WENT SEEKING A POET.

She went seeking a poet
O'er hills far away—
The maid with the bright, happy face;
She went seeking a poet,
And for many a day
Roamed longing for his biding place.

And she pictured the beauty
His home would contain,
And his smiling content on the hours;
Oh, she pictured the beauty,
Again and again,
Of the poet's home, garland of flowers.

And she dreampt he would love her,
Her poet ideal,
The maid with the bright, sunny face;
Ah, she dreampt he would love her,
And to her would kneel,
And to her heart sue for a place.

But, at length, when she found him,
  'Twas in garret, and pale
On a couch, and with deep sunken eye.
She knelt, not the poet;
  Ah, she knelt low to wail,
While her dream with the poet did die!

ON THE FARM.

The cow—a good concern of usefulness,
A source of gain and blessing—
And that which to a hungry stomach
Gives comfort and satiation.

Hard by the brook in midday heat
She chews her cud 'neath shadowing tree;
Nips in the calmness of content
The sweet green grasses at her feet
And switches gadflies with her tail
Or bawls, perhaps, unto a friend
Adown the swale among the fern.

"How pleasant this is," and the cow-bell rings
As she shakes her head to rid the gnats.

"Come, merry milkmaid, art thou so free
And happy at heart as I dare be
Here in the cool shade by the brook
Listening to caw of lusty rook?"

Lo! the sun moves on and shadows are growing long,
Comes merry milkmaid down the glen singing
  a sweet love-song.
The sky is red away at the west,
And the birds are silent in their rest;
'Tis eventide and the lover comes down
From the high, high hill all purple and brown;
He sings a song the maid doth sigh
And stops to listen while he draws nigh,
And a song comes to her lips anon,
And she sweetly sings as she hastens on:

"The cricket sings its evening lay,
The firefly gleams in the dying day;
O, my heart, thy joy's complete,
Wait, O, wait thy love to meet;
For the world is fair, fair and bright,
Wait, my heart, so glad and light.

"The shadows fall, the sun is red;
Sink low, sink low apace to bed;
For the world is fair, fair and bright,
Wait, my heart, so glad and light."

Hush! do not disturb their joy
Their hearts are pure in love;
Leave them alone in their trysting-place
'Neath the nest of the moaning dove.
Each is the light of the other's soul;
They're lost in love's sweet witchery;
Woos the lover; sighs the maid;
Meet their lips in ecstasy!

"O! where's the maid, the sorry maid?
I've waited long her coming!"

Apace the madam seeks the glen
And calls and calls at every jump:
"O! where's the maid; the cows are up
And wait in barnyard long and weary!"

Alas! the lover starts from wooing;
The madam's pother starts the maiden,
And thus they part till eventide
Doth draw them thither once again.

WHEN SALLY LENT THE BABY OUT.

When Sally lent the baby out
  To her sister, Daisy Gad;
I never felt in all my life,
  So miserable and sad,
And Sally went a-crying,
  And I walked to and fro
A-wishing he was home again—
  Our little baby, Joe.

She only lent our little boy
  Out for a half a day;
But, oh, it seemed a month or two
  That he had been away.
And Sally fretted till at last
  She had to go to bed,
And I sat down beside her
  And nearly wished I's dead.

And doleful silence creeping thro'
  The cheerless rooms did rob
Our hearts of all their happiness;
  And poor wife Sally's sob
Was all that broke the silence,
  Save the clock above the bed,
And it seemed to me a-tolling bell—
  A-tolling for the dead.

But all at once we heard a knock
  And we jumped for the door,
And there was smiling baby Joe
  As happy as before.
I never felt in all my life
  So thankful and so glad,
And the way that Sally kissed him
  You'd have thought that she was mad.

But as I said, I never felt
  In all my life so sad,
As when wife lent the baby out
  To her sister, Daisy Gad.
Of course I told the story
  And amused my hearers smiled;
The only one with sympathy
  Had lost a little child.

NEW YEAR'S EVE., 1890—11 P. M.

Thro' yon clear welkin, vast and calm—
 Bestudded galaxy of night—
I lift a happy, trusting heart
 In thanks to thee O, tender Might.

The old year has not lost its mirth ;
 It seems as happy at its death
As in its tender infancy
 When first thou gavest unto it breath.

And thro' it all I'd little cause
 To chide it, for it blessed me well ;
Tho' little thankful oft, has smiled
 On me from happy new year's bell.

Yet there has been somewhat of grief,
 That mine be not uncommon lot ;
But it has only sweetened the
 Rare blessings I feel worthy not.

Few tears it portioned unto me
 To mingle with peace and hope and song.
Such years are few, indeed, I fear
 In life—too often sad and long.

But this has flitted by and seems
 Gone ere it fairly reached its bloom ;
It seems a transient honeymoon
 Of happy, loving bride and groom.

My deepest grief is parting ; tho'
 I can not think I err, and yet,
Perhaps, 'tis better to rejoice—
 The joy remember—pain forget.

But let me for the gifts of love
 And tender care, this new year's night,
Lift up a happy, trusting heart
 In thanks to thee, indulgent Might.

EARLY TIES.

Oh, sing not of the early ties
 That to a sacred past belong ;
Wake not the love that fate defies ;
 Oh, sing to me some other song.

Remains for aye the fire within ;
 But oh, I pray thee, let it be ;
Left smouldering it breeds no sin,
 Which quickened was consuming me.

There's somewhat in thy dreamy eye,
 Where depths of tenderness repose,
That lifts the cold mist that does lie
 O'er idol fairer than the rose.

But waken not the subtle hopes ;
 Sing not those half-forgotten songs ;
Tho' memory sadly o'er them gropes,
 Oh, leave my heart where it belongs.

A SUMMER LAY.

Drowsily humming over the clover—
 Midsummer rover ;
For sweetness hid in the summer flowers ;
Scarlet and yellow is the low, bloomy fallow
And seamed with the brook from the forest
 spring,
And hearts like the weather are light as a
 feather,
For love bides a-wooing within everything.

When thou art past, oh, dearest of all times,
 Will not some love-rhymes
Linger a while to remind us of thee ?
Bobolink's sweet song, we love all day long,
Will we remember when winter is drear ?
And light as a feather will hearts beat to-
 gether
As when music, sweetness and summer were
 here ?

OH, ASK ME NOT.

Oh, ask me not that beauty's smile
 To me no charm unfolds ;
The heart would answer to revile
 The vision it beholds.
Oh, sing not thou the sweet old song
 We sang in former years ;
'T hath mingled with regret so long
 'Tis full of bitter tears.

There's little that can charm the eye
 When love hath scorned its grace ;
There's little meaning in a sigh
 When beauty hides her face ;
But, oh, the woe that stings to death
 Is the woe of faithlessness :
Oh, cherished hope thy dying breath
 Doth curse and yet doth bless.

A CONFESSION.

I see her face, I see her form,
 Her eyes that passion-lit were brown ;
 Her bosom rise and fall, while down
Her member coursed the flashes warm.

Her faltering answer to a friend,
 Who made remark upon an air
 Which classic, filled the brilliant sphere,
Showed weakness that a doubt would lend.

Entranced, and yet within a truth,
 And yet within a wrong, and yet
 Within a shame with no regret—
The vanity of passioned youth.

And holding still within my hand
  The warm and thrilling member soft,
  I felt that strange quintessence oft
Of passion few that e'er withstand.

Thrilled on the bliss of blisses, yet,
  O, chide me not that I were weak;
  My dumb tongue would have joyed to speak,
But failing left me no regret.

And then the crowd stirred listlessly,
  And left her by a pillar, pale,
  Long-gazing as one deep in bale
And heeding not what she would see.

But when at length the spell was o'er,
  The brilliant throng dispersing, she
  Cast one sad, lingering look on me,
Sighed, "May I never see thee more!"

SUNDAY AFTERNOON.

Oh, quiet Sunday afternoon,
  So full of sadness, peace and rest
  That fill the wayward, vacant breast
And grant the longing heart a boon.

Some wander thro' the old church-yard
  And weep o'er old, familiar names
  On time-worn slabs, while conscience blames
The worldly heart for small regard.

O'er wavy, lazy-seeming fields,
  We think we hear some old friend call,
  And longing, gaze o'er rise and fall
Of ripening ears that summer yields.

And say, "Could summer of my life
  Be fruitful—yield abundant good:
  O'er thankful, thankful to be should
This hallowed peace be ever rife—

"That may the peace o'ercome the strife;
  May sorrow be the strength of hope's;
  Joy tread where melancholy mopes,
And wisdom fill and bless my life."

Thus to the weary of their dole,
  The quiet Sunday afternoon
  Comes as a sweet, and precious boon—
Rest for the hands—peace for the soul.

MARY AVERY.

When the spring-birds sang at early day,
  An' soft winds were muskily blowin',
I met Mary Avery with basket an' asked,
  "Oh, whither, sweet girl, are you goin'?"

She said, "I am goin' to Gilpins's Mill
  For brown-flour for our Sunday bakin'."
"Oh, Mary," said I, "will you not give one hope
  To a poor heart that feels all forsaken?"

She said, "Pray whose heart is in such a plight?
  I know none that out-weighs a feather!"
"Sweet Mary," said I, "well you know whose it is,
  For 'tis months I have loved you together."

An' then with a sigh she looked far away,
  An' a tear o'er her pink cheek went streamin';
As we crossed o'er the stile, the sweet word that she said,
  Set my heart in the most blissful dreamin'.

An' now 'round the door our sweet babies play,
  An' love with us ever has tarried;
An' we bless the day, tho' years have rolled by—
  The bright, happy day we were married.

WHY NEED I SIGH.

Why need I sigh, tho' a wild mistress strays
In gayer hour to love deserving blame,
When tired to loathe the fancies of my lays;
Since eyes of beauty languish in their fame?
Deserving much of independent lore,
I fain approve the purpose of her wile;
But may I die before I shall restore
The honor lost in ways of sinful smile!
A mistress wild, a love-lorn youth beset
Ignoring kind remonstrance to take heed,
Who needs reviling and more pity yet
And little mercy and of love less need.
But why this be, wild love's designs reflect,
By furtive means, relinquished love's respect?

NOVEMBER.

The rifty winds in revel scud
  Along the dusty road,
And old November whistles sharp and clear;
There's not a wild-flower nor a bud,
  That mellow summer wooed,
On frowsy hill or in the woodland sear.
The twisting stream has run so low,
  The yellow fallen leaves
A-drifting, almost cloy its silvery thread,
And where the roses used to bloom,
  At early morn instead,
We see the hoarfrost glitter o'er their graves.

The water-lily and the flag
Have withered by the pool;
In chilly blast the stiff reeds are amoan;
And where the ivy, green and cool,
Grew spreading 'round the quag,
There's only left the dreary, barren stone.
But down the hollow where the spring's
Low purling on to death,
There quivers yet a lonely golden-rod,
With nature's kindly shelterings
From autumn's frosty breath,
And nourished by the noon rays on its sod.

But, O, I see not anywhere
A gladness in the scene;
The summer birds have flown with song and
young,
And whatsoe'er my heart did ween,
Alas, in vain and drear,
And tremble low, sad regrets from my
tongue;
But while I pause beneath the oak
Familiar names I trace,
Carved in the old tree's bark in days of love;
I hear the tender words once spoke;
I see each happy face;
While overhead does moan and moan the
dove.

O, THOU.

O, thou, in thy beatific sphere,
With naught to beard thy endless reign,
Look deep within our charnel-house
And draw the goodness from the stain.
Our contour is of mighty king—
The embers of long-cherished fame,
Which, in some epoch of the past,
Left but his picture, not his name,
With fineness to the finger tips!
Score-fold the region of the air,
Gemini-lit, hath cycles run:
Thy idiom doth teach us fear!
Reach down! the poet knows thy touch!
Tune thou his heart to sing thy praise,
In words ignescent, o'er the world,
And weary souls from darkness raise.

THE FALSE LOVER.

A blush suffused her dusky cheek;
Her midnight eye shone like the gem;
With purest feeling of the soul;
With true love for her diadem.

It crowned her heart; it tranced her soul;
It*led her singing o'er the meads,
And far o'er many a summer hill,
And down the stream with sighing reeds.

Soft all the summer day she sang:
"I love my love; I love my love,"
And all the mellow twilight sang
The same sweet song as on she rove.

But when the night came dark and vast,
She ceased her song and sad withal,
Turned within the garden gate
And gazed within the silent hall.

There seated in his comely prime,
With golden locks and happy face,
She saw the youth, and by his side
His aged mother in her grace.

Low speaking to herself she said:
"If it be true he false does prove—
If it be true, O, woe is me;
For dangerous thoughts are born of love!"

In sadness gazing thus she saw
Him rise with mantle on his arm,
And thro' the long and silent hall
He trod with little thought of harm.

Without the creaking gate and o'er
The lonesome hills he took his way,
And close behind the Indian maid
Followed in her sad dismay.

And murmuring, "He is false they say,
O, woe is me! I love him so.
Tho' happy, happy all the day
At night I feel my dream is woe!"

And gayly on his way he sang
An old love song he sang to her;
So plaintive, sweet it seemed, and fell
So softly on her listening ear.

She paused and leaning 'gainst an oak,
Wept to it as it softly fell:
"The same sweet song he sang to me,"
She said, "O, sad, sad is its spell."

Then following close again—too close,
He heard her moan and turned his head
And peered back o'er the dewy hills;
"I thought I heard a moan!" he said.

And listening, he a moment stood:
"The wind, perhaps, in its unrest!"
Then hastened on, but sang no more;
Sprang some strange feeling in his breast.

But when at length he reached the bridge
That spanned the dark and troubled stream,
The summer moon sweet in her sheen,
Smiled down awakened from her dream.

Lo! on the bridge the new love met;
He clasped her to his heart with kiss!
With tender vows his love did prove,
Tho' loving her in secret bliss.

From craggy ledge the Indian maid
  Gazed down upon them; wept, " 'Tis true!
He's false to me, O, let me die!
  Since living now is but to rue."

She, weeping, watched them till at length
  With tender kiss and long embrace,
They parted, and a troubled cloud
  Passed o'er the bright moon's silent face.

And then that subtle passion strong—
  That passion of revenge and ire—
The strongest passion of her race—
  Sprang up and burned with fiercest fire!

The lover paused midway the bridge.
  "One thrust," she said, "and all is o'er!"
And stealing from her hiding place
  She quickly glided to the shore.

A moment's pause—a dagger's flash—
  A hurried step—a thud—a groan!
The waters parted in the stream—
  The Indian maiden stood alone!

She stood a moment gazing at
  The waters in their wild unrest,
Then leapt with wild cry in the flood,
  With dagger sunken in her breast!

YOU HAVE PRAISED ME BY CHIDIN'.

  You have praised me by chidin',
    An' censured by praise;
  You have led me confidin'
    Into weary days;
  You have proffered the favor
    That would lift me to fame
  Where bitter tears flavor
    The old-time good name.

  Do not tempt me with glory,
    Tho' its pictures are grand.
  Teach me some simple story
    O' truth's honest hand.
  I pray you believe me:
    Rather than praises rare,
  I would ask, only breathe me
    Some words in your prayer.

LADY ALICE.

Oh, in your soft and glintful eyes,
  Little Hoosier lady, Alice,
Every time your lashes rise
I see a blissful paradise;
The rapture lifts me to the skies—
  Little lady Alice.

And every time I touch your hand,
  Little Hoosier lady, Alice,
Strange feelings I ne'er understand
Come to my heart and take command;
Save you all else fades from the land—
  Little lady Alice.

And every time I kiss your lips,
  Little Hoosier lady, Alice,
My soul a rarest nectar sips,
That thrills me to the finger tips,
As on my longing heart it drips—
  Little lady Alice.

OVER IN THE COUNTY GREEN.

Over in the county green, county green,
  county green,
Where the youth grows tall an' lean,
  An' the maid grows stout;
There I bought a sweeny mare,
There I learnt best how to swear,
There, and truly I declare,
  Is the devil's flout!

Over in the county green, county green,
  county green,
Where the pumpkin grows an' bean,
  An' the hickory tall;
There the raccoon winked at me,
There the horned owl blinked at me,
There the cur dog slinked at me—
  Devil take 'em all!

THE MOTTO:

"DEAR LOVE OF MINE, MY HEART IS THINE."

These words are graven on my heart
  Though old in story they may be—
"Dear love of mine, my heart is thine,"
  They keep me ever near to thee.

Though care should come and life be full
  Of weary days, still I shall say:
"Dear love of mine, my heart is thine,"
  Thou art my comfort and my stay.

To-day, I saw thy first gray hair—
  But true love never dies of age.
"Dear love of mine, my heart is thine,"
  No less of love does time presage.

With all the happiness of love,
  Oh, let us crown our soul and heart—
"Dear love of mine, my heart is thine,"
  Thine till us death doth part.

SWEET LITTLE BABE.

Sweet little babe! Heaven sent thee to me
To dance upon my knee and coo and smile
And drive away dull care—my heart beguile
As back to Babyland I stray with thee.
Thy little hands can more than soothe—can bless!
Thy little dimpled hands, so soft and white,
Have led me far away from dreary night
Into the light of perfect happiness.
And, yet, O, precious little tender dove,
Of loved simplicity and innocence,
My heart doth in affection pain, and tears
Bedim mine eyes, when brooding moments move,
With thou and me in fated severance,
Imagination on to woeful years.

FAREWELL, OLD POEMS.

Farewell old poems! I must cast thee aside—
Cast thee aside in a careless way—
Cast thee where dust and mould will hide
The many hours thou received each day.
Aye, nights, too: night hours were many,
When the old lamp's flicker shadowed the wall,
How often I've sat concealed from any
And poured out my passion at thy call.

But those halcyon days are gone, sweet verse;
The passion lives; but thought has varied.
Time changes all for better or worse—
Time changes, old poems, but be not worried:
Be not worried, old poems, but lie
In the dusty old attic all silent for years;
Aye, many years may sadly roll by;
But thou'lt know again of joy and tears.

'Tis sad, old poems, to cast thee aside;
Ah, that I could linger awhile with thee;
Ah, that I could linger in the old attic wide
Where thou hast been all in all to me.
Farewell, old poems! mind not my tears;
My duty is labor; I must list to its call!
I may know thee again in after years;
If not, thou art my soul, my thought, my all.

GENTLE MAIDEN, IN THINE EYES.

Gentle maiden, in thine eyes
  Show the pureness of thy soul,
Purity's thy paradise,
  And from out but troubles roll.
Let, I pray thee, never guile
  Bide within thy snowy breast,
Nor give to vanity thy smile,
  Maiden, if thou wouldst be blest.

I've a woe within my breast
  That will leave not at the grave!
From the woe I have confessed,
  Thee, O, maiden, I would save.
Pray, O, maiden, that there may
  Be nor guilt nor shame for thee;
That thy heart may be for aye
  Blissful in its purity.

THE WINDIN' BLUE.

Oh, leave me by the windin' Blue,
  The bloomy summer's dyin'.
Oh, leave me yet a little while
  In tender thoughts a-sighin'.
The dove is moanin' in the wood,
  The faded leaf is fallin',
An' lonely for its truant mate
  The whip-poor-will is callin'.

Oft here with lighter heart I've trod,
  Nor dreamed o' heart forsaken,
When gay these banks in bud an' bloom,
  To summer's smile did waken;
But joys that wakened with the bloom,
  Like summer, now are dyin'.
Oh, leave me by the windin' Blue
  In tender thoughts a-sighin'.

Ah, sweet the thoughts o' fondest ties
  That hapless, here I cherished;
But oh, the tender thoughts o' them
  Sink with the hopes that perished.
The summer's noddin' in its seed,
  The birds are southward flyin'.
Oh, leave me by the windin' Blue
  In tender thoughts a-sighin'.

THO' WOMAN'S SMILE.

Tho' woman's smile my heart beguile,
  I'll never, never marry;
But for the bliss of woman's kiss,
  I'll ever, ever tarry;
  But never, never marry;
  No, never, never marry;
But for the bliss of woman's kiss
  I'll ever, ever tarry.

Tho' woman's love may constant prove,
  I'll never, never marry;
But for a place in her embrace,
  I'll ever, ever tarry:
  But never, never marry;
  No, never, never marry;
But for a place in her embrace,
  I'll ever, ever tarry.

MORE.

More than to vex a tender heart,
   As by a wintry form-forced mind—
To use thy virtue and be kind,
Or mix regrets with song and art.

More than transplanted in thy worth,
   Where thoughts, mature, bend to thy faith
Which, loyal, ranged above all death,
Crush down the vanity of earth.

More than to move with changes slow
   Wrought on thy cold and lovely face,
Where profit lingers to embrace
The burdens of thy deep-set woe.

MY WEE BIT MAID.

I found a wee bit at my door
   Wrapped in an Eider blanket;
It keeps me walkin' many a night;
   But, oh, I can not spank it—
I can not spank my wee bit maid;
   Than all else she is dearer;
A-lookin' in her face is like
   A-lookin' in a mirror.

Then, oh, my wee bit darlin',
   May blessin's fall upon you;
No matter who your mammy is
   So daddy deigns to own you!
You fill the house with many a flur',
   An' wakeful night reproves you;
But, oh, my wee bit darlin' maid,
   Your daddy dearly loves you.

The neighbors with their furtive winks,
   An' nods an' quips were pryin',
An', Mattie Joe, my good old aunt,
   Was mortified to dyin';
But, oh, the wee bit maid I love
   In spite o' joke or noddy;
More sweet than any joy in life
   Was when she called me Daddy!

I DREAMPT I WENT A-ROVIN'.

I dreampt I went a-rovin',
   O'er bloomy hills so gay;
I dreampt I went a-rovin',
   A-rovin' far away;
An' the maidens that I met with
   Had such pretty eyes an' cheeks,
I dreampt that in their country
   I tarried many weeks.

First, I courted this one,
   An' then I courted that—
The last was always sweetest—
   Some lean an' some were fat.
Oh, I courted till my money
   Had dwindled to a bit,
An' then a spell came o'er me
   That ended in a fit.

So there I lay a-kickin',
   A-kickin' left an' right,
An' the pretty maids stood o'er me
   An' wept with all their might;
An' the one I loved the most o' all
   Knelt by me in my pain,
When all at once I got a nudge—
   "Wake up!" yelled Mary Jane.

THE PRESENTIMENT.

The hours passed slowly with the day,
   And all the beauty of the woods
Hung in a mist of rainy blight;
   But all around the dreary cot,
The scene did shift unto her moods;
   She combed her hair of wavy light
And sang, "To-day I read my lot."

Lo! thro' the window flew a bird
   And winged its way across the room.
Where, fluttering, fallen to its death,
   It lay on snowy-pillowed bed.
She wept, Anora, "'Tis my doom!"
   She wept anon with quickened breath:
"I read my lot—my heart is dead"!

She, turning sadly to the woods,
   Gazed thro' her tears into the mist:
Long silent, then in fullest trust
   That woe was hers, made moan:
"These are the tokens often kist;
   These are the jewels doomed to rust,
Thine all, poor heart, thine own!"

Sad, when the wan moon grieved the sky,
   She lay her down beside the bird;
She warmed it in her soft white hands,
   And held it to her throbbing heart;
But when the silent vastness stirred
   Her fated soul with strange commands,
She shuddered at her part.

Thus bitterly she wept the while:
   "False love! false love is his!
Oh, woe is me, and bitter tear,
   And broken heart and sigh,
Oh, yesterday my life was bliss
   With not a grief, not any fear;
But now, alas! I die."

EDITH.

Lo, on the snowy-pillowed bed,
Where comfort woos the weary soul
And other joy exceedeth,
Lay in the mellow afternoon,
'Mid fluffy lace and scents o' musk,
My lovely sweet-eyed Edith.

There, with her dainty foot drawn up,
I traced her perfect symmetry,
And kist her twice and thrice.
There was my blissful resting place—
Upon her breast so soft and white—
None other half so nice.

When thro' the hall and soft and sweet,
The music from the fountain came
To haunt her in her dreaming,
A smile broke thro' her tempting lips;
She spoke my name while thus asleep
In dreams of blissful seeming.

Oh, love is all there is o' strength,
And love is all there is o' worth
Within a man that's noble;
And be he blest with woman's love
He's noble even to divine,
And strength and worth are double.

'TWAS EVER THUS.

Hope came to me yesterday
When the sky was bright;
Hope came to me, but was gone
Ere the comin' night.
An' I heard a strange voice say
'Neath the moon an' old an' pale -
"Hope's gone wanderin' thro' the vale—
Vale o' yesterday."

An' I said, 'twas ever thus
An' ever will it be,
There never dwelt within a heart
A perfect love for me:
I never held for one brief day
Within my grasp joy's temptin' cup,
But fate has sternly took it up
An' dashed it far away.

THE HOOSIER BOY.

Oh, he was a gallant Hoosier boy
That rode at the break o' day;
Oh, he was a brawny Hoosier boy
So handsome an' so gay.
Up from the lowland at mornin'
An' far o'er the gay green hill;
Oh, the pain at my heart when we did part
At the sound o' the bugle shrill.

Oh, he was a lovin' Hoosier boy
That gave me the ring o' gold;
An' true was the heart o' the Hoosier boy
As ever a breast did hold.
Far away to the field o' battle;
Far away to the southern plain;
But, oh, for the love that from me did rove
To never return again.

Oh, brave was the heart o' the Hoosier boy
That carried the old flag high;
An' faithful the heart o' the Hoosier boy
That fought but alas, to die!
An' oh, for the days that are not;
An' alas, for the hopes so vain;
Yet love binds my heart to the Hoosier boy
That will never return again.

AGAIN WITHIN THE FACTORY WALLS.

Again within the factory walls
I see the faces worn and pale,
And above the din of the wheels that spin
I hear again the saddening wail—
Working away from the early day,
On till the day is dying;
There's trouble enough for the weary soul;
Trouble enough and sighing.

And there the maid who never knew
The joys of home or mother's love,
With many a tear and silent prayer,
Sighs to the spinning wheels above—
Working away from the early day,
On till the day is dying;
There's trouble enough for the weary soul;
Trouble enough and sighing.

And there the widow with her babe,
Perhaps a-sleeping by her side,
With hollow cheek does sadly seek
To earn their bread since papa died—
Working away from the early day,
On till the day is dying;
There's trouble enough for the weary soul;
Trouble enough and sighing.

And sadly there the fallen one
With broken heart does seek to gain
Her scanty meal, that she may feel
No more is added to her stain—
Working away from the early day,
On till the day is dying;
There's trouble enough for the weary soul;
Trouble enough and sighing.

And there's the maid with sunken breast,
And oft she turns her head to cough;
Sometimes she smiles when hope beguiles
Or sings as one that's afar off—

Working away from the early day,
  On till the day is dying;
There's trouble enough for the weary soul;
  Trouble enough and sighing.

And there's the unknown gifted one
  Who strives beneath grim duty's rod—
From poverty to ne'er be free
  Till she is summoned by her God—
Working away from the early day,
  On till the day is dying;
There's trouble enough for the weary soul;
  Trouble enough and sighing.

WHEN WINTER.

When winter with his frosty breath
  Comes freezin' up the river,
An' cold the moon thro' scuddin' clouds
  Shines down in fitful quiver,
An' sedge along the bottom land
  'Way in the midnight's moanin',
An' on the hill the long-armed oaks
  Are groanin', deeply groanin',
Oh, then the poor, Lord pity most,
  When winter with his frosty breath
Comes cuttin' with his sword o' death!

When winter with his icy breath
  Comes sweepin' o'er the valley,
'Tis not the rich man by his hearth
  That fears old winter's sally;
'Tis not the jolly, brawny bud
  So full o' warm blood leapin';
But it's the poor that feels the sting,
  So cold an' hungry weepin'.
Oh, then the poor, Lord pity most,
  When winter with his icy breath
Comes cuttin' with his sword o' death.

When winter with his arctic breath
  Wraps up in his embraces
The hill an' valley, wood an' stream,
  An' on the window traces,
An' all the sky is in a frown—
  Come, with me pray nor canty,
The Lord, unto the poor may deal
  From measure never scanty—
Oh, pray the poor he'll pity most,
  When winter with his arctic breath
Comes cuttin with his sword o' death.

LULLABY MEDLEY.

Sing a song of sixpence
  A pocket full of rye,
Sing it to the baby
  Whenever it does cry.

Rock a baby Bunting
  Your papa's gone away
To catch a little rabbit skin—
  That's what the song does say.

Ring around a rosy,
  With baby for the rose;
The sweetest little flower,
  As everybody knows.
He sings about King William,
  Who was King James's son,
And fire on the mountain,
  Run, boys, run!

London bridge is falling,
  O, let the old bridge fall.
Dame Crump had a little broom
  She hung upon the wall.
Mary had a little lamb
  That followed her to school;
But the teacher didn't like it
  'Cause it was against the rule.

Make a Jacob's ladder
  With a piece o' paper string;
Give it to the baby
  For it's such a pretty thing.
Don't you wish, my little baby,
  You were in a high tree-top
Rocking in a cradle
  And the cradle wouldn't drop?

Then rock a little baby;
  Rock-a-baby-by,
We'll sing about the black birds
  Baking in a pie,
And little Johnny Horner,
  And Mother Hubbard, too.
O, go to sleep my baby,
  While mamma sings to you.

A CHARACTER.

I'd give thee consolation, friend,
  Thou knowest I've a kindly heart;
But fearful of the grief I mend
  I shrink from what I would impart.

Why cryest thou? is truth athirst?
  What profits, brother, vain desire?
Man endeth at perhaps his worst
  When risen to his hopes or higher.

Great men—great poets—thinking men,
  Go thro' a thorny world in vain.
Thou cryest—smileth I, but when
  Will our fair ships return again?

Cast thou a mite; cast I a great;
  But will the beam drop to the strong?
Come, leave the reckoning unto fate,
  And sing with me some sweet old song.

O, royal bones, O, slumbering bones—
  Doubt full of cant, and full of ire;
What claimest thou? why rollest stones
  Against the door of cleansing fire?

O, brother, there is yet vast good;
  Life's blest with many a golden truth.
My heart tho' old hath what it would—
  The tender lessons of its youth.

And true humanity is ours,
  And nobler yet our lives are cast—
May, with each season of the flowers,
  Grow fairer, purer till the last—

Snow-white and blest and risen higher—
  High in the zone of blessedness.
O, teach me not thy vain desire
  To rob me of my happiness.

WHEN DAWN COMES ON.

When dawn comes on with all its loveliness
And sparkling dew is yet upon the flower,
While in the gables twit the merry birds
And nature smiles upon the happy hour—
O, may I know Thee as a perfect friend;
And may I trust Thee with no cause for fear—
Lord in thy mercy teach me wisdom's ways,
Nor sin throughout the day allow to sear,
And thro' each hour of toil be ever by
My side and lead me ever on aright,
Wind round my soul the robes of perfect faith
And open wide mine eyes to perfect light—
When dawn comes on with all its loveliness
Thus ask I of the Lord my soul to bless.

A SONG O' DUSK.

In royal purple clusters deep
  The sweet clematis hides the wall
An' far across the slantin' lawn
  Low sings the waterfall.
The hedge-row quivers in the soft
  June breezes full o' summer musk
While 'round the eaves the martins dart
  An' sing o' comin' dusk.

Way o'er the hills the scarlet sky
  Reflects the last smile o' the sun
An' those strange songs o' night, scarce heard,
  Start up, that fancy spun.
Deep in the pine tree o'er the well
  Low moans the voice o' yesternight
An' in the green vine o'er the door
  Rasps faintly some strange sprite.

Long musin' sits without the door
  An old man hoary-haired an' bent.
His thin pale lips let go these words:
  "I would I were content;
Yet I'd not live life o'er again.
  Life slips from me on fleetest wing.
Was not life's mornin' yesterday?
  What will the morrow bring?"

Ah, sweetly falls the gentle dusk;
  I glance across the misty field,
Far where the forest rims the east
  The young moon is revealed;
An' turnin' west I see the star
  In which reflected once a face
'Tween it an' mine the troubled main
  E'er rolls. Lord give her grace.

WHEN MILD NIGHTS WERE BLOWIN'.

When mild nights were blowin' in early September
I strolled with my love 'neath the wood's thorny boughs,
We sang the old songs I shall ever remember
An' hallowed our hearts with the sweetest o' vows.
The stars were a-blinkin' while we were a-thinkin'
With joy o' the days that our words framed in bliss;
But never, oh, never to come but to sever
The fond ties forever with one clingin' kiss.

Ah, well for the days that have passed an' forever,
An' vows that are broken an' love that has flown;
In the sands o' regret my grief I'll endeavor
To bury so deep it will perish alone.
But if in dejection to fond recollection
I cling for a moment an' cease to adore,
Oh, bear with me kindly if unwise I blindly
Should drink at the fount in the valley, No More.

I MET A MAID.

I met a maid on Davison's Hill
  When sharp the wind blew very,
An' she was smilin' at the wind
  With lips an' cheeks o' cherry;
But, O, the wind did blow her gown
  Hard 'gainst her limbs an' showed me
Her perfect shape an' loveliness—
  The picture truly wooed me.

"O, pretty maid," I said to her,
　"Let's walk along together;"
She smiled an' let me take her hand,
　An' talked about the weather;
But, O, the wind did blow an' blow
　As if to raise a blister,
So stoppin' 'hind a portly oak
　For shelter, thrice I kissed her.

Nor she at kissin' took offense;
　But said, "O, how it blows, sir!"
I said, "Indeed it does, my dear,"
　An' held her closer—closer
Till—O, I'll tell you nothin' more,
　Save that the Lord was clever
To give us such an element.
　May it blow on forever!

PLEASANT RUN

You thrifty, frisky, twistin' creek
　You flash a glance at me
As thro' the golden, noddin' grain
　Your smilin' face I see;
An on you go an' sing an' spin
　As by the wood you send;
I catch the sweetness of your voice
　And smell your musky bud.

You bend the water-lilies low
　As swiftly on you hie,
An' dartin' thro' the sunny glade
　The violets look awry;
An' leapin' o'er a mossy break,
　Where shiny red-eyes dart,
You lend a sweetness to your song
　That lingers in the heart.

An' 'round the old oak's snaggy roots
　You gurgle in your glee,
An' eddy, leap an' fret your banks
　In your wild revelry;
An' far adown your limpid source,
　An' joy does thrill my soul,
I catch a glance thro' thorny boughs,
　O' the old swimmin' hole!

I hasten on to gain the spot
　With heart a-beatin' high,
Forgettin' age an' stiffened joints
　An' many a cause to sigh;
You lead me on with smile an' song
　As you led me long ago
When no grief was deeper seated
　Than you washed out with your flow.

I see the boys a-plungin' in
　Your temptin' cup o' bliss!
An' long again with leap an' shout
　Your smilin' face to kiss;

But, oh, your waters, warm an' clear,
　Would chill my old bones through;
I can only come an' look an' sigh
　An' drop a tear in you.

WHEN COMETH MORNING.

When cometh morning with her train
　Of mellow, floating robes of light,
I grieve me that in deepest night
My spirit's light was light in vain.

I grieve me most at stilly morn,
　Ere thro' the mist of early day
The first bird twits its homely lay
Or cushat moans its song forlorn.

I grieve me that the virgin morn,
　Ere scarce awake, shall tainted be—
Smile on the sins we daily see,
And ere the evening virtue scorn.

And solve the problem unto shame,
　That God, alone, shall teach us love,
Tho' scornful finger points above,
And curses link this holy name.

And hold the truth of noble things
　A secret trust of hardened age
That gives the deepness to the page
That myriad doubtful meanings rings.

And thwart the noble heart's design;
　See genius fettered till it dies,
While marks of sorrow ring the eyes
That once were thought-lit to divine.

See little portioned unto love,
　And little unto charity;
Unrighteousness sweep like a sea
To drown the good for which Christ strove.

I grieve me that in deepest night
　My spirit's light was light in vain—
While sweetly dreaming that again
The day with purity was bright.

THE WAY, THE TRUTH, THE LIFE.

Thou art the way, O, let us flee
From sinful paths and follow thee;
For thou wilt give the weary rest,
Aye, thou wilt love us far the best.
Then let us sing: Thou art the Way,
And we shall follow thee each day

Thou art the Truth. Thou dost impart
The lesson to make pure the heart,
And keepest us in sweet accord

With thy true wisdom; dost afford
A safeguard for our soul; nor care,
Nor sin, nor harm shall enter there.

Thou art the Life. The rending tomb
Proclaims thy might! Aye, unto whom
No power's denied, oh, let us trust,
Not to the things of sordid dust
That clingeth to a transient breath
And sinketh in their sin to death.

THE EMIGRANT.

We parted, though loving
And tears dimmed our eyes.
We breathed a prayer to ease our care,
To give us strength, and make us wise
In choosing of the narrow way;
That God would lead us—man and wife
Unto a brighter day.

We parted, though loving.
'Twas poverty's cry.
We'd hungered on till hope had gone
And life, through struggling, longed to fly
And end its misery in the grave,
Where tired heart would cease to pain
And fevered mind to crave

We parted, though loving,
'Twas duty's loud call.
To stay was woe. 'Twas sad to go;
But man from duty should not fall
And leave some loved one in the slums
With sunken eye and hollow cheek
To wait death's funeral drums.

We parted, though loving,
And I took my way.
Wet, cold or hot, clime mattered not,
I wandered on, until one day
I was borne here by wind and wave,
And made a home; but when word came
It was about her grave.

THE FARM IN AUTUMN.

The dreary days have come, alas!
  The crops are in the fields are brown;
The summer birds have flown away;
  The scarecrow in the garden's down.

The old cow bawls around the bars;
  The sharp wind whistles o'er the sky;
The chickens sadly mope about
  Or stand on one leg in the dry.

The old horse drowses in the barn
  Or lazily nibbles at the hay;
The watch-dog quoiled up in the straw
  Is very hard to drive away.

As by the fire the farmer sits
  At eve with wife and children fair,
The old Seth Thomas clock strikes eight.
  He kneels and offers up a prayer:

"O, have we cause to ever fret
  Since You have yet denied us not?
O, keep us humble day by day
  And well contented with our lot."

A SONG.

Blithely o'er the summer lee,
  You and I together.
What care we how the world may go
  So its bright and pleasant weather.
Happy the song and merry the laugh
  From our hearts light as a feather;
Life is gay as we fly away—
  You and I together

All the world is a sweet love scene;
  No care for us does tarry.
You are my hope and you are my star
  And you are my own sweet Mary.
Here is a rose for your silken hair
  And here is a kiss, my fairy,
And here is a ring, O, tenderly sing:
  To-morrow we shall marry.

THE HAUNTED MILL.

TORN DOWN IN THE SPRING OF '92.

Oh, the grim old mill on Davison's hill,
  Deserted long ago,
Stands silent and wide in its mouldering pride
  And frowns on the stream below;
And the rats run o'er its sounding floor,
  And the snakes crawl o'er its stones,
And its pallid host is a midnight ghost
  That moans, and moans, and moans!

At the foot of the hill not far from the mill
  Stands a long-armed sycamore,
And its dead arms wave o'er a lonely grave
  That the weeds have covered o'er,
And 'tis said at night, if the moon is bright,
  You can see, if it's calm and still,
The ghost come up from its grave to sup
  And go to the dark old mill.

And the rafters high they creak and sigh
  When the storm is wild at night,
And the bats fly out and around about
  At some strange and weird light,
And a hollow laugh you'll hear and half
  The old mill seem to fall;
Then moan, and moan, and groan, and groan
  Re-echo from wall to wall!

When it rains and blows, the story goes,
   And 'tis said the story's right,
The ghosts go there from far and near
   To pass away the night.
And the cock does crow and the dog whines low
   And the owl hoots in the tree,
While they rattle their bones o'er the old mill stones,
   Till the Arsenal clock strikes three.

CHARLIE.

Charlie put on his silk-yoke shirt
   An' his moleskin breeches,
An' Charlie put on his white necktie
   To show his style an' riches;
But when he came to Bloomin'dale
   Whose glens were gay an' balmy,
He met a maid from Brooklyn Hights
   The first time from her mammy.

Oh, Charlie was so boon an' smooth—
   A wily-mannered Hoosier—
He g'lanted her thro' bloomy glen
   An' vowed he'd not misuse her.
He pinned a wild-rose in her breast
   An' called her sweet an' lam'y,
He put his arm around her waist
   An' kist her for her mammy.

He took her to the high-top cliff
   On Sunday, neat an' shaven,
With scentin'-oil upon his locks
   O' curly hair so raven;
The folks did cut her with their eyes
   An' said she shamed her duty
She loosed her han'k'chief o'er her breast
   An' killed 'em with her beauty.

'Twas down the glen an' o'er the hill
   An' thro' the wood with Fanny
Gay Charlie took her paisley shawl
   An' spread it in a cranny.
The stars were blinkin' in the sky:
   He called her sweet an' lam'y.
She thought that heaven was ne'er so nice;
   But grieved she left her mammy.

A SCENE.

Retreat embowered, where all is dreaming,
   Where life was love and love's sweet lay
Tranced tho' each joy and blissful seeming
   To fly too soon to yesterday.

To these sad changes swiftly flying,
   Lit by bright eyes that are unseen,
Return the sweet, vain hopes long dying,
   To gaze once more where love has been.

Came oft the longing hearts at even,
   Close side by side, sweet joys to wed,
Where souls let in the light of heaven,
   In mellow twilight o'er the dead.

OH, PRETTY MISS.

Oh pretty miss the bloomy spring
   With wild-flower is a-comin';
Ere long the bees, o'er apple trees
   In blossom, will be hummin';
An' with your sleeves rolled high, I hope
   To see you same as las' year
A-workin' round the flower-beds
   An' singin' as I pass here.

A spring like this wooed into bliss
   Is nothin' to your beauty!
Oh, pretty miss give me a kiss
   An' you'll have done your duty.

Oh, pretty miss, the Hoosier hills
   The warm winds are a-frettin';
The bright sun sends the happy glens
   A compliment befittin',
An' 'round the wood's a streak o' green;
   The cloyed stream is a-breakin';
Oh, let the light o' your bright eyes
   My poor heart, too, awaken.

I'M MOST TOO YOUNG.

A Hoosier boy came wooin' me
   With many a smile an' sayin',
An' many a sigh an' glance o' eye—
   Hard for my love was prayin'.
Tho' tender grew my heart for him
   I could not ask him tarry,
For mother says I'm most too young
   To marry, oh, to marry.

Oft from the pasture at the morn
   I hear him gayly singin';
The selfsame song, the whole day long,
   That thro' my head is ringin'—
A song o' love he sang to me;
   But I was quite contrary,
For mother says I'm most too young
   To marry, oh, to marry.

When last he met me in the lane
   He was so very clever,
An' in my ear spoke words so dear
   I can forget them never.
An' tenderly he kist my hand,
   But I was rather wary,
For mother says I'm most too young
   To marry, oh, to marry.

"Oh, little girl," he said to me,
"Don't think me overweenin',
I love you so, oh, could I know
Your heart an' all its meanin'."
An' tho' I knew I's most too young,
I gave my heart to Harry,
Yet mother says I'm most too young
To marry, oh, to marry.

MY COUNTRY AND FLAG.

Oh, let me voice my country's heart
Where thrall and fetter have no part;
Oh, let me sing of freedom's joy
That tyrant hand shall not destroy.
America, my home, sweet home,
My heart from you shall never roam;
Sweet home beneath my own roof-tree
Where ever is sweet liberty.

To you, old flag, that proudly waves
O'er loyal hearts and soldiers' graves,
O'er all this fair, glad land of ours—
This paradise of peace and flowers—
My country full of goodly things
To glad the heart—oh, loudly rings
My voice in love, for you alone,
Are dear old flag, my own, my own!

BEYOND THE HILLS.

Beyond the hills where ever it is bright
Nor sorrow is nor gloom nor ever night—
Far, far beyond the range of mortal sight—
There is a place of perfect rest and light.
And all the sorrow and the useless tears
Shed and endured thro' all this stretch of years,
And blame and censure and all sordid fears
Turn to sweet fruition when that land appears.

THE OLD VILLAGE BELL.

Oh, the old village bell I remember so well,
It hung on a post by the door,
And many a time thro' fancy its chime
Takes me back to the bright days of yore;
For too sweet is the joy for time to destroy,
Too dear are the echoes that dwell
In memory yet for me to forget
The musical old village bell.

Ding, dong! ding, dong! I hear it sweetly ringing.
Ding, dong! ding, dong! sweet thoughts to me it's bringing.
Of days of happiness, its echoes gladly tell.
Fond memory takes me back again
To the dear old village bell.

Oft in fancy I rove thro' the cool, shady grove
Where the wild-bird so sweetly did call,
Or steal to the nook by the murmuring brook
Where the wild-roses hung on the wall.
These pictures are dear that for many a year
Kind memory has cherished so well;
But dearer to me, and forever will be,
Is the echoing old village bell.

In sorrow and tears, looking back o'er the years
To the bright days of boyhood and home,
I would give all the earth, should it be my vast worth,
To return again never to roam.
But there only remain in hopes that are vain,
The sweet recollections I tell,
That oft to my ear bring the music so dear
Of the welcoming old village bell.

TWILIGHT.

This is my hour of perfect bliss—
When twilight mellows all the west;
He comes that I may sweetly rest
My head upon his breast—
That I may give him vow for vow,
And being loved, more loving grow,
While every passion murmurs low
The rapture of his kiss.

HERE IS A SIGH.

Here is a sigh for the hopes that perished;
Here is a tear for the tender love;
Here is a prayer, may it fly to heaven,
Fly where my angel dwells above.

Oh, the days go by with their dreary duty,
An' my brow is seamed with the weary years,
An' friends remark my hair is turnin'—
I say 'tis age, but my heart says, tears.

There's little o' peace when the soul does hunger—
When the light that lighted the soul has fled;
There's little o' joy when the heart but lonely
Clings to the hopes forever dead.

Here is a sigh for the hopes that perished;
Here is a tear for the tender love;
Here is a prayer, may it fly to heaven,
Fly where my angel dwells above.

DADDY DAN DANGLESHANKS.

Muckle's your chuckle,
Daddy Dan Dangleshanks;
Muckle's your chuckle,
Daddy Dan Down.
You come all the way
From Terry Hall neighborhood,
Muckle's your chuckle
Since you've been in town.

The houses reach up
Nigh to the blue heavens;
The streets are so smooth
An' the maidens so sweet,
An' truth a full score o'
Miles you've been walkin'
An' never once thought
It was done with your feet.

Muckle's your chuckle,
Daddy Dan Dangleshanks;
Muckle's your chuckle,
Good Daddy Dan.
The sights you have seen
Have set you to jiggitin'!
You'll go home a-thinkin'
You're quite a wise man.

JORDAN B. THACKER.

Jordan B. Thacker liked good drinkin' liquor,
Jordan B. Thacker, a very fine man,
An' Jordan B. Thacker, to trade an' to dicker,
Would go to the village behind his gray span.
His farm was a fine one that spread wide an' mucky
An' many a fine beast did browse on its green,
For Jordan B. Thacker was wealthy an' lucky;
His beat as a trader was sure never seen.
But this was his answer when drinkin' o'er muckle,
If askin' his name when acquaintance began,
With a bow to the ground an' a wry look an' chuckle,
"I'm Jordan B. Thacker—a very fine man!"

One day at the village a-tradin' he lingered
Till night drew her curtain an' shut out the light,
An' Jordan the glass so often had fingered
That he was befuddled an' jolly good tight.
He left his grays tied to the hitchin'-post neighin',
An' started afoot to return to his home;
But the night waxed so dark for the wild clouds a-flyin'
Shut out the moon an' amiss he did roam.

The big trees did moan as through the woods Jordan
Trudged along singin' his song as it ran—
"Happy-go-lucky", an' this for the burden,
"I'm Jordan B. Thacker—a very fine man!"

An' old owl sat high in a tree top a-blinkin',
The mice bein' scarce an' luck had gone wrong,
She sat there a-warmin' her wits an' a-thinkin',
When Jordan B. Thacker came singin' along;
But the old owl aroused by this jolly intruder
Broke forth with her song of "too whoot!" an' "too whoo!"
But Jordan mistakin' her song thus construed her
As one askin' "Who are you?" in language most true.
So low to the ground, in keep with his manner,
He bowed with a smile on an exquisite plan,
An' tipped his plug-hat an' waved his bandana,
Sayin': I'm Jordan B. Thacker—a very fine man!"

EAST OHIO STREET.

Oh, pleasant east Ohio street
So bloomy, cool an' shady.
My heart's delight on moonlit night,
Is strollin' with my lady
Along your smooth an' happy way,
When summer time is merry
With little children glad an' sweet
An' loves boon an' cherry.

But oft I've strolled along your way
When over-worn by labor;
An' oft I've strolled with heavy heart
Unknown to kindly neighbor;
An' oft in stilly midnight hour
I've strolled alone an' lonely
When all the world seemed harsh an' cold
An' you had comfort only.

Oh, pleasant east Ohio street,
I never can forget you—
Your spreadin' trees, an' grassy yards,
An' beauties that befit you.
I've known you many a happy hour;
You've soothed me oft in sorrow;
My brightest hopes sprang from your bloom;
I'll trust them till the morrow.

WE MADE HER A GRAVE.

We made her a grave 'neath the cold sod o' winter,
When wild winds were moanin', and dreary the wood,
An' silent the stream—no song-bird to hint her,
We laid her to rest in her young motherhood.

Oh, little we thought as she roved care unminded,
Thro' summer's green glens an' autumn's gay bloom,
That ere winter's cold icy robe was abandoned,
It would wrap her in death in its silence an' gloom.
The eye kind an' glintful, the hand warm an' lovin',
The voice sweet an' gentle, the heart true an' brave,
Lie closed, cold an' silent—no impulses movin'
The calm, holy bosom at rest in the grave.

But, oh, for the heart whose lonely commotion
Yields only the throbbin's o' deepest regret,
As it bows 'neath the weight o' life's fated portion,
Too bitter—too painful to ever forget.

IF DARING DEEDS.

If daring deeds my lady please
I'll ride away, I'll ride away,
I'll ride away at early day
Where guns are loudly roaring.
But, if with me thou wilt agree,
I'll bide awhile, I'll bide awhile,
I'll bide awhile in thy bright smile
Thy lovely eyes adoring.

YOU 'MIND ME OF YOUR MOTHER, BOY.

You 'mind me of your mother, boy,
An' days o' long ago—
You mind me of your mother, boy,
An' joys I used to know.
Your brow is broad an' white, boy,
Your eye the deepest blue ;
May I never question that, boy,
Your heart's as warm an' true.
May I never question that, boy,
Your heart's as warm au' true.

Like yours, her eyes were blue, boy,
Her hair a golden sheen ;
Like yours, the merry dimples
'Round her cherry lips were seen,
An' she was blithe an' gay, boy ;
But that was long ago.
You 'mind me of your mother, boy,
An' joys I used to know.
You 'mind me of your mother, boy,
An' joys I used to know.

I, too, was happy then, boy,
But now I'm sad alway,
For your mother's smile is gone, boy,
Could I but recall the day.

You lead me by the hand, boy,
As I led her long ago—
You 'mind me of your mother, boy,
An' joys I used to know—
Of joys I used to know, boy,
But again shall never know.

O'ER THE HILL TO MARY.

The balmy win's o' spring are blowin',
The lark is singin' high above,
My heart has gone, an' I'm a-goin'
O'er the hill to Mary love,
To Mary love, to Mary love,
O'er the hill to Mary love ;
The win's may blow, but I mus' go
O'er the hill to Mary love.

The bloomy glade is gay an' cheery.
I'll pull a wild-flower as I go
To deck the golden hair o' Mary
Who lives down in the valley low,
The valley low, the valley low,
Who lives down in the valley low.
To deck the hair o' Mary fair
Who lives down in the valley low.

Her song is like the wild-bird's sweetest,
An' she's as tender as the dove,
An' she's the fairest an' the neatest,
My own sweet-heart—my Mary love,
My Mary love, my Mary love,
My own sweet-heart—my Mary love.
The win's may blow, but I mus' go
O'er the hill to Mary love.

THE TOMB.

O, tomb, thou holdest not eternal life,
But death—the passport to the soul's long peace.
The tears shed o'er thee reckon not of rife
Despair, but grief that only with thee cease.

THE HOOSIER HILLS.

Oh, the Hoosier hills, oh, the Hoosier hills,
Where the red fox plays an' the wild-bird trills,
Where the wood-dove moans an' the wildflower blows
An' the tuneful rill in its gladness flows,
Where the heart's as free as the dronin' bee,
Oh, there, oh, there is the place for me.

Oh, the Hoosier hills, oh, the Hoosier hills,
With love for them how my bosom thrills,
An' my thoughts fly back to my boyhood days,
To the old-time friends at the old-time ways,
To the still graveyard on the old hill top
Where the weary road of life did stop,
Where the dove moaned low an' the tears
    did flow
O'er the hearts, o'er the hopes in the long ago.

Oh, the Hoosier hills, oh, the Hoosier hills,
My heart never strays from their springs an'
    rills
An' their broad roof-trees an' their musky
    flowers
An' their quiet shades an' their bloomy bowers
That the heavens bend o'er with an' open door.
Oh, there let me rest when I am no more.

SLOWLY BY.

Slowly by, slowly by, woe-days, so slowly,
While the heart in its pain bows to you lowly.
But the eyes cannot weep for the heart's token,
Nor the lips cannot speak vows that are broken.

Slowly by, slowly by, woe-days, so dreary.
Who in the laughing eyes reads the soul weary?
What in the words of mirth hints of woe
    spoken?
Only the heart above knows the heart broken.

I'M GOIN' BACK SOME DAY.

I'm goin' back some day
    To the Mississinewa,
Where the wild-bird sings the sweetest
    An' the banks are green an' gay.
I'm goin' back some day
    To the Mississinewa.
I'll take my old bob-tail nag
    An' go joggin' back some day.

A false love led me here,
    It led me here to sigh;
But the love that will lead me back again
    Is a love that will never die.
I lay on a wild-rice bed
    When my false love was astray
An' dreampt my old love call me back
    To the Mississinewa.

Oh, I never shall forget,
    If I live to the world's last day,
The girl I left on the gay, green banks
    Of the Mississinewa.
But she was poor an' so was I
    An' I said that I must go,
So I rode away on my bob-tail nag
    To the banks of the Ohio.

On the banks of the Ohio
    I stopped at a rich man's gate,
An' the rich man's daughter took my hand
    An' I said, I've met my fate.
I bought her a weddin' ring,
    I bought her a ring o' gold,
But before we had been married a year
    Her love for me was cold.

Oh, I never shall forget,
    If I live to the world's last day,
The girl I left on the gay, green banks
    Of the Mississinewa.
So I'm goin' back some day
    To the Mississinewa.
I'll take my old bob-tail nag
    An' go joggin' back some day.

CHARLEY BRUNETT.

I wrote this song for a young Mexican girl who related to me the story of her faithless lover by the above name. She set the piece to a plaintive, sweet air and used to sing it over and over at evening accompanied by her guitar.

Charley Brunett, I'll never forget
Your gay song and laughter; I sigh in regret,
Charley Brunett, that fate did us sever,
Forever, forever, O, Charley Brunett.

Charley Brunett, my heart was beset
By the ravishing bliss of the maze of your net,
Charley Brunett, with hope for the morrow,
To find only sorrow, O, Charley Brunett.

Charley Brunett, O, Charley Brunett,
I'm praying to linger one hour with you yet,
Charley Brunett, from you ever parted
To die broken-hearted, O, Charley Brunett.

THE MISFIT.

Your pants don't fit you, Jakey;
    The tailor was so shaky
He cut them too tight about the knee,
    They're too loose in the spank and
    They're too short in the shank and
They show your white socks, Jakey,
    Don't you see, don't you see?
They show your white socks, Jakey,
    Don't you see?

The tailor took your measure
    With a wise look at his leisure
And he said, "I see, dear fellow, that you
    are low-cut shod!
I'll cut them long and stylish

For your low shoes," said he smilish'
And receipted your good money
With a nod, with a nod,
And receipted your good money
    With a nod.

But he went out with the boys,
And he filled himself with joys
That in a liquid form he took quite free,
Which unjointed all his nerves
And his scissors squared the curves,
And you're a misfit victim,
Don't you see, don't you see?
And you're a misfit victim,
    Don't you see?

BOB GRAN'PAP.

Bob Gran'pap was a good man,
  He lived to be quite old
By coolin' off when he was hot
  An' warmin' up when cold.

He kep' an old brown jug well filled
  An' drank from a silver cup
The stuff that used to cool 'em off
  An' likewise warm 'em up!

In winter it would warm 'em up,
  In summer cool 'em off,
An' when 'twas neither hot nor cold,
  He took it for his cough.

An' to keep his circulation right,
  Also a level head,
He took a pull when he got up
  An' when he went to bed.

Thus he kep' his temperature just right
  Till a hundred years had past,
Then with a blossom on his nose
  He passed away at last.

OH, SISSIE, YOU'VE A HAPPY TURN.

Oh, Sissie, you've a happy turn
And would you sing a song to me?
My heart does ever sadly yearn
  For what can ne'er belong to me;
But question not, oh, question not;
  But, Sissie, sing a song to me
To cheer my heart that sadly yearns
  For what can ne'er belong to me.

Your eyes are of the heaven's own blue;
  They speak of soul too pure for me;
'Twould break my heart were it untrue,
  Yet it would sin endure for me.

But ask me not that I repine;
  But, Sissie, sing a song to me
To cheer my heart that sadly yearns
  For what can ne'er belong to me.

If heart defiles the heart it loves,
  'Twere better far that it love none.
Oh, Sissie, kindly that heart proves
  That in its sin lives all alone.
But think not of these griefs the while
  But, Sissie, sing a song to me
To cheer my heart that sadly yearns
  For what can ne'er belong to me.

I'LL THINK NOT OF THOSE GRIEFS THE WHILE.

I'll think not of those griefs the while
  That love hath taught to me;
I pray thee give me yet one smile,
  Since parting now must be.
I've held thy dainty hand in mine—
  Caressed thy snow-white brow;
Thou smiled on me in rapture then,
  O why refuse me now?

I know that love oft fills the heart
  With hate when hope is vain.
But O I pray thee, ere we part,
  To smile but once again.
The moon smiles in the gloaming
  As in hours forever gone.
O smile on me a last farewell,
  My lost love—only one.

THERE'S SOMEWHAT IN THY DREAMY EYE.

There's somewhat in thy dreamy eye
Where the dusk of sadness lingers,
Bell Ellen, of the warm love-light
I knew in days agone
  When haply I have heard thee sigh,
  And held thy dainty fingers
  And fancied that my heart the while
  Had fairest idol won.

But, O, forgive me, ere we part,
Tho' love inspired the feeling,
Bell Ellen, and forget me
Since thy heart's another's now.
  Tho' vain the longing in *my* heart,
  I pledge thee lowly kneeling—
  I pledge again the old-time love
  And leave a broken vow.

OH, WILDING, THINE'S A PRETTY FACE.

Oh, wilding, thine's a pretty face,
  And wilt my wish thou offer me?
I come to thee o'er many a hill
  A rarest joy to proffer thee.

Thy beds are neat and carpet swept,
  The fire crackles on the hearth;
But in thine eye's a brighter light
  And neatest is thy slender girth.

Oh, should I dare thy frown disdain
  And take and give in even change
Thou wouldst often look for me and sigh,
  And sigh for joy so sweet and strange.

But I will leave thee, pretty maid,
  And leave thee also naught to rue;
But thou wouldst hold me with thine eye
  To chide I do not dare and do!

WHO KNOWS?

Who knows what's done in the dark?
    Love's a flame:
Who can tell by such a light
    Who's to blame?
Forty gallants dare and fly,
Forty maidens sit and sigh:
Should we laugh, or should we cry?
    Ask not I—ask not I.

Who knows just how far to go
    In the dark?
Hapless Fate may meet us there
    With his mark!
And old Daylight joy to yell
What the good Dark ne'er would tell—
Saint is sinner—heaven is hell!
    Toll the bell—toll the bell!

BY KILLARNEY'S BLUE WATERS.

At evening alone by Killarney's blue waters
  I wept for a love that can never return;
The fairest to me of all earth's fairest daughters,
  Had vanished away to that far, happy bourne.
The tide flowed along in a murmur of sadness
  And my burden of grief it seemed longing to bear;
But I turned to the sky, when a bright face of gladness
  Did smile me to rest as I gazed on it there.

Oh, now far away from dear scenes of Killarney
  My heart wanders back to its gay hills and streams;
The warm hearts that wait with a welcome for Barney
  So often, so often I see in my dreams:
But there is one spot in my heart's sacred keeping
  That's dearer to me than all else e'er can be,
'Tis the low, grassy mound where my Kathleen lies sleeping,
  Sweet Kathleen who smiled from the heavens on me.

O, SINCE YOUR HEART'S ANOTHER'S NOW.

O, since your heart's another's now,
  The songs I loved alway,
Fall full of sadness on my ear,
  From your fond lips to-day.
You sing of love—but mine has flown,
  You sing of hope—I've none;
You sing to me of heart that's dead,
  And that I have alone.

Now I repine. Once as a flower
  You smiled beneath my gaze,
But, heedless of the golden hour,
  I strayed in other ways;
But thought should fortune smile on me
  I'll linger not apart,
But, when at last I sought my flower,
  'Twas on another's heart.

MEDREAMPT I KIST THY HAND ADIEU.

Medreampt I kist thy hand adieu
  And wandered far apart;
But wheresoe'er I wandered to
  It was with paining heart.
Medreampt I entered castle gate
  And host bowed low to me;
But all the while my paining heart
  Was sighing, love, for thee—
    Sighing, love, for thee.

Medreampt I trod in marble hall
  Where beauty's eyes did shine;
Methought they shed the light of heaven
  Save when compared to thine.
Medreampt that wealth had made me proud—
  I was one of royalty;
But all the while my paining heart
  Was sighing, love, for thee.—
    Sighing, love, for thee.

THE THREE LOVERS.

I sat me under a willow tree,
  Under a weeping willow wept,
Three young maidens lost their love,
  Three young soldiers heart-pierced slept.

One I saw of the maidens fair,
  One with a wealth of tresses gold,
Bathe in blood her tender breast,
  Cleft with dagger bright and cold.

And another saw I there,
  Jet black locks and pale and fair,
Die of broken heart and lie
  Prostrate on her lover's bier.

Third no less to beauty given,
  Tresses brown in cypress wreath,
Gaze and turn—nor tear nor sigh—
  Reason flown she knew no grief.

Thus 'twas why I sat and wept
  Under a weeping willow low.
Pest and famine are sore, I said,
  War the essence of all woe.

ALICE BAINE.

When blushin' hung the jennetins late in September days,
I left my love a-weepin' in her woe,
An' far o'er many a Hoosier hill I wandered from her gaze,
An' far o'er many a river I did go.

O, many a weary day has come an' gone,
An' many a night I dream o' her in vain;
An' I'm weepin' bitter tears as I wander on and on,
Far away from my own sweet Alice Baine.

When blushin' hung the jennetins late in September days,
With tender word I wooed sweet Alice Baine;
But she was little spoken an' quiet in her ways,
An' I thought her cold an' told her she was vain.

But I was blinded an' my heart but hardened at her tears;
I turned from her an' left her stricken pale;
An' far o'er many a Hoosier hill I roved to ease my cares,
An' far o'er many a stream an' pleasant vale.

But when I touched the silvery sands that rim the surging main,
'Twas then repentin' that my hard heart bled,
An' cryin', Alice, Alice! my own sweet Alice Baine,
Too bitter is the word that you are dead!

When blushin' hung the jennetins late in September days,
I left my love a-weepin' in her pain,
An' now she's lost forever, forever from my gaze.
In silent death sleeps my sweet Alice Baine.

ANIEN.

I

Let the world frown, 'twas cold from beginning;
Let it go bickering on till the last;
Let the grim sophist haunt tender hearts
Till love is forgotten—a word of the past.

Let the cold formalist wheedle the soul;
Naught is his love but for things that decay.
The tenderest feelings, the purest thoughts,
He spurneth with coldness and casteth away.

Let my soul fly above this grim earth-god
Seated where justice struggles to live;
Let my heart throb with a purer conception,
Or wither to dust or whate'er death may give.

To kneel at the shrine of the dark monster Death,
Is all that poor mortal can trust to as sure.
Our laughter and tears, our sorrows and joys,
Compose but a death-song we strive to endure.

What is a life when to hope it's a stranger?
'Tis but a grim blank—a mere breeder of crime.
It knows but of pain and a future of sadness,
Whilst battling the rocks in the shallows of time.

Aye, vanity came and vanity lingers,
And man sips her cup—alas, some must fall.
Life's but a clasp on the belt of deception—
Wealth a mere term for the name of a thrall.

Ah, let the vain hopes burn in despair,
And passion sink low and the ashes blow wide;
Yet must the hearts that have known pain so long
Meekly submit to the things they're denied.

O Grief, with thy dark-circled eyes of dejection!
O saddest Regret, what soul hast thou moved?
O deep-seated Woe, I wed thee forever!
Yet greater the pain in the heart that I loved.

The heart that I loved in the home of a despot.
Riches and poverty counted as one!
Vainly, O, vainly the tired heart battled
The whim of a parent— a *higher-born* son.

II

I knew thee when the bloom of spring
   Had settled on the vine;
I knew thy smile in summer
   When the berries ran with wine.
I knew thee when the orchard
   Had a deeper golden hue,
And when the bee was drowsy
   And the summer flowers were few.

I knew thee in the morning
   When thy maiden robes were fair,
And the ever-coming blushes
   Leaping kist thy chestnut hair.
I knew thee at the noontime,
   When thou lingered by the brook,
'Neath some cool and balmy bower
   That the summer sun forsook.

I knew thee in the evening
   When the deepest passions move,
And thy maiden heart was quickened
   With the sweetest hopes of love.
I knew thee in the love-light
   That thy tender passion shed,
When thy heart was sweetly wedded
   And the future gave no dread.

I knew thee when thy joy
   Leapt in sweetest flame of love,
And thine eyes portrayed soul-pureness,
   Aye, as that which reigns above.
I knew thee when thy laughter
   Cleft the sweetly perfumed air,
And quickened into gladness
   Every being that was there.

I knew thee when there lingered
   Just a little tinge of care
On thy brow; thine eyes were margined
   With the circle pain leaves there.
I knew thee when it deepened
   To the the darkness of deep woe—
When thy parent-murdered passion
   Struggling, spoke and bid me go!

III

O, sweet Anien, tender Anien,
The world was too cold for thee.
It has frozen thy tender heart,
          Anien.
Thy life was too pure to ever be
Mingled with others, live as we,
Alas, alas! too cold a part,
          Anien.

O, sweet Anien, tender Anien,
The light of thine eye grew dim.
There lingered no smile on thy lips,
          Anien.
The world was too cold and drear and grim,
And life was like a shallow whim,
That through our higher senses slips,
          Anien.

O, sweet Anien, tender Anien,
Thou art lost for aye and aye!
Thou sickened at the world's cold art,
          Anien,
And mockery that is wrought in clay,
And given being thus to prey
On victims of a tender heart,
          Anien.

O, sweet Anien, tender Anien,
Thy heart was fed on sighs.
Thy life ran out in bitter tears,
          Anien.
Thy soul knew but thy bitter cries,
Till lost in glories of the skies,
There dawned the peace of eternal years,
          Anien.

IV

May the blood of crime be ever,
Evermore upon the guilty,
Till the dread of death's more awful
Than e'er death can be itself.
May the cherished hopes that lingered
In the maiden heart so tender
Stand as specters at the window
Of the soul that killed those hopes.

Aye, kindly be the parent,
That rather looks to duty
Than to worldly wile of station,
That the purer heart does loathe;
Aye, kindly, nay, thrice kindly,
Be the parent that had rather
Give his child unto a beggar!
Than to sell his child for gold.

Years will bring no balm or healer
To his heart, for grief shall wed it.
Nothing but sad retrospection
Will reward his future years;
Though his smile be bright as ever—
Clothe in mockery the echoes
Of his heart, still deepest misery
Shall haunt him aye and aye.

May his cold, proud heart be ever
Haunted by her tender pleadings;
May his deep-set eyes forever,
Shrink before her child-like form;
May he hear each night those rending,
Agonizing cries of misery,
That re-echoed through his marble
Floored statuary hall.

SUPERSTITION.

Superstition, thou art a demon!
Dark and subtle as the feudal law.
When once thy ban has sunken
In poor man, alas, then thy bitterness
Is felt. Thy victim is led hither and yon,
A slave to thy inclinations.
Demon! hell-born, ill-starred,
Despotic, demon! thou dost
Lead man o'er a path
More solitary than the path of death.
Would to God 'twere death in thy stead—
That we know comes to all ;
But, alas, what know we of thee?
Thou art, O, hell-born, the blackest
Imp of Satan's whole train;
And thy offspring, scattered
O'er the earth to muddle reason,
Blind sight, and dwarf courage, as black.
Foul incubator of damnation!
I pity thee, that thou shouldst
Bear the name, but much more
Envy thee one so good.
If there were now a Solomon
With his magic ring or cap,
It would be my sole purpose
To beseech him to transform thee
Into a mighty stone, and sink thee,
Never to arise, in the mighty depths
Of the ocean; that, there thou shoudst lie
Supine and lost for all time—
 Eternally!

SCRAPS.

'Tis but a skull, alone and empty,
Left to its fate of nothingness.
There once the bright eye beamed
And the smile of affection dwelt.

I love those good old hymns
 That I in childhood hours did learn.
For those old hymns so soft and sweet,
 How oft my heart does yearn.

IS THERE REWARD?

If I, with all the power
 Of a willing soul and anxious mind,
Labor and toil unceasingly,
 Shall I then reap nothing but the wind?

Shall I, if kind providence
 Leads my mortal frame on to the last,
Laden with acts of kindness,
 Be then rejected for kind deeds past?

If it be thus, why not rest
 The brain, hot fevered with weary thought?
Why need we heart—aye being,
 Why are we here, a figurehead for naught?

LOVE'S YOUNG DREAM.

A dream that all my being thrilled with joy—
A dream sublime that leadeth heart and mind,
Came to me in the calmness of an hour,
And with a blessing rarely humankind.
For, sweeter than the breath of any flower,
Played mellow, balmy breezes o'er my soul,
And all the crumbling ruins of the past
Were cities fairer built, and never dole
Came in. O joyous day that could not last!
I pay thee homage in far sadder hour
Than when I, wayward in love's old-time
 ways,
Unmindful of the sweetness of thy bower,
Repented silently of sad delays—
O dream, sweet dream! no sadness can destroy.

A LITERARY MAN.

He's supposed to be a gentleman
 Worth thousands. His income,
So great from books and manuscripts,
 He stows away at home.
The needy stranger hunts him out:
 His signature's immense;
Subscription papers daze his eyes—
 Perpetual consequence.

Periodicals! He takes them all.
 Books with requests: "Please read,"
(An advertisement. Hist! be mum.)
 Come regular, indeed.
Manuscripts! Great Scott! why, man,
 The postman's worn the door
Half-way through the panels
 Just by knocking, nothing more.

They come from east and west and north
　And south and in between
For his opinion of them, though
　They're always good, they ween.
The editor has rejected them;
　But that's all right; you see
The literary man don't care,
　And they help kill time, may be.

He's to sit down any minute,
　If a poet, and knock off a rhyme
On any subject, no matter what,
　'Bout the past or present time.
All that he wants is the subject
　For an eulogy, ode or prologue,
And he's to do it up like machine work
　In the floweriest language in vogue.

He's to write up a bucolic lover,
　A mother-in-law, aunt and a niece
And the fourth of July and Christmas
　All together or piece by piece.
He's to write for fairs and picnics,
　Make dinner speeches, too.
He's to attend all the celebrations,
　And subscribe for each object in view.

He's called on by his admirers
　To correspond, who say:
"We have no claim on your time, dear sir,"
　Then follow six foolscap, they
All interlined with pale blue ink,
　(Long letters and pale ink are twins,)
And he's expected to read the thing
　Clear through from where it begins.

POVERTY.

Poverty drew her direful shroud
　Around my life and shut it out
From all things else save misery.
　Poverty! O, what is it?
You whose hold on plenty is firm,
　And heaven smiles on you,
　　Can answer not.
Within where starving vitals prey
On weakening mind, on weakening heart,
On weakening body, weakening soul,
　Can only answer it.
Down, down its victim sinks;
To starvation's shrine he kneels!
A weakened, ghastly sight of woe,
　A dupe of misery.
'Tis one of hell's entanglements,
　Set here for man, its prey.
A heinous, damnable design
　　Of Satan to destroy.
Roll on, you hell-brewed scheme of woe,
Reap full your gluttonous want;
Reign o'er weak victims while on earth,
　Then sink to hell—your home!

THE FAIRY OF SIN.

I ascended the hill—the prospect was fair;
Lo! the fairy of sin was lingering there!
The propitious moon shone everywhere,
And the song of the brook was sweet and clear.

"O art thou theist, sinner or divine?
The winter is past and thy heart is warm.
Tell me, dost thou to Themis incline,
Or blind to good and harm?"

My horse in the thills pawed the turf hard by,
And champed his bit in a restless way.
The still was broke by his frequent neigh,
And I longed for the coming day.

"I wear a cypress" said the fay, "death's symbol!
Cometh not near, 'tis the home of death!
No mortal here liveth, but here do tremble
The voice of sin and the devil's breath!

"I hear the cushat's mournful note.
True, spring is come and my heart is warm;
But a demon clings to my tender throat,
And I feel the touch of the foul death-worm!

"Leave to thy home, this is not, stranger, for
　thee.
I court not Themis, neither am theist.
Leave ere the sickening death-rattles take me,
And I here die to rot—nor devil resist!

"Then the pismire and death-worm shall have
　me,
And the goshawks cope with the ghouls,
While my soul with its foulness and booty,
Sinks to hell in its tantrums and howls!"

SHE SANG A SONG.

She sang a song with tearful voice
　An' set my heart a-painin',
An' listenin' on with easy ear
　My heart began complainin'.
Oh, Jennie, sing no more, said I,
　My heart is full o' sorrow,
An' I must go along, my dear,
　I'll stop again to-morrow;
An' I must go along, my dear,
　I'll stop again to-morrow.

I kissed her on the oaken porch,
　With tender word she blessed me.
My heart seemed nearly breakin' an'
　Sweet Jennie most distressed me,
Till soft the moon light on her face
　Showed me a tear o' sorrow.
An' when I said good night, she said,
　You'll stop again to-morrow?
An' when I said good night, she said,
　You'll stop again to-morrow?

I turned from her an' clicked the gate;
　She watched me from the door;
An' then I stopped to ease my heart
　An' called her out once more.
Oh, Jennie, take my heart, said I,
　So heavy with its sorrow,
I cannot carry it away;
　I'll leave it till to-morrow;
I cannot carry it away;
　I'll leave it till to-morrow.

I held my Jennie close to me,
　An' felt her wild heart beatin'.
I kissed her o'er an' o'er again,
　An felt our glad tears meetin'.
Oh, Jennie, take my heart, my love;
　'Tis yours in joy an' sorrow,
An' I'll ne'er take it back, my love,
　For ne'er does come to-morrow;
An' I'll ne'er take it back, my love,
　For ne'er does come to-morrow.

A JOY OVERTOOK ME.

A joy overtook me last night in my dream
And spilt my descent to the throne.
I awoke with a sigh of regret it did seem
　So real, yet I lay all alone.

I thought of her beauty, her sweet words of love;
　Her hot kiss that thrilled all my soul.
Could regret pay the longing? nay, heaven above,
　Ne'er a joy of such equal could dole.

Yet, stained with the error of innocent youth,
　I languished in restlessness there,
And cursed with the curse of unbearable truth,
　The sin to which mortal is heir.

OLD AMITY.

As I went over Amity Road,
　With many doubts, and many fears,
I met an old man with hair in his ears—
　A strange old man with a heavy load.

I said, "May I help you along, good man,
　For your back is bent with your heavy load,
And whoever travels over this road
　Should always help whoever he can."

The old man viewed me with squint and scowl,
　And at length he said, "Pray who be thee,
That would descend to thus help me—
　Even me, at whom the dogs but growl?"

I answered, "Is this not Amity Road,
Where friendship and peace go hand in hand?
Come, good man, I'm at your command;
May I bear a portion of your load?"

In sorrow the old man shook his head,
And through his wrinkles there coursed a tear;
"No, no!" he said, "this load I'll bear
Alone and weary till I am dead!"

While at the village I asked if pelf,
Or food or clothes the old man bore.
They shook their heads—"We know no more,
Than he's old Amity himself."

A DIRGE.

Do not weep, the day is done,
　Life has cast its burdens off.
Do not weep, the race is run,
　And the heart's at rest.

Do not weep, for all is well;
　Cease thy grief, believe 'tis wise.
Do not weep, hearts cannot tell
　What is best for all.

Do not weep, though life is past,
　Let the links of love be strong—
Do not weep, but hold them fast
　Ever in thy heart.

Do not weep, and grieve the soul,
　For in heaven all is joy.
Do not weep, but let there roll
　To thy bosom peace.

BURY THE PAST DEEP.

Why need the heart through bitterness relenting,
Cling to the past and try to soothe a woe—
Woe that the heart has battled with consenting
To cease the strife and let the victory go?

Far better, far, that life had been at dawning,
Sealed up and sunk in innocence' sweet calm,
Than thus be battling from the red of morning
Until the night of death without a balm.

Then let the woe that's past be well forgotten,
Pamper the heart with sweetest hopes you know,
Full soon the tomb shall hold us while we rotten,
Far sooner those who'er battling with their woe.

THE ORPHAN.

She wept away the weary day,
  Her cheek was pale, her eye was gloom,
Her sweetest wish was but for death,
  And for her heart the silent tomb.

"Oh, let my spirit rest," she said,
  "Oh, let me know there's love for me,
If not on earth, in heaven: oh, sweet
  'Twould be to rest, oh, God, with thee.

"I care not thus to linger on
  And know but sorrow and despair.
I long to burst this earthly chain,
  And free my soul from earthly care:

"Live in the realm of purest love,
  Where never hope can be destroyed,
Where there's no pain, nor sin to mar
  The happiness thou hast employed.

"Oh, let my weary soul be free;
  Oh, give to me a better part.
I'm tired of the weary hours
  That pain my sick and throbbing heart.

"Receive my soul; it longs to fly
  To that perpetual light that's given
Unto the care-worn, longing soul,
  That enters into heaven."

THE DISAPPOINTMENT.

The shoemaker rode in his buggy one morn,
  With his fair servant by his side.
He was drest in his seventh-day coat and fresh shorn
  Were his locks which by age were much pied.

His fair servant smiled, and the shoemaker said,
  "Three years has it been since my wife
Past away, and since so long she's been dead,
  I've tired of my single life.

"And," thus he continued, "my children at home
  Should have a good mother, you know,
To teach and to love them that they ne'er may roam
  And bring to me regret and woe."

His fair servant smiled and looked buxom withal,
  And cleared her throat stammered and blushed.
Long since had she set her cap, in fact all
  Her thoughts on the shoemaker rushed.

Extended the shoemaker, "Libbie," said he,
  "You've been faithful (She swallowed her heart!)
Since my wife past away. I believe you to be
  Ever dutiful—true in your part."

Her nod was reply; she could say not a word.
  "So, this morning," the shoemaker said,
"I thought I would ask you (a shriek!) if you've heard,
  That to-morrow I am to wed?"

REJECTED.

Love and Hope have flown away!
Wellaway! lackaday!
Longer yet they might not stay.
  Poor heart o' mine!
What is life when love's astray?
  Poor heart o' mine!

Shall I weep or shall I pray
Night and day, night and day,
Till love comes again this way?
  Poor heart o' mine!
Alas, or has love gone to stay?
  Poor heart o' mine!

Ah, well, I'll just pull off my boots—
I'll sleep it down while old Time scoots!
She said she wouldn't live an roots!
  Poor heart o' mine!
And druggists they are all galoots!
  Hang her, by dang!

MY LOVE.

Bright at the close o' day her eye
  Shines like the evening star,
Whither away from my own true love,
  Whither away so far?

Out in the world at the beck o' fate
  Away from my true love's breast;
Little care I how the world goes on
  So she only loves me best.

Sing of her heart so constant and good
  That never a chidin' knew;
Sing merry-makin' voices all,
  Sing of her heart so true.

She calls me her brawny Hoosier boy,
  So lovin', brave an' good.
Oh, I would that I had a little o' good
  That flows thro' her precious blood.

Oh, she is the light o' the world to me,
  An' my soul drinks deep from her eye—
Drinks deep o' the love in her tender breast—
  A haven o' purity.

THE DECEIVER.

A proud ambition still and dead
As the gray stones ocean-washed and cold.
The towering thoughts of a cultured mind
Gone like a sun-touched vapor's fold,—
    'Tis well to sigh.

They were sweet. They led me vain.
They were mine, oh, proud, proud wight ;
But I've cast them now at a shrine to mould
And feed the worms of eternal night—
    'Tis well to sigh.

She was proud, of beauty given,
To me ten-fold more than any.
That were all her charms untold ;
Mask removed, like many, many—
    'Tis well to sigh.

Still I deemed it wise to love her,
Tho' but ruin was her giving ;
Rather not to love you had cast me
Into fires eternal living—
    'Tis well to sigh.

Had our passionate season ended
Without fruit of nature giving,
Sweet, perchance, her love, now hatred,
May have blossomed ; still be living—
    'Tis well to sigh.

She, deceiver 'reft of promise,
I, an ill-starred rueful being.
Naught for either but the chidings
Of a cold world fleeing, fleeing—
    'Tis well to sigh.

SHE WROTE ME A VERSE.

She wrote me a verse with a rhyme at the end,
  And it was a queer little bit.
'Twas about a sweet flower that it inclosed ;
  But love was not mentioned in it.
    But I ne'er grew unhappy ;
      For its meaning I strove.
    Some said it was hatred ;
      Some said it was love.

She wrote me a verse with a rhyme at the end,
  And it was an odd little bit.
About a sweet flower, the For-get-me-not,
  That was daintily wrapt up in it.
    Some said if the meaning
      I could not define,
    To go find the sender
      And claim her as mine.

She wrote me a verse with a rhyme at the end,
  And the meaning was hard to define ;
So I took in my fear the advice of my heart
  And claimed her forever as mine.
    With a smile on her lips
      And a tear in her eye,
    Our hearts beat together
      With love ne'er to die.

WHEN COLDLY NEEDY FRIENDSHIP'S VOICE.

When coldly needy friendship's voice
  First touched my heart with care,
The happiness I'd treasured long,
  Flew wildly otherwhere.

I looked within the heart of hope ;
  For peace I looked in vain ;
I found that hope had turned to grief
  And peace had turned to pain.

I dipt down deep in pleasure's tide ;
  But found no comfort there ;
There, too, did mingle grief and pain,
  And sorrow and despair.

I strove and gained of wealth my want ;
  But trouble more it gave.
Fond love denied me not its bliss,
  Yet happiness did crave.

Where is the happiness, old friend,
  That once I called my own ?
He answered with a tearful voice,
  "Take comfort ; there is none !"

VAIN HOPE LIES DEAD AND COLD.

Vain hope lies dead and cold
  In love's fair hall ;
Life's chamber of the heart
  To death yields the pall.
Two hearts have parted
  And left love to die
In the ashes of passion
  And the fire of the eye.

I love you—I love you !
  The echos come back,
Tho' the hearts hear the echos
  Never swift wings aslack.

They say not farewell;
  Nor does tear dim the eye;
  Nor is last parting kiss
    Offered, nor even sigh.

But, alas, comes the day
  In its brightness above,
When the breeze fans love's ashes
  To sweet flame of love.
But where are the severed hearts?
  Under dark ocean wave,
And the other on yonder hill,
  Low in her grave.

A VOICE.

I'll never drink of happiness;
  No rest from pain for me;
For mine's a woe more deep by far
  Than the lower graves of the sea.

I haunt a place in the old churchyard
  Where the noise of life does cease,
Where the only sound that breaks the still
  Is the sigh of the midnight breeze.

Woe is me! O come not near,
  Leave me in my sadness;
Tread not on this doleful spot
  That robs life of all gladness.

Here is not the home of joy;
  Here are pain and sorrow;
Here is all that makes a life
  Wish not for the morrow.

Hasten from my dire abode,
  O listen unto me—
For mine's a woe more deep by far
  Than the lower graves of the sea.

CLAIM THINE OWN.

Precious thoughts from sorrow rise,
  Wiping woe-marks from the eyes.
Gladly on, yes, gladly on
  Thou canst lead thy sweetest joy—
Slumber in calm peacefulness,
  Nor sterner facts destroy.

Duty labors, duty waits,
  And with hope and firmness mates.
Give not thou to sighing
  For those who're left behind.
Ah, they'll love thee in the future—
  Call thee noble—call thee kind.

Cherish all that's dear to thee,
  Nor fear the surges of life's sea.
The day of youth, fast dying,
  Doth lead us far away—
Away where youth's ambition,
  Never knew the light of day.

Call not thou on yesterday;
  Let thy regrets pass away.
Work will bring a blissful ending
  To thy long and weary part.
Claim thine own—naught too good for thee—
  Fame and wealth and loving heart.

A DREAM.

And thus I dreamed a pleasant night
  When myriad stars did stud the sky.
My heart seemed gone far hence and I
  Lay in a calm of mystery,
When, in the sadness of a song,
  Set to a heart that hope had long
Led on, nor knew its destiny,
  Youth's ambition dauntless, great;
Hight sublime of fame and wealth;
  Glorious majesty of self,
Told me the story of their fate;
  Portrayed the gauntness and ill health,
And sordid action of the soul—
  I cried, O, charity for the whole.!

THE MAIDEN.

"These truly are thy happiest days,"
I said to the dreaming maiden;
"Smile innocently thro' the maze
Low floating o'er thy far off gaze;
These truly are thy happiest days."

When love sought out her trusting heart,
I said to the sighing maiden:
"Sweet visions hope did set apart,
Doubt cometh now and sad thou art;"
When love sought out her trusting heart.

Lo, when the bridal wreath was made,
Said mournfully pale maiden:
"I long to return to the sun-lit glade,
Where my sweet hopes lived and my young
    heart strayed."
Lo, when the bridal wreath was made.

ROSELLA WILE.

Rosella Wile, sin is so sweet—
  Sweet lips and red wine;
Thine eyes are divine.
Dreaming of love, dreaming of bliss;
  Sin charms my soul away
With thy sweet kiss.

Rosella Wile, rest on my heart:
  Lips meet in long kiss;
Sure heaven is this;
White arms entwined, soul lost the while!
  Oh, sweet the sin of love,
Rosella Wile.

I THOUGHT THE WHILE.

I thought the while that love was flown,
What trouble, heart, you put me to.
You rob me of a joy I rue;
You turn from tenderness to stone!
Let me alone—let me alone.

The moon waxed old the while I yearned;
A hot flame flashed athwart my breast
And soothed me unto tranquil rest;
But left my heart-strings pained and burned!
Love had returned—love had returned.

YE FRISKY WIN'S.

Ye frisky win's that fret the trees
  An' nip the blossoms from the boughs,
Ye bring to me a happy thought
  That leaves me with a bitter tear
For broken vows.

For Elsie's hand was soft an' white,
  Her voice was coo, her eye divine;
She languished in my absence oft
With thought that I should stray an' she
  Should not be mine.

But now she sleeps on yonder hill;
  Her gay deceiver far apart—
He came, he wooed, he ruined, fled!
An' I forgave her, but she died
  Of broken heart.

Ye win's, ye bring a happy thought
  Of blossom-time of days of yore,
But, O, it turns too soon to grief
An' makes me weep for one I knew
  But see no more.

I'M WEARING LONG DRESSES NOW.

Now don't ask me, Charlie, to do such as that,
  For I'm wearing long dresses now,
And really now, Charlie, it wouldn't be pat,
  For I'm wearing long dresses now.
My mamma says I must be *ever* so nice;
And quit playing tom-boy, and take her advice;
So after this, Charlie, you'll politely bow,
For I'm wearing long dresses now, you see?
  I'm wearing long dresses now!

Yes, I've grown to be quite a shine ladee;
A blushing, bewitching fine ladee,
And I'm acting, you see, as such, you'll agree,
Since my dresses much longer are madee!

Sometimes I can go for a stroll in the park,
  For I'm wearing long dresses now.
You must act very civil if you are my spark,
  For I'm wearing long dresses now.
You must say, "why, Miss Brown," with a smile all serene,
"May I help you to strawberries, soda and cream?"
Just nice things now, Charlie, I only allow,
For I'm wearing long dresses now, you see?
  I'm wearing long dresses now!

DEARIE MARY LINDOMEE.

Dearie Mary Lindomee, watching, waiting o'er the sea,
Far off where the mountains rise up to kiss Italian skies.
Sweet her harp she plays at eve—dearie Mary Lindomee,
And her song does not deceive—'tis of love and constancy—
  Dearie Mary Lindomee.

Dearie Mary Lindomee, from thee severed e'er to be—
I an exile doomed to roam far away from love and home;
Yet in fancy I can hear, dearie Mary Lindomee
Singing by the fountain clear of her love and constancy—
  Dearie Mary Lindomee.

GENTLE REFINA.

Gentle Refina, thine eye is blue,
Thy heart is tender, thy love is true.
Gentle Refina, to know as I
Thee pure as angel none could deny.

Gentle Refina, thy winning smile,
Thy witching accents haunt me the while.
Gentle Refina, love such as thine
Can not be other than love divine.

TO WHITE RIVER.

O, oft your bloomy banks I've strolled,
  An' oft I've rowed your waters long,
An' I have seen you roarin' bold
  An' gently ripplin' in your song.
Yes, oft with joy I've strolled your banks
  When spring was in her charmful dress,
An' oft when winter's ruthless pranks
  Had bound an' stole your tunefulness.

I love your waters an' your banks,
  Tho' many a fault is beckoned you,
I love you all the more in thanks
  For many a good that's reckoned you.
O, oft I've sung you happy song,
  An' oft I've mourned you my regrets;
An' hallowed once your banks along
  To stroll with love heart ne'er forgets.

DREAMING.

I saw the tall ships sailing by
To the port beyond the sky,
  Where the zephyrs waft a rare perfume
  And time is peace and eternal bloom,
Nor friends e'er bid good-bye.

My heart was sad as the ships sailed by
And I gazed with tear-dimmed eye,
  For I thought of a face forever gone;
  My throat was cloyed, but the ships sailed on
To the port beyond the sky.

NAN'S GONE WITH A WESTE'NER.

Nan's gone with a Weste'ner!
  A man who wore a broad-brim hat;
Nan's gone with a Weste'ner!
  That's what the folks are wonderin' at.
His mustache was nine inches long—
  Nan's gone with a Weste'ner!
He sang sis' Nan a breezy song—
  I'll bet he gets the best o' her!

Nan's gone with a Weste'ner!
Nan's gone with a Weste'ner!
Nan's gone with a Weste'ner!
  An' I'll bet he gets the best o' her!

Nan's gone with a Weste'ner!
  A lasso hung across his back;
Nan's gone with a Weste'ner—
  His saddle-horn was big an' black!
He said he lived in Idaho—
  Nan's gone with a Weste'ner;
But I think his place is down below!
  An' I'll bet he gets the best o' her.

Nan's gone with a Weste'ner!
  She wanted to be a cowboy's bride;
Nan's gone with a Weste'ner
  With two big pistols at his side!
His Texas pony wasn't slow;
  Nan's gone with a Weste'ner!
She on behind he let it go;
  But I'll bet he gets the best o' her!

DREAMING OF THEE ALWAY.

Dreaming of thee alway, love,
  But never to see thee more,
For thine were the wings of unseen light
  That from me thy beauty bore,
That bore thee far away, love,
  So far away from me,
That I wait not thy return, love,
  Nor again thy face to see.

Dreaming of thee alway, love,
  Dreaming of thee alway,
Thro' the silent watches of the night
  And the hours of the toilsome day:
And at twilight I sing thy songs, love,
  To our babe upon my knee;
But they have not the sweetness of yore, love,
  But a sadness now for thee.

Dreaming of thee alway, love,
  Dreaming alway of thee,
And we stroll thro' the scenes of the past, love,
  And sit by the stream in the lea,
And we gather the lilies at morning, love,
  And at evening we kneel to pray—
I am dreaming of thee alway, love,
  Dreaming of thee alway.

FIELDS OF HOOSIERLAND.

Oh, vernal fields of Hoosierland,
Seamed with the smile of many a stream,
My heart was born to worship thee,
My lips to sing thee songs of praise.
  Oh, pleasant fields of Hoosierland,
  I sigh for thee and sigh and dream
  Of that dear home that was for me
  In good old-fashioned Hoosier days.

Oh, vernal fields of Hoosierland,
Thy soft green grasses were my bed,
Thy cooling waters were my drink,
Thy perfume filled my infant breast.
Oh, happy fields of Hoosierland,
I'll sing thee praise till life has fled;
Thou parlor of my heart—I think
God's choicest blessings on thee rest.

A CHARACTER OF CREED.

He railed against his creed to worship God;
He saved an enemy to save a friend;
Belied himself and then belied his lie;
Misproved a foe and thereby proved his guilt;
Sought woman's love while faithless deeming
    her;
Gained wealth and said no man was great and
    poor;
Sought wisdom with the thought it was a curse,
And cursed a man for what he did himself.

WOMAN OF DARK EYE.

Woman of dark eye and hair
    Of a golden light,
Oft I dream and while with thee,
Yet thy face I ne'er shall see,
Only in vain fantasy—
    Woman of dark eye and hair
    Of a golden light.

Woman of dark eye and hair
    Of a golden light,
Oft thy dainty hand I kiss,
Gaze into thine eye in bliss,
Where a love-light ever is—
    Woman of dark eye and hair
    Of a golden light.

Woman of dark eye and hair
    Of a golden light,
Long I've grieved I took ungiven,
Ere the musk died at the even,
More than life from thee and heaven—
    Woman of dark eye and hair
    Of a golden light

A SKILLFUL SAILOR.

A skillful sailor ne'er was made
    By calm, smooth seas and summer skies,
Nor wealth uninterrupted gained
    Can crown our hearts with heavenly ties.
Adversities, like ocean storms,
    Must dot our pathway o'er life's sea,
Then hearts with gratitude sublime
    Will anchor in eternity.

DIRGE.

The bell in the old church tower—
A solemn voice on the evening air.
The low, sweet songs of the nuns
And the lifted heart and the fervent prayer.

Awake, O heart! to that solemn call,
Nor fall from the love of a tender heart—
From a time-tried love with a sad, sad lot—
From a love-born soul in a bitter part.

A dead, cold heart with life's warm blood
Is worse, by far, than the silent tomb,
And lips with a blue rimmed pall of woe
Breathe out sweet hopes to eternal gloom.

ANDOINE.

Lo! fairy-like, in soft-fold robes,
They wandered o'er the silvery sands
With silken tresses wreathed in flowers,
    And sang:

"O song, sweet song o' the summer sea;
    O song, sweet song o' the sea,
Thou dost thrill our hearts as softly thou
    Art wafted in ecstasy.

O song, sweet song o' the summer sea;
    Thou dost soothe with a mystic spell!
And mingled with the dancing waves,
    The mermaid voices well.

O song, sweet song o' the summer sea;
    O song, loved song o' the deep,
Thou dost teach but love to our young hearts
    Till for love we longing weep."

Far up the cliff an old man bent
And hoar with age looked sadly down,
And by him stood a youth, as fair
As ever maiden's heart broke for;
And goats fed near and lazy ass
And oxen in a ferny brake
Lowed, and there bleated yet apart
From these, with faithful dog, the sheep.

Long gazing down the old man's silence broke.
He spoke as if he spoke unto himself:
"Andoine! Andoine! Andoine!
O thou miserable! O thou miserable!
Andoine! Andoine! Andoine!
O thou miserable! O thou miserable!"
And then the youth as tenderly,
As ever mother to her new-born babe,
Soothed the old man with kindly word
And took his arm and led him on.

Slow winding down the rugged steep
Anon they paused to rest and gazed
Down and listened to the song—
Sung by the maidens, of the sea—
While fell a blush o' mellow light
From out the west upon the twain,
And then the sun dropt down
And sweet, calm twilight settled o'er the scene.
Then wended on old age and youth,
And following, the sheep and goats
And lazy ass, and, yet behind,
The heavy-footed oxen slow.

At length they reach the level plain
And greet the maidens in their glee,
Who roundabout the youth with kiss
And many a long and sweet embrace,
Each in her turn, ring with their merry chat.
The only lover for them all!
And he to love them all as one.

First one does in her rapture kiss
His shapely hand, and then likewise
Another falls upon his neck,
And yet another strokes his hair;
Another yet o' lovely limbs,
In highest admiration speaks,
Till he is kist a hundred times.

The old man deep within his grief,
Stood trembling, gazed and made his moan:
"Andoine! Andoine! Andoine!
O thou miserable! O thou miserable!
Andoine! Andoine! Andoine!
O thou miserable! O thou miserable!"
And then the youth broke from the maids
And soothed the old man with a kiss,
And led him on with kindly care
And reached the castle with the night.

With many a brilliant lamp high swung,
The castle glittered to the sky,
And thro' the musky air o' night
Stole forth sweet strains o' music low,
Or, wafted by the timid breeze,
Lest it should lose somewhat o' its
O'er-precious burden to regret,
The flute-like noted song o' love.

Clad in a silken velvet robe,
Wine-colored to the mellowed blush,
That ever and anon suffused
And leapt from maiden's cheek to cheek,
And raven hair shot full o' darts
O' luster; hanging long and curled;
And eyes lit bright with passion fond
O' love; low seated on a silken rug;
His fingers jeweled; he pefumed
With rarest musk o' faintest sweet,
The youth sat smiling in his joy.
And over by the window low,
Where sweet-breath vines twined roundabout,
The old man sat and dozed in fumes
O' wine, and slobbered on his breast!
While thus the maidens sung:

"O for a token, token,
  Only a token o' love;
Only a token o' love we beg o' thee.
Ne'er shall be broken, e'er constant will prove
  The vows we make to thee so faithfully."

And chorus accompanied by their
Sweet-toned and golden harps:—

"We have never concealed it,
  Darling, darling,
We have never concealed our love for thee;
Time has revealed it; gladly we yield it,
Ever true to you, darling, we shall be,"

And thus they sang, and flitted by
The hours far in the happy night,
When, slumber overcame the merry hearts,
And wrapt, the old man with the rest,
In dream they lay on long-pile rugs
O' many patterns, rich o' stuff and shade.

And thus I saw them on the foreign isle.
The old man sad and rich—sad for his son
Whom beauty led astray—rich o' the world,
And richer yet o' love that doting son bestowed
So bountifully 'mid the happy times
That love and beauty twain did while away.

I did not see the morn break o'er the scene;
But once a maid, far in the night, did sigh
And call the youth by name and ask for drink;
And once the old man swore a royal oath
And chuckled in his dreams o'er his own
  quips;
And then the castle clock chimed three.

I cast a long and last glance o'er the hall—
On beauty all divine o' mould and real,
On beauty dark, with tresses o'er her breast,
On beauty light, with golden hair hung down—
With here a head at rest upon an arm
All lily-white, bare bosom, limb o' art;
Or there another resting in rare lace
O' fleecy robe, bewitchingly misplaced,
From which peeked beauty ravishingly sweet—
When clapping loud his wings the cock did
  crow!
And I from pleasant dreaming did awake.

A PRAYER.

The daylight fades behind the summer hill,
The tuneful fountain leaps beneath the stars,
My weary soul to rest from fated wars,
Lies down with hope resigned to Thy will.

HAPPINESS.

Religion first to purify the soul,
  Next love to cheer and beautify the life.
The sacred blessings of a devoted wife,
Man's hitherto unfinished happiness make
  whole.

O, THOU MERRY MAID.

Believe me, O, thou merry maid
  Whom beauty favors, fancy free,
Thine eyes reflect the soul of thee
  In beauty that shall never fade.
Leaps to thy lips thy happy heart
  In mirth and merriment and song
Which, O, I pray, may all life long,
  Of thy pure self be greater part.

MAY MORLEY.

May Morley, May Morley, your eye is so glintful,
Its love-light has kindled a flame in my breast,
And wherever I go tho' to you never hintful,
My heart throbs for you in its wildest unrest.
You smile on me tenderly, gentle May Morley,
You smile on me tenderly when I am near ;
But there is a sadness in your smile, May Morley,
A sadness that oft trickles down in a tear,
A sadness that oft trickles down in a tear

Your eyes speak to me of a tender emotion,
Your lips tell of love that never grows cold,
You sing me a song of truest devotion ;
But never to me of your sadness you've told.
May Morley, May Morley, oh, if you were longing
For my love, how quickly I'd speak ; but I fear
I only remind you, perhaps, of another
Whose memory oft brings you many a tear,
Whose memory oft brings you many a tear.

MOREEN.

Moreen, fair Moreen, dreary the day
When from my side, love, thou art away :
Naught can inspire my heart with content,
But thee, fair Moreen, in thy languishment.
Soft in the gloaming, dream-songs of thee,
Ever are bringing their sweetness to me.
Moreen, fair Moreen, haply thine eye
Told thy love dying, too should I die.

Moreen, fair Moreen, when to thy bower
Sweet thoughts returning, blessing the hour,
Where late thy bright smile thrilled all my soul,
All to me heaven thy charms unfold.
Far hence thy love-lit eye is my star,
While I am singing to light guitar—
Moreen, fair Moreen, haply thine eye
Told thy love dying, too should I die.

HOOSIERLAND BALLADS.

THE HOOSIER.

Don't ye try to act the Hoosier
  Ef ye haint a Hoosier borned ;
Don't ye try to act the Hoosier
  Fer ye'll do it to be scorned ;
'Taint no use ; they's sompin' 'bout him
  'At ye'll never nimitate,
'Cep'in' 'at yer borned a Hoosier
  An' brung up in the state.

Fer a Hoosier's sich a meller,
  Easy, breezy sort o' man,
With a heart as big as heaven,
  Ef ye reckon by 'at plan,
'At jes to jump into his place
  An' fill his clothes out well,
I reckon 's 'bout the hardest job
  'At on a bein' fell.

They haint much style about him,
  Ner his lang'age, tobeshore ;
But he's faithful in his fr'en'ship
  An' he's honest to the core,
An' he's tender, an' he's merciful,
  An' he's full o' hope an' song ;
But he's roarin' woe an' thunder !
  W'en he's puttin' down a wrong.

He haint teched up with no etiket,
  Ner kivered up with shams ;
He's as open as the weather
  With his smoke-house full o' hams ;
An' his sympathy flows freer
  'N the water from a spout,
Ner it haint dammed up by money
  W'en it's 'bout a-bustin' out.

Ye may have yer kollege l'arnin'—
  Speak as oily as a witch
In ol'en times, an' write, mabbe,
  Fer past yer day an' sich,
An' act the plays the poets writ
  An' jine yer p'ints right well ;
But to try to act the Hoosier—
  Yer a heap less'n a smell.

Ye'll like about ten cents a-bein'
  Hardly worth a s'cat
(A-drawin' it down fine, ye see,
  To show ye whur yer at,)
W'en it comes to tryin' to make a
  Hoosier out o' sompin' else
'Sides a Hoosier, jes as well set down
  Tell yan air north pole melts.

No, don't try to act the Hoosier
  Ef ye wasn't borned fer one,
Fer while yer doin' all the tryin'
  He's a-havin' all the fun,

A-livin' au' a-blessin' all
  This happy Hoosierland,
An unadulterated critter
  From the Lord Almighty's hand.

Ye may try to talk the Hoosier,
  Ye may try to write the Hoosier,
Ye may try to act the Hoosier,
  But ye'll fail as shore as fate;
For they's sompin' 'bout the Hoosier
  'At ye'll never nimitate,
'Cep'in' 'at yer borned a Hoosier
  An' brung up in the State.

STARCHY SMITH.

Starchy Smith, Starchy Smith,
  Clever feller to be with.
Set a-straddle uf a chur,
    Joke an' smoke;
    Smoke an' joke.
I've nigh bu'sted many a time,
Hearin' him repeat a rhyme
'Bout some feller on the pike
Courtin' gyrls an' the like.
Folks says he writ it hisself;
'N, agin, some says 'at Belf
Goodhue got the blame thing up
Jes to spite Amandy Gibbs—
Never mind, it tickled ribs,
'At air rhyme, w'en Starchy Smith
Undertuk to please therewith.

Starchy Smith, my goodness he
Lays clean over you er me—
Speakin' 'bout, ye understand,
    Dressin' loud;
    'S awful proud.
Seen him sawin' wood fer Mat
Slaughters, in a silk plug hat,
Shoes a-shinin' an' his clothes
Brushed to death, the sayin' goes;
Workin' there with no shirt on;
Jes a bosom pinned in so
All the balance wouldn't show;
Cuffs the same—sleeves clean gone.
A feller 'u'd think Starchy he
Bein' so proud, his ancestry
A lot o' kings an' queens, mebbe.

But I reckon 'at haint so;
All his folks has lived, ye know,
Right here at Mahaleysville
    Some'rs near
    Sixty year.
Fam'ly on'y middlin' folks;
Mostly all the wimmin smokes;
Nuthin' 'bout the ole man Smith
'At 'u'd link 'im to a king;

Havin' ager in the spring
An' shootin' rabbits in the fall,
'S 'bout all he's distinguished fer,
'Thout it's bein' awful tall
An' so dreadful, mortal slim
His shadder is ashamed o' him.

But givin' Starchy his jus' due,
Tell ye what, they's mighty few
Fellers with a bigger heart.
  Ef he's stiff,
    What's the dif'?
'S well be 'at as t'otherwise;
Sour apples makes good pies;
Toughest timber best sills, too—
Speakin' adgeways now to you!
Fer doin' favors neat an' trim
They haint none willin'er 'n him,
An' w'en a ole friend draps off,
Starchy's heart does git so sof'
'At it 'mos' runs out in tears—
Meltin' sof' while it a'pears
Kivered up with high-tone airs.

No, Starchy haint like none his kin
No light 'at ye take him in.
Ole Doc Bragg says Starchy is
    Mixed up so,
    Style an' woe
Compounds 'bout what he 'u'd call,
"Liver-wise an' spleen content!"
Riddle it an' I'll haul
Out my pockets, ever' cent,
An' jes treat the whole blame crowd,
Glad to know why Starchy's proud;
Glad to think they's some 'at knows
Sompin 'bout the feller's woes;
Glad 'at woe to mix it with
Style make men like Starchy Smith.

NAPOLEON AND ABE POOL.

Ah, friend, you see, Napoleon was
  The greatest general ever known.
Whole nations trembled at his power—
  His scepter swayed from cot to throne.
Now tell me, friend, oh, if you can,
Did e'er you know a greater man?

"Wol, I donno, 'thout it was
  Abe Pool 'at lived on Crooked Crick,
Nepolyun might o' made folks shuck,
  But w'en Abe fit the town turnt sick."

But, friend, you see, Napoleon took
  The famous city, Moscow; yes,
Marched a myriad-score of men
  Thro' Russia's dismal wilderness.
Now tell me, friend, oh, if you can,
Did e'er you know a greater man?

"Wol, I donno, ye see Abe tuk
  'Is town a dozen times, I s'pose,
An' as fer marchin' men about,
  W'y Abe jes led 'em by the nose."

But, friend, you see, Napoleon loved
The battle-field, and lived for naught
Save war. Oh, mighty conqueror!
  Who but he such conquests wrought?
Now tell me, friend, oh, if you can,
  Did e'er you know a greater man?

"Wol, I donno; ye see Abe Pool
  'U'd druther fight 'n sleep er eat.
Nepolyun might o' fit right well,
  But I haint never saw Abe's beat."

THESE POETS.

I've heard 'bout these fellers
  Called poets—men 'at write,
An' does a heap o' thinkin'
  An' knows an awful sight,
An' makes a man feel bloo 's all
  Git out, an' 'n turns roun'
An' makes 'im feel so happy
  You can't hardly hold 'im down.

Now, a man out hur on Rock Crick,
  Like me, don't stand no show
A-runnin' onter poets.
  I don't believe I'd know
A poet ef I seen one,
  Fer a man 'at's allers ben
Uster common folks an' ager
  Haint no jedge o' them air men.

Nute Swaggs told me 'at he knowed one
  In '60, but he said
The feller j'ined the army
  An' got shot in the head
At Gittysburg in '63;
  But Nute said there's no doubt
But what he's like the poets
  'At us fellers hears about.

Nute said he'd allers reckoned
  'At poets wus all rich,
An' sort o' big-bug-like, ye know,
  Er allers passed fer sich;
But, w'en he seen 'is feller
  He concluded poets stood
A better show o' livin'
  Shuckin' corn er choppin' wood.

No; I've on'y heard 'em talked uf
  I haint never saw none yit,
Though they say they'r thick 's skeeters
  In the swamps; but ef I git
A chance ter see a poet
  I'll be hanged ef I don't try
Ter treat the feller decent—
  'At's thur pay—er mighty nigh.

DON'T YE MAKE FUN OF NO POET.

Don't ye make fun of no poet,
  Ner his peculer way o' thinkin',
Ner his peculer way o' writin',
  Ner his lang'age, mild er rough;
Don't ye come a-talkin' to him,
  'Thout ye've sompin' good an' pleasant;
Ef ye haint, jes let the feller be;
  He's havin' trouble enough.

Ef ye don't like his style o' thinkin',
  Ner don't like his style o' lang'age,
Ner the verses he has writ to try
  To drive away yer cares,
Don't be too quick to condemn him;
  Mebbe some'll allers bless him,
An' a feller writin' poetry
  'S often writin' it through tears.

It haint often 'at a feller's
  Writin' poetry fer money,
Ef he is he haint no poet,
  Fer 'at haint a poet's pay—
He's in luck ef he's a-gittin'
  A few tears an' a ole rosebush
An' a effytaf an' tumestone
  After he has passed away.

So don't ye make fun of no poet,
  Ner his peculer way o' thinkin',
Ner his peculer way o' writin',
  Ner his lang'age, ner his song;
Fer they's sompin' 'at's a-drivin'
  Of his pen an' he can't he'p it;
Jes ye treat the feller decent
  An' try a-he'pin' him along.

GYRL I LOVED.

Gyrl I loved wa'n't no beauty,
  Ner stuck up like some ye see,
On'y a fairly good-lookin' gyrl,
  Yit, folks said she's too good fer me.

Gyrl in love, as a gineral thing,
  Haint got no ears ner got no eyes:
Gyrl gittin' married takes a big risk,
  Yit she tuk the risk an' we's married likewise.

Thar's heap o' talk 'mongst the Wileyville
    people—
  I'd ben drinkin' some in my time;
Fact, hed ben, as many man's ben—
  'Thout a friend an' 'thout a dime.

This wus my home 'mongst these people
  I hed knowed sence I's a chile,
Yit, I coldn't p'int out one 'mongst 'em
  I owed a friendly word er smile.

"It's lazy Joe," I'd hear 'em say;
"He's out o' clothes an' full o' drink.
Lazy Joe—his grave is dug,
An' he's a-totterin' on the brink!"

Sickness come an' they carried me
To the poorhouse, an' one day
Mary come to read the Bible
An' to sing to me au' pray.

I jes thought my heart 'u'd break
W'en she tuk me by the han'
An' shet her eyes an' prayed I might have
One more chance to be a man.

Fact is, boys, I hed a chance;
In three ye'r I owned a farm—
In the meantime married Mary
An' love still keeps our ole hearts warm.

Forty ye'r sence we was married;
The Lord has blessed us won'erfully;
Yit I know 'at Wileyville folks wus right
W'en they said she wus too good fer me.

RED-HEADED BEN.

Red-headed Ben? I've knowed 'im
I reckon twenty ye'rs,
Er mabbe more 'n 'at, I can't
Jes figger, but it 'pears
I've allers knowed red-headed Ben;
But men sometimes begin
To nu's' a feller's fr'en'ship
An' time haint counted in.

Red-headed Ben wus lazy—
'Thar's nary man I know
'At ever seen red-headed Ben
At work—he wouldn't throw
A stick o' wood in winter
On the fire, an' they say,
He'd hardly scratch a sore
'At wus eachin' night an' day.

But men all has thur failin's,
An' Red-headed Ben hed his,
Yit, thar wus sompin' in his manner
'At more 'n ouct has ris
A feelin' 'at wus purty hard
Fer me to understand;
'Twus sompin' *more* 'n fr'en'ship
An' the shakin' uf the hand.

Onct I found a scrap o' paper—
'Twus a verse er two he'd wrote;
'Twus sompin' 'bout a true heart
Underneath a ragged coat,
An' sompin' 'bout a feller
Bein' too slow fer the times,
But he turned out in the endin'
A great man fer makin' rhymes.

The piece it wus so techin'
'At my ole eyes swum in tears,
The first time, too, I reckon,
In morn 'n twenty years,
An' my ole heart wus softer
Fer a good deal longer time
'N it ever wus before
By the readin' uf a rhyme.

I'm no jedge o' human nater,
'At is, sizin' up a man,
Jes by readin' uf his features,
Though they say thar's some 'at can;
But thar wus sompin' good an' pure
In the make-up uf ole Ben,
'At haint in half the preachers
Ner these loud professin' men.

An' 'at's the very reason why
I've allers ben his friend,
Though I reckon I's the on'y one
'At he could ricommend.
He wus lazy, p'or an' ragged—
Small pertaters—very small;
But w'en we've rounded up hereafter,
May be bigger 'n us all.

NEVER HAPPY.

'Pears like some men's never happy
'Thout they'r in a stew;
Pesterin' an' gee-an'-hawin',
Can't make nothin' do—
Can't git nothin' to work nohow,
Fix it as they will;
Growlin' w'en they'r makin' money
Er a-standin' still.

Parley half a day to try to
Buy a currycomb,
Er a yard o' yaller fact'ry—
Better stayed at home.
Growl like blazes ef the wheat crop
Falls a leetle slack,
Er ef corn has dropped a leetle
Er ef it's ris back.

Go to town to the elexion,
Like 's not git tight;
Whoopin' 'round the publik square
Er try to raise a fight.
Er a-swoppin' hosses 'n a
Kickin' 'cause they swopped,
Git to barkin' up the wrong tree
An' about git dropped.

Carried to the 'squire's offis
Thinkin' they'll die,
Child'en cryin' an' the wimmin
Faintin', mighty nigh.

'Squire haint long in decidin'
  On the foresaid case,
Whisky's 'fects air jes a-b'ilin'
  Over in thur face.

Strip thur coat an' go to darin'
  Airy man in town,
Er turn in, 's like 's not,
  An' knock the 'squire down.
Ends up in a jury axion,
  Bunged up eyes an' sich,
Mabbe they'll come out in whole clothes,
  Mabbe not a stitch.

SCLISTY ELLEN'S COURTSHIP.

Well I remember though ye'rs has passed by,
The crab apple orchard an' swing;
I blush w'en I'm thinkin', but oftener sigh
Fer the sad disa'p'intments they bring.
'Twus in mild September, the 16th I think,
O' the ye'r,—I declare I've fergot !
I'd ben with a passel o' gyrls fer a drink—
The weather wus dusty an' hot.

'S we walked thru the orchard Melindy Spry said,
"Come on, Sclisty Ellen," to me,
"We'll git in the swing while Samanthy instead
Of a gyrl be our feller, ye see."
We'd scarcely got seated, Melindy an' I,
W'en a cough made us jump with a bound;
We's all in confusion an' come purty nigh
Fallin' out o' the swing to the ground !

My goodness ! I'll never fergit how I felt;
Cy Ditmore hed heerd all we'd said !
I thought in my soul I'd certainly melt—
The blood 'peared to rush to my head.
Jes 'n Cy come up; we's all in a stew;
An' says, "Ef ye'ir needin' a man,
Instead o' Samanthy, I'll 'comedate you
An' be mighty well pleased ef I can."

I reckon we's all 'bout 's well pleased 's Cy,
Fer they wa'n't airy gyrl in the town,
But what would a-jumped at the chance. So, says I,
"Mr. Ditmore we're glad ye come down."
He smiled sort o' like an' 'peared bent on sompin',
But, goodness ! us gyrls didn't know
Jes what 'u'd crop out, fer he'd talk an' he'd grin
An' swing us 's high 's we'd go.

W'en we got thru a-swingin' I remember so well,
'S we walked to the house, side by side,
He nudged me as ef he hed sompin' to tell

An' jes 'n my hat come untied.
Cy spoke up an' says, "Sclisty Ellen let me
Tie yer hat," an' 'n went on to say,
W'en the gyrls hed went by, "I'd like to," says he,
"Hev the pleasur' o' callin' some day."

I don't s'pose they's ever a gyrl in the world
Felt worse tuk under 'n I;
I got so frustrated my head fairly whirled,
I's allers so timid an' shy ;
But I managed to say, "It 'u'd please me a sight
Ef ye'll call anytime," an' says Cy,
"Ef ye haint no engagement fer nex' Sunday night,
I'll call," an' 'n "thank ye," says I.

Nex' Sunday I's workin' a ha'f day I guess,
A-fixin' an' braidin' my hair;
In the evenin' I put on my new lawn dress,
The weather was pleasant an' fair;
I h'isted the winders an' placed the setee
By the organ, clost to the door,
I lit a new candle an' laid two er three
New rugs about on the floor.

Cy come an' the time passed so pleasantly by,
We talked of the orchard an' swing,
Nen begin tellin' riddles, me first an' nen Cy,
'S long 's we thought of a thing.
Nen I played on the organ two er three times
An' sung, "Gentle Sister, Draw Near,"
Cy looked thru the album an' read all the rhymes
So soft like 'twus soothin' to hear.

By 'at time we'd fairly got under headway !
We's both settin' on the setee.
Cy wus 'bout to propose, I could tell by the way
He wus talkin' an' lookin' at me ;
But, goodness ! jes 'n Bill Simmons's goat
Shot thru the ha'f-open door,
An' its head got mixed up with the tail o' Cy's coat !
An' he never come back any more.

THE SHIVERREE.

I's never much on courtin',
  Never keered a whit, but still
A man'll sometimes stumble on
  A thing agin his will.

Be ketched w'en not a-thinkin';
  Beats the mischief how they'r drawn
Round a gyrl with awk'ard moshun,
  Tel they slip the halter on.

An' it tickles me to see 'em
　　Jes as timid as a mouse,
Marchin' up the i'le on Sunday
　　Of some country meetin'-house,
Standin' up afore the preacher
　　In a rattled sort o' way,
A-answerin' his questions
　　Hardly knowin' what they say.

Nen the shakin' hands an' kissin',
　　An' the thousan' things 'at's said
'Bout, ye know—congratulations,
　　Tel they'r tucked away in bed.
Nen thar comes 'at mortal dreadin'—
　　Ever' noise makes 'em quail!
Fearin' from the tin can rattle
　　They'll be ridin' on a rail.

Fer longside the sway-back wood shed,
　　Thru the gloom in silent glee,
Sneaks a score er two o' boys
　　Fixin' fer a shiverree.

Louder'n a clap o' thunder,
　　Bu'stin' on the evenin' air,
Comes the sound o' washin' biler,
　　Tin cans rattle ever'where.

An' I tell ye it's provokin—
　　'Nough to make a preacher swear,
To be a-straddle of a fence rail
　　Ridin' in the evenin' air.

MY SON NUTE.

My son Nute—jes got back
　　From kollege—'s a wonder.
Thinks 'at he's 'bout 's smart
　　'S reg'ler slycoon thunder.
Gradiate—knows a sight o'
　　High-tone words a feller
Sees on cirkus bills an' downs
　　A mighty handy speller.

Doctor—knows how many bones
　　Ye'ir got in yer whole body,
An' how many j'ints an' nirves
　　An' mussels—he's a prod'y!
Knows all yer in'ard orguns
　　An' how they'r citywated,
An' the reason 'at yer teeth draps out
　　W'en ye git sallyvated.

Knows latten names fer all the 'urbs
　　'At the ole woman's dryin',
An' how ter git thur virtue out
　　By stewin', bilin', fryin';
An' what they'r good fer curin'—
　　Catnip makes yer fever lower;
Ruburb's death ter yaller janders;
　　Tansy knocks the ager, shore.

Las' week Mandy, she's my wife,
　　Tuk sick an' says I to her,
"Les give Nute a show an' see
　　Ef he can raily cure."
I knowed what ailded Mandy—
　　She hed a gum-bile comin',
An' a woman with a gum-bile
　　Jes keeps ever'thing a-hummin'!

"Yes, give Nute a chance," says she,
　　"Ter show his doctor l'arnin'."
So Nute he felt her puls' an' says,
　　"Stick out yer tong', 'n turnin'
Says ter me, "W'y pap," says he,
　　"W'y, mother's got a fellen
An' needs some arnicky," says he,
　　"Ter drive away the swellin'."

"A fellen!" Mandy says, says I,
　　"What did ye call 'at swellin'?"
Says Nute, "A fellen, pap," says he,
　　"A jinnywine ole fellen!"
Wol, drat-my-cats! I thought I'd bu'st,
　　So I cut out fer the stable
An' jes hung on a hoss troft
　　An' laft tel I wa'n't able!

They idy! Nute a gradiate
　　'At cost a thousan' dollars,
An' his credenshuls "Doctor,"
　　Wearin' chiney-laundried collars—
A-comin' home an' struttin' roun'
　　'Sef he knowed all worth tellin',
W'en, dang my skin! he didn't know
　　A gum-bile from a fellen.

CROWS IN THE MEDDER.

The crows air in the medder,
　　An' spring is down thar, too,
An' after the long winter
　　They's lots o' work to do.
The boys has went to plowin'
　　An' air yellin' "gee!" an' "haw!"
While the crows j'ine in the chorus
　　With thur "caw, caw, caw!"

W'en I git up in the mornin'
　　At the airly red o' day,
An' look out on the medder
　　Over yander green an' gay,
An' hear 'em crows a-callin'
　　In thur ole familer glee,
Though it's coarse an' rough fer t'others,
　　It's sweet music onter me.

Of course they cause some trouble
　　W'en it's sproutin'-time fer corn;
But ef trouble's allers light as 'at
　　I'm shore I'll never mourn.

An' I've noticed w'en they's lots o' crows
The crops air never small;
But the Lord agreed to feed us,
An' He's goin' to feed us all.

Yes, the crows air in the medder
An' spring is down thar, too,
An' after the long winter
They's lots o' work to do.
I kin hear the boys a-singin'
An' a-yellin' "gee!" an' "haw!"
While the crows j'ine in the chorus
With thur "caw, caw, caw!"

WISE MEN.

They's men 'at knows a awful sight, 'pears to
    me—
Knows so much they don't average right. D'y
    see?
'At is, too much fer one, not 'nough fer two,
'S I heerd say. Brains fairly leakin' thru
Ever' pore! Body wonders they haint rich,
Knowin' jes how ever' thing ort be done.
Reckon sich men's 'em jes lives fer fun—
Satisfide in knowin' it all. They hitch
A ole weatherboarded plug to a post
In harvest-time—weather hot 'nough to roast,
Crop an' harvest fiel' be dang! thur in town,
The loudest men, too, you kin set 'at down.
"Come in to tell folks sompin' fit to hear!"
An' they haint tuk a paper in ten ye'r.

LITTLE EMMY ROSE.

She had sich a purty face,
    Little Emmy Rose,
An' a right smart, too, o' grace,
    Little Emmy Rose.
Her hair wus brownish an' her eyes
Wus gray as Injin summer skies;
But, my! she hed so many bose—
    Little Emmy Rose.

Monday, Charley went ter see
    Little Emmy Rose;
Tuesday, Will said "O, take me,
    Little Emmy Rose;"
Wednesday afternoon come Smith,
One she hed the trouble with
'Cause she hed so many bose—
    Little Emmy Rose.

Thursday, Eddy Brown called on
    Little Emmy Rose;
Friday, Jim said, "I'm clean gone!
    Little Emmy Rose;"
Sunday, 'n she made it pay,
All o' 'em 'u'd call 'at day;
Goodness! she hed lots o' bose—
    Little Emmy Rose.

Finally one day, in the rain,
    Little Emmy Rose
Sought fer shelter, but in vain,
    Little Emmy Rose
Jes got soaked clean thru an' thru,
Cracky! she was ugly, ugh!
After 'at she hed no bose—
    Little Emmy Rose.

'Cause her bose foun' out an' said,
    "Little Emmy Rose
Wus false from toe clean to'er head!"
    Little Emmy Rose
Now jes sets an' cries an' cries,
An a-wipin' on her eyes,
An' a-wipin' on her nose—
    Little Emmy Rose.

HER SONG.

Come, dear, and sing me one of those sweet
    songs
For which a lover's heart in sadness longs;
Of which the burden is, "My love is true."
As merry as, forsooth, some roundelay
That Comus sang upon the wedding day
Of Juno—full of pleasing words and few
Interludes, that I, an ardent lover,
May the secret of thy heart discover.
"A gyrl out in the country," ran her song,
"Mashed a town-feller folks said wus a dude,
An' yaller legged chicken wus his food,
An' her father let his board jes run along.
Now, ef he loves this charmin' critter still,
I think he'd pay her father his board bill!"
N. B. He paid it.

WISHT I'D A-MARRIED.

Wisht I'd a-married an' worked at my trade,
'Stid of a-went a-writin',
Fer they's room fer complaint w'en a man's
    po'rly paid,
An' with hard times is allers a-fightin'.
W'en I think o' the dimes I've lost makin'
    rhymes,
I git ruther hot in the coller;
But sadder 'n 'at is the thoughts o' the times
W'en my word wus good fer a doller,
An' 'at pill 's the hardest ter swoller!

Wisht I'd a-married an' worked at my trade,
'Stid of a-went a-writin';
But I courted the Muse an' the tune 'at she
    played
Growed more an' more invitin',

Tel it seemed I could soar 'round with her
  evermore,
An' t'other work I fairly hated;
But the idy o' livin' so dog-fennel poor,
  Wus a thing 'at wa'n't intimated—
  Wus sompin' 'at wa'n't cal'lated.

Wisht I'd a-married an' worked at my trade,
  'Stid of a-went a-writin';
Fer I've writ tel I reckon my eyesight's 'bout
  played,
An' my hair is a-goin' a-skitin'.
Jes well state the facts while I'm chawin' my
  wax—
My experryunce is, down here on Lick Crick,
Ef a man writin' poetry kin pay his poll tax,
  He's a man 'at kin beat Andy Bickwick—
  He's a man 'at's a-havin' a picnic!

INDIANY WEATHER.

Git out my las' ye'r overcoat
  Fer I mus' go to town.
Gee whiz! the win's a-blowin'—
  Haint the snow a-comin' down?
Ole Indiany weather jes
  Beats all 'at's cert'in shore;
W'y yistiddy 'twus warm anough
  To open ever' door.

An' yistiddy I's goin' roun'
  All day in my shirt sleeves,
An' the chip birds wus a-singin'
  Yander in the smoke house eaves;
An' I ketched ole Nero lookin'
  Fer a shadder to lay on,
A-pantin' with his tong' out
  'Sef his win' wus purt nigh gone.

An' yistiddy the chickens wus
  A-singin' roun' the barn;
'Twus jes the sort o' weather
  'At a man haint wuth a darn;
An' while I's settin' out a-lookin'
  At the wheat fiel' over thar,
Fust I knowed I's sweatin'
  An' it way in Jinewar.

Yes, git out my las' ye'r overcoat
  Fer I mus' go to town.
I 'gin to think 'is winter
  'Twa'n't wuth while to take it down;
But ole Indiany weather jes
  Beats all plum out o' sight!
Yistiddy the doors wus open
  But to-day we'll shet 'em tight.

BILLY WITTY.

Billy Witty, 'tain't no pity
  You hev moved to town.
Got the folks a-laughin' tel
  The'r jes a-fallin' down.
Boys a-yellin' roun' the publik
  Square 'at you air in;
Laughin' tel the'r sides air akin
  An' you hardly haint begin.

Billy Witty, 'tain't no pity
  You hev moved to town.
Settin' on the court house fence
  An' runnin' nabers down,
Ben 'bout all 'at's goin' on,
  'Cep' seein' Blev Good lick
Newby Sprowls fer talkin' patent
  Rights tel he wus sick.

Billy Witty, 'tain't no pity
  You hev moved to town.
Place wus gittin' lank an' onery
  'S a long-ye'rd houn'.
Men 'at 'fesses bein' funny 's
  Gittin' awful slow,
Tellin' same ole jokes they's tellin'
  Twenty ye'r ago.

Billy Witty, 'tain't no pity
  You hev moved to town.
Got the folks a-laughin' tel
  The'r jes a-tum'lin' roun'.
None like you kin wake 'is ole town
  Up an' make 'er clim'!
You kin smoke a five cent segar
  On me ever' time.

SINGLE HARNESS.

Never keert much fer to marry,
  Courted some, though, now an' then;
Ben to many a apple cuttin'
  'Ith a gyrl, like other men.
Swung 'er, too, 'bout 's handy
  'S the nex' un on the floor,
To 'at good ole tune, the Rye Straw,
  Tel the sweat begin to pour.

Hardly ever wus pertic'ler
  W'en it come to choosin' gyrls;
Liked the looks o' Betsy Miller
  'Ith 'er long an' yaller curls.
But 'ith me, somehow er t'other,
  Shapin' things to make a match,
Never worked so smooth an' oily
  W'en it come down to the scratch.

T'other fellers, game an' plucky,
  Sailed right in an' stood the'r chance,
An' to-day's got strappin' boys
  Big anough to wear my pants.
But I've worked in single harness;
  Ben about 's well off, though,
Yit, sometimes it makes a feller
  Fell 's blue 's indygo.

OLE HOSS, NANCE.

They's no style about 'er
  O' course 'at 's all so,
But I pet an' like 'er,
  An' to say she could go,
Comes as fer from guessin'
  'Er speed as I know.

W'y she could throw dus'
  In any nags eyes.
The fus' I knowed it
  Wus when ole Bill Wise
Wus keepin' toll gate down hur
  An' makin' cross ties.

Ole Bill wus one o' these
  Blinkity sort o' men—
Allers foolin' aroun'
  An' nine times out o' ten,
Break sompin' er uther
  He never could men'.

Foolin' roun' 'ith ole clocks,
  It beat all holler!
He sp'ilt a watch o' mine
  'At cos' six dollar
An' los' a leather chain
  I bought o' Mart Swaller.

But 's I wus a-sayin',
  W'en Bill kep' the gate,
I'd ben to town one day
  An' started home sort o' late,
An' I'd whipped Nance up
  To a purty purt gait.

W'en I got to the jog
  In the road by White's Mill,
I stopped to water ole Nance
  An' up rode ole Bill,
An' bantered me to race 'im
  'S fer 's Knobb Hill.

Bill kep' on a-banterin'
  An' I'd sort o' smile,
Thinkin' Bill's hoss
  Could trot a mile
Quicker'n mine,
  By no little while.

But nothin' 'u'd do
  But a race, an' says Bill,
"I'll give ye ten yards
  An' we'll start from the mill
An' I'll beat ye all holler
  'Twixt thar an' the hill."

Now 'at sort o' riled me,
  An' it 'peard like ole Nance
Knowed jes what he said,
  Fer she started to prance
An' caper about
  Like a gyrl at a dance.

So I straddled ole Nance
  An' rode up to the mill,
White stepped off the groun',
  Says I, "Take it, Bill,
Ye'll need more'n 'at
  Ef ye beat to the hill!"

Bill tittered an' laft
  'S I turnt Nance aroun',
An' rode up to the mark
  While Bill tuk the groun'—
Ten yard on the start—
  An' we's off 'ith a boun'!

Ole Nance 'ith 'er tail up—
  Now didn't we sail!
An' the win' whisseled thru me,
  An' my ole coat tail
Stuck out 's straight
  'S a new popler rail.

An' Bill wus a-yelpin'
  An' kickin' an' swearin'!
It beat all to flinders,
  W'y people come tearin'
To the'r doors 'ith the'r mouths
  An' eyes open a-starin'!

An' the dus'—w'y Great Caeser!
  Riz up like a kite,
An' the hogs in the mud holes,
  Jumpin' up in the'r fright,
Run like wildfire—
  Skeert to death at the sight!

But, Nance, seemed to me,
  She's jes tickled all over;
'Twus more fun fer her
  'N a paster o' clover
Sprinkled 'ith May apple
  Blossoms all over.

An' to make a long story
  Short an' more pleasin',
Bill wus woss beat,
  Outside o' all reason,
'N a man in a pair o'
  Tow pants w'en it's freezin'!

Well, Nance af'er 'at
　　Could beat anything
In the shape o' hoss flesh
　　On a mud road er ring
Of a fair groun'. W'y, man,
　　She went by ever'thing.

An' now I don't reckon
　　She'd be very slow
Ef it wa'n't fer bone spavin—
　　It pesters her so
An' keeps her from showin'
　　Her mettle ye know.

An' often I set on the
　　Fence while she's eatin'
'Roun' in the orchard
　　Af'er comin' from meetin',
An' think o' ole Bill,
　　Now passed worldly greetin'.

Nance, an' me, too,
　　Will foller 'im soon;
Our time haint fer off;
　　But I reckon our spoon
Has ben in the puddin'
　　'Bout 's long 's they's room.

LINEN CLOTHES.

Ef they's one time more 'n anuther
　　A man feels cheap an' mean,
It's when he puts on linen clothes,
　　'Spech'ly ef he's lean,
An' starts out fer a picnic,
　　A show er a hoss race,
An' strikes a shower 'bout the time
　　He's nearin' to the place.

How it makes his spirits flatten
　　An' drap clean to his feet,
An' his temper git so sour
　　It's mighty hard to beat;
An' his face look sad an' yaller,
　　His 'pearunce sompin' like
A las' ye'r's skeer crow jes pulled thru
　　A hog hole on the pike.

When he pulls up at the doin's
　　He feels as cheap as dirt,
An' looks 'bout as lonesome
　　As a pocket in a shirt;
An' he'll shy 'roun' an' try to dodge,
　　The wimmin folks; but, 'shaw!
'Tain't no use, he'll meet a passel
　　Ever gee er haw.

An' when his clothes air dry they look
　　As wrinkled as a shuck,
An' shrunk an' drawed all out o' shape—
　　It's jes a feller's luck.
An' he'll have a dozen grass stains
　　On his pants, an' his coat-tail
Will draw up to his gallesses—
　　'Twus never knowed to fail.

He'll shy 'roun' a while, an' 'n
　　As like as not cut out,
A-feelin' mean an' onery
　　As a feller could, about;
An' it'll strain his christianity
　　To blot out in a ye'r,
The language 'at he uses
　　To express his idys clear.

WRITIN' SAME AS ME.

Nuther feller in our town
　　Writin' same 's me;
Like to form his 'quaintance
　　Fer he's way up in G!
While I'm jes sort o' danglin'
　　Roun' the windy adge o' C.

He knows all the high-tone folks,
　　Jes chuck full o' fun an' jokes,
An' they say one thing is shore,
　　He kin make a feller roar—
Make you laugh tel you 'mos' die,
　　An' turn roun' an' make you cry!

Draw his chin down, like's not
　　Nimitate some b'uty spot,
Er a ole man, er mebbe,
　　Sompin' else, jes 's he
Takes a notion, don't you see?
　　Feller slick 's slick kin be—
Writin' jes the same 's me.

SKINNER'S RIDGE.

Folks at Skinner's Ridge don't often lead a feller out:
People's mostly law-abidin' livin' thereabout.
Feller stands a mighty little show ef he ain't square;
Up an' git, er dangle to a saplin' anywhere.

Comes along a man las' summer—'peard to be all right.
Hed on store-clothes 'at fit him mighty nigh skin tight,
An' a diamon' pin, I reckon, big as an acorn,
An' a pair o' shoes as p'inted as a powder-horn.

Got a'quainted in two days with ever'body
    there;
Said he's from the city, jes come out to git the
    air—
Banker, health wus sort o' failin'—allers in a
    smile;
Liked the place an' liked the people, guessed
    he'd stay awhile.

First he stopped with Big Ben Miller—keeps
    the "Ridge Hotel;"
Fin'ly went to boardin' with ole Uncle Cy
    Milwell.
Good man, owns five hundred akers, trades in
    stock an' sich;
Carries his money in his pocket—powerfully
    rich.

Banker settled right down on him—stuck to
    Uncle Cy
Tel he foun' out all about his business mighty
    nigh.
Folks they sort o' felt oneasy, but what could
    they say?
Banker 'peard to be a-actin' square in ever'
    way.

Things run on two weeks er better, still the
    feller staid;
'G'inst 'at time the folks wa'n't feelin' half so
    much afraid.
Gyrls wus fixin' fer some doin's 'bout with all
    their might;
Goin' to ask the banker to the meetin'-house
    'at night.

"Course he'd go ef Uncle Cy 'u'd," an' I reck-
    on there
Wus more fixin' 'mongst the gyrls 'at night 'n
    anywhere.
Folks begin to gether, but the banker an' ole
    Cy
Didn't come er send the people any reason
    why!

Tell ye things got mighty cloudy—whispers
    ever'where.
'Twa'n't long 'fore a dozen fellers up an' out
    o' there!
'Bout ha'f ways to Uncle Cy's house—sort o'
    lonesome place—
Told the tale. Cy's pockets empty, cut about
    the face!

Banker? Well I guess the feller up and jes
    made tracks;
Leastwise, 'at's the supposishun—no use
    statin' facts.
Man kin think an' have his idys spite o' all
    soft soap—
Anyhow, the meetin'-house has got a new
    bell-rope.

'SQUIRE EVILSIZER'S OFFIS

'Squire Evilsizers's offis,
    Over Wincy's store,
Haint a very purty place.
    Man kin see heap more
Style, ef style he's lookin' fer,
    Most any whur, I guess,
'N's desplayed in Evilsizer's
    Offis in full dress.

Roomy, 's bout the on'y charm,
    An' airy—'spechly so
Long 'bout 'is time o' ye'r
    W'en they's ice an' snow.
Brick fell down the chimbley onct
    An' the draf' hit got a choke;
Long 'bout 'is time o' ye'r
    You'll find hit full o' smoke.

They's a map o' Igo Township
    Takes the place o' glass
In the winder, whur a feller
    One time made a pass
'Ith the poker w'en 'e tried to
    Black the marshel's eye,
An skeert a lot o' wimmin'
    Tel they fainted mighty nigh.

They's a bookcase nimitated
    By two aig crates nailed
'G'inst the wall, an' full o' law
    An' ecity curtailed.
They's a picter, too, o' honest
    Ole George Washin'ton,
An' Abe Linco'n an' a motto
    Is the other un.

An' ole 'Squire Evilsizer—
    Never leave 'im out,
Er ye'll sp'ile the 'scripshun o' the
    Offis 'thout a doubt.
He's the piece o' furnyture
    More preshusher 'n gold;
Big o' heart an' small o' pocket—
    He's the offis, boys, all told.

OLE MARTIN MILLS

Ole Martin Mills, ole Martin Mills,
'Ith his claw-hammer coat 'at his body scace
    fills,
An' his broad, pleasant grin. He's a good man
    to call
An' spin off a joke er a story to all.

Fer many a ye'r has ole Martin Mills
Lived all alone at the foot o' the hills,
Cooked his own dinner, kep' his house, too,
I s'pose 'bout 's good 's a woman could do.

Courted 'bout ever' gyrl 'roun' here;
An's kep' the thing up fer many a ye'r;
But nary a mitten! W'y, law, goodness, me!
The gyrls hankers af'er ole Martin, ye see.

Reason? Great Ceasar! they's reason anough.
Yes, he's ole, an' looks sort o' rough;
But, money! W'y, men, they's no end to his
    wealth,
An' the gyrls knows 'at age 'll soon tell on his
    health.

But they say a thing happened in ole Martin's
    life,
An' he vowed 'at he'd never be tied to a wife.
What it wus I don't know, he never 'u'd tell;
But they's one thing sartin, he's stuck it out
    well.

Still ole Martin seems 'bout 's happy an' free
'S a man ever expects in 'is world to be.
He's foot-loose; kin go, no matter w'en,
'Thout bein' hampered like us married men.

Ole Martin Mills, ole Martin Mills,
Lives all alone at the foot o' the hills,
Never wus married; never will be;
Ole Martin's head's 'bout level, ye see.

HOSS AUCTION.

Hangin' 'roun' the ole hoss auction
    Man kin see a sight.
Fellers bettin' an' disputin'—
    Excitin' as a fight!
See ole plugs stringhalt an' wheezy,
    'Bout in the las' stage
Uf the bots, ringbone er spavin—
    Hard to tell the'r age.

Heer the auctioneer a-shoutin';
    See the ole plugs trot
Up an' down the dusty road er
    'Roun' the ole hoss lot.
Heer ole Uncle Billy Mayfield's
    Little squeaky laugh
W'en a bid is riz a quarter
    Er anuther ha'f.

An' the man 'at rides the hosses—
    Pants tucked in his boots—
Cal'lates to skeer a ole plug
    Tel it fairly scoots
Roun' an' makes a feller reckon
    It haint half as ole
As the ole plug railly is
    Tel af'er it is sole.

Hangin' 'roun' the ole hoss auction
    Many man's got rich.
Nen a man kin learn a sight
    'Bout medicine an' sich,
Jes by hearin' old hoss doctors
    Talkin' 'bout disease,
An' o' this er that er t'other
    Uf the'r recipes.

An' a man fer cheap amusemint
    Can't find any place,
'Cordin' to my cal'lashuns
    Uf the forsaid case,
'At kin hol' a candle to a
    Hoss auction. W'y, men,
It'll beat a fight er cirkus
    Nine times out o' ten.

EVEN TEMPER.

'Tain't no use ter grumble,
    Ner 'tain't no use ter fret;
A man won't live no longer
    By a-gittin' all upset.
It's the man o' even temper
    'At is allers shore ter win,
An' the man 'at's allers kickin'
    'At's a-gittin' taken in.

The hog 'at's allers squealin'
    Gits the smallest shur o' slop,
An' the man 'at's allers growlin'
    Never raises half a crop.
An' of'en w'en a feller
    Gits a lickin', it has been
The man at' talked the loudest
    Jes afore the fight begin.

It's a fact—the man 'at carries
    The fattest pocket-book
Is the quiet, stidy-goin'
    Feller ever' time; but look
Whurever ye'r a mind ter,
    'Tain't of'en 'at ye'll find
A man 'at's wuth 'is feedin'
    Ef 'e's any yuther kind.

I've seen men 'ith lots o' money
    Rooster over men 'ith none,
An' it tuk a heap o' pashunts
    Ter put up 'ith all they done;
But the po'r man 'at said nothin'—
    Jes done well what he's about—
'U'd turn 'roun' 'fore a great while
    An' buy the rich man out.

Nen 'tain't no use ter grumble,
    Ner 'tain't no use ter fret;
A man won't live no longer
    By a-gittin' all upset.
Never let a sour temper
    Try ter tote ye thru 'is life,
Fer ye'll fin' it mighty risky
    'Thout a pistol er a knife.

STICK TO FARMIN'

Makin' money hain't so easy.
  Men'll fret an' fool about
All the'r lives an' nen be po'rer
  Nan when they first started out.
Ever' one's a snatch-an'-grabbin'.
  Beats Sam Hill! W'y, I declare,
Man's relashun to finances
  Hain't the thickness uf a hair.

Let me say while we're a-talkin',
  'Fore ye sell yer little farm,
An' by moovin' to the city
  Think ye'll live jes like a charm.
Think 'at ye'll invest in sompin',
  Make a fortune 'ithout work,
Wear good clothes an' be a big bug,
  Do yer business thru a clerk:

'At the stone 'at's allers rollin'
  Gethers no moss. Men 'at fails
Is the men 'at lets the future
  Swoller 'em teeth un' toenails!
My advice is stick to farmin'.
  Stick to it thru good an' bad,
I'll bet a peck o' rotten apples
  Ef ye don't ye'll wisht ye had.

OLE UNCLE BILLY.

Ole Uncle Billy wus a man
  Chuck full o' good intenshuns.
He'd give a feller his jus' dues
  Regardless of dimenshuns.

He bought a farm on Hickory Ridge,
  Sompin' like sixty akers,
An' started up a settlemint
  O' good, square, honest quakers.

He supervised a new dirt road
  From his place to Lick Skillet,
An' fenced in widder Thomson's farm
  An' he'ped her boys to till it.

He built a spankin' new log church
  An' daubed the cracks 'ith hardpan;
He made the fire-place so big
  It roared like a wheat-fan.

An' all the t'other things he done's
  Too numerous to menshun;
But the thing I aimed to speak about
  Wus a country school convenshun.

'S nigh 's I remember now,
  A man named Asher Givin'
Come to the settlemint one fall
  To teach school fer a livin'.

He went aroun' from house to house
  A-huntin' up a scholar
Rigged out in bran' new store-clothes
  An' paper cuffs an' collar.

But, nary scholar. Some 'u'd say,
  "We hain't no time fer schoolin'."
While t'others snubbed him off, er said,
  "We don't uphold sich foolin'."

'Twa'n't long afore he's tired out
  An' weary an' down-hearted,
An' they say the feller railly cried
  W'en from the Ridge he started.

But, it's cur'ous how the win' does change,
  It's the same 'ith luck, I reckon;
Leastwise, a man kin never tell
  What minnit it'll beckon.

Fer of'en w'en a man's fagged out
  An' his reason gits to squirmin',
An' its cal'lashuns on his face
  Air 's plain 's any sermon,

Some one 'll come along 'bout then
  An' read him like a letter,
An' nen turn in 'ith all the'r might
  An' he'p make matters better.

'Twus 'bout 'at way in Asher's case,
  Leastwise, ole Uncle Billy
Come joggin' down the road to mill,
  Woman-fashion, on his filly.

His head wus bent 's ef in thought,
  But 'cashun'ly he'd whistle
A few notes uf the "Rye Straw,"
  Er the "Rabbit an' the Thistle."

But fin'ly glancin' at the sun
  He urged his nag on faster,
An' lookin' on ahead apiece
  He seen the lang'age-master.

He's settin' on a popler log,
  His body well nigh double,
An' Uncle Billy at a glance
  'U'd a vowed he' in some trouble.

So, nudgin' up his nag a bit,
  "Halloo!" says Uncle Billy,
An' nen the teacher riz his head
  An' lookin' sort o' silly,

Says, "Howdy, sir; I didn't know
  'At any one wus comin'."
An' nen he sort o' looked confused,
  An' on the log kep' drummin'.

"Ben to the settlemint, I s'pose,"
  Says Billy sort off handed,
An' nen he slid off uf his nag
  An' by the teacher landed.

An' stoopin' down to brush his pants
  Whur the hoss hair made 'em reden,
He made a few remarks about
  The way his nag wus sheddin'.

Now Uncle Billy hed a knack
  O' gittin' 'roun' a feller
Sort o' onbeknowns to them—
  His manner wus so meller.

So settin' down long side him
  Soon they fell to conversashun;
'Twa'n't long 'fore Uncle Billy knowed
  The teacher's situashun.

The teacher told him all about
  His mother—widder Givin,
An' his little sisters three who 'pended
  On him fer a livin'.

An' nen about how hard he'd tried
  To keep 'em all together—
To pay the mortgage on the'r home
  An' keep 'em from the weather.

An' nen the tears begin to come,
  An' Uncle Billy's dander
Riz higher 'n a ten rail fence—
  Mad 's a naked gander!

So jumpin' up an' sayin',
  "Ef you want a school fer teachin'
I'll knock it out o' 'at air Ridge
  'S shore 's gospel preachin'!"

"An' I'll p'int 'em out a lesson
  'At 'll be a little chillin';
An' take 'em down a button-hole
  Er two ef you air willin'!"

So straddlin' uf his filly,
  Though it never carried double,
He got the teacher on behin'
  'Thout hardly any trouble.

He turnt the nag toward the Ridge;
  But he never intimated
To the teacher what his idy wus
  Ner what he cal'lated.

But comin' to the new log church
  'Ith its new laid puncheon floor,
He told the teacher to slide off
  An' open up the door.

Nen mountin' on a hoss-block
  'Ith a mighty firm intenshun,
He begin to call the people up
  To hold a school convenshun.

Soon wimmin, men an' chilen
  'Ith the'r heads thru winders shootin'
Er a-dartin' thru the doorways
  Up the dusty road come scootin'!

An' I reckon 'twa'n't ten minnits
  'Fore each person, clean er rusty,
Congregated at the church-house
  All excited, hot an' dusty.

Nen dismountin' from the hoss-block
  Uncle Billy tuk the pulpit
An' begin in lang'age forcin'
  'S a war-time minny bullet!

He showed 'em how they'd trifled 'ith
  A good, square, honest feller,
In a way 'at knocked the'r feelin's
  From the roof clean to the celler!

Nen in lang'age somewhat milder
  Told 'em uf the teacher's mother,
An' his little sisters, three, 'ith none
  To he'p 'em but the'r brother.

An' I'll bet tha'r wa'n't a dry eye
  In 'at whole congregashun
W'en Uncle Billy finished up
  His techin' suplicashun.

An' he made the teacher up a school
  Right thar an' nen—instanter!
Each man planked down his Chilen's fees
  'Thout a word o' banter.

An' Asher—well I reckon
  He's the happiest mortal creature
'At ever started out in life
  To be a country teacher.

So droppin' on his knees he said,
  "God bless ole Uncle Billy—
God bless 'em all fer 'is good work—
  God bless 'is place so hilly!"

An' nen they all riz up an' felt
  Too happy to consider!
But the purtiest part come af'erward—
  W'en Billy married the widder.

www.ingramcontent.com/pod-product-compliance
Lightning Source LLC
Chambersburg PA
CBHW020134170426
43199CB00010B/741